THE ARAB PRESS

Contemporary Issues in the Middle East

THE ARAB PRESS

News Media and
Political Process in the Arab World

WILLIAM A. RUGH

SYRACUSE UNIVERSITY PRESS • 1979

.

Library of Congress Cataloging in Publication Data

Rugh, William A
  The Arab press.

  (Contemporary issues in the Middle East)
  Includes bibliographical references and index.
    1. Press—Arab countries. 2. Journalism—Political
aspects—Arab countries. I. Title. II. Series:
Contemporary issues in the Middle East series.
PN5359.R8   301.16'1'0953   79-13950
ISBN 0-8156-2191-4
ISBN 0-8156-0159-X pbk.

Manufactured in the United States of America

TO MY PARENTS

Roberts Rugh

and

Harriette Sheldon Rugh

William A. Rugh, counselor for public affairs at the U.S. Embassy, Cairo, was a Council on Foreign Relations Fellow and has served in Saudi Arabia as Director of the American Cultural Center in Jidda, of the English Language Center in Riyadh, and as Embassy Public Relations Officer.

CONTENTS

TABLES

PREFACE

THIS BOOK analyzes the news media as institutions, to see what forms they have taken in the independent Arab states, how the self-governing Arab societies have chosen to control them, and how they relate to the political processes in the Arab world. The material and observations presented here have been gathered over a period of more than fourteen years of living in the Arab world or working on matters related to it. In the 1960s, first as a student of Arabic in Beirut and then working in Egypt and Saudi Arabia, it became apparent to me that the press and other mass media performed functions in Arab society that were extremely important. With the spread of television throughout the area, and the growth of newspaper publishing even in the less advanced parts of the Arab world, the mass media have taken on even greater significance.

It is clear that the Arab mass media participate very actively in politics. Their commentaries, how they report the news, and what they report or omit are matters that Arab politicians, government officials on all levels, and many others watch carefully on a day-to-day basis. And because the Arab world consists of eighteen countries which are independent, sovereign, and different, but which all share a language, a culture, and a sense of common destiny, the people tend to pay an unusual amount of attention to what is being said in other Arab countries —through the media—about significant concerns. In the spring of 1979, for example, the radio, television, and newspapers amplified and helped to shape the intense debate about the peace treaty which Egypt and Israel concluded in April, as well as the lively discussion about developments in revolutionary Iran. It is important to know what determines how Arab editors and reporters deal with these and other events.

No systematic analysis of the mass media in the Arab world exists, in any language. Western authors have not dealt with Arab media as a subject in itself since 1952, when one American writer produced a book on five (of the now eighteen) Arab countries.[1] There are several books in Arabic on the Arab press, but they are all single-country studies except for one, and that is a purely catalog-descriptive survey with no analysis.[2] The others tend to be either politically biased apologia or historical studies that do not deal with the contemporary situation. There is no up-to-date book analyzing the role and function of Arab media, what motivations and constraints influence the behavior of Arab journalists, and what governmental and other influences affect the media. It is the purpose of this book to examine those questions, and particularly to look at the relationship between the mass media and the government in the Arab countries to see how much freedom the Fourth Estate enjoys.

The countries dealt with in this book are the eighteen nation-states where Arabic is the official language and the mass media are primarily in Arabic, and where the people clearly consider themselves part of the Arab cultural community. These are: Algeria, Bahrain, Egypt, Iraq, Jordan, Kuwait, Lebanon, Libya, Morocco, Oman, Qatar, Saudi Arabia, the Sudan, Syria, Tunisia, the United Arab Emirates, and both Yemens (Arab Republic and People's Democratic Republic).[3]

The system of transliteration of Arabic words and names used in this book is based on the simplified one used by the Foreign Broadcast Information Service (FBIS) of the U.S. government, which avoids the sublinear dots and other special marks but still conveys the proper original word to speakers of the language.[4] Wherever a name has a different spelling that is in common use, such as Gamal Abdul Nasser, that one is used instead.

I would like to acknowledge the generous assistance from several sources which made this book possible. First of all, the Council on Foreign Relations gave me a fellowship for the academic year 1972–73 specifically to undertake this study. I was able during that year to survey all of the existing literature, read broadly in the Arab press, and make an extensive tour of nearly all of the Arab countries, interviewing more than 150 key journalists, editors, information ministry officials, and others. The Council arranged for a group of experts to discuss an early draft of the manuscript, and Council staff, particularly Dr. John Campbell, provided helpful advice. Professor W. Phillips Davison of the Columbia University Graduate School of Journalism read some drafts and made invaluable suggestions for revision. And many colleagues in the United States Information Agency and the Department of State have shared their knowledge and understanding of the subject with me over the years. All of these people have helped in many ways to make this a better effort, but any remaining flaws must be attributed solely to the author.

Finally I wish to acknowledge that my wife, despite her own full schedule of scholarly activities and research, leading to a Ph.D., was able to give me the greatest possible support and encouragement throughout the years that this study was in progress.

Cairo   WAR
Spring 1979

INTRODUCTION

W<small>HY SHOULD WE STUDY</small> the Arab news media? The news media have taken on increasing importance in recent years everywhere in the world. The growth of television viewing and radio listening audiences has been dramatic, and newspaper readership has expanded similarly. One cause has been rapid technological innovation, such as the transistor revolution which has extended the reach of the media. Another has been the population explosion which, together with the trend to urbanization has resulted in the concentration of large groups of people in places where they have easier access to mass media. Increasing literacy, too, has brought forth a larger newspaper-reading public.

This book is about the press as it functions in Arab society. It describes and analyzes the organization of the press and its relationships to the government and the political process.

By "press" we mean essentially the fast news media, i.e., the daily newspapers, radio, and television. We will make some references to other printed media such as weekly and monthly magazines. But non-news mass communications media such as motion pictures have been excluded because their role in society is somewhat different, and a study treating them in sufficient depth would be a book in itself.[1]

The news media play a larger role in the daily lives of people everywhere. These media are consequently regarded by politicians and governments as having greater political importance than ever before. It is true that the acquisition and distribution of news has been seen for a long time as a vital function in society which has political significance because the news items may have political impact very quickly on large numbers of people. Most societies have wrestled with problems of media controls and freedom, and have dealt seriously with questions of media-government relations.[2] But as the technical means of communication have improved, governments and political leaders have judged these problems as increasingly critical because they think the power of these instruments to affect the political process is growing. Thus in the third quarter of the twentieth century, the typical news-handling institution is likely to be of great interest to the government and the public because it is a complex organization that involves great expense and because people regard it as important politically. The way government and society deal with this institution is significant for an understanding of that government and society as well as of the mass communication process.

A basic assumption of this book is that news media institutions do not exist independently of their environments but rather take on the "form and coloration of the social and political structures" within which they operate.[3] There is an intimate, organic relationship between the media institutions and society in the way those institutions are organized and controlled. Neither the institution nor the society in which it functions can be understood properly without reference to the other.

This is certainly true in the Arab world. The news media there, in fact, are particularly interesting in this regard because of the roles they have played during the third quarter of the twentieth century as most of the Arab countries gained their full independence and developed their own national institutions. Arab media systems have taken on their current institutional forms only recently, and these forms can only be explained by reference to the underlying political realities in the society as a whole.

The spread of communication facilities in the Arab world has been remarkable. By the middle of the 1970s, every Arab country, including even the poorest ones, had built its own television system, and a majority had satellite ground stations capable of transcontinental television transmission. By that time, all Arab countries were active in radio broadcasting for both internal and external audiences, and in many places the programming was extremely varied and rich. Egypt's international radio broadcasting services, for example, are designed for many different audiences, and their total hours of air time are the third highest of any country in the world, greater than any Western nation. And all eighteen Arab countries not only publish their own newspapers and magazines but each one has its own news agency. The amount of news, commentary, and other information and interpretation turned out by these media every day is enormous.

These media have become quite important in the lives of most of the 140 million people who live in the Arab world. Growing literacy has given many access to the printed media, but television viewing and especially radio listening have burgeoned as cheaper transistorized receivers became available. The story is told in Saudi Arabia of an American oil-company geologist, crossing a barren expanse of desert in 1969, who encountered a lone bedouin tending his flock of camels and stopped to try out his own Arabic. When the bedouin asked where he had come from, the American solemnly pointed to the sky and said, "I've just come from the moon." Without batting an eye, the bedouin replied, "Oh, then you must be Neil Armstrong." The story may be apocryphal, but it is certainly true that the details of the American lunar landing became known even by the least educated people in the remotest parts of the Arab world by means of transistorized radios. At the same time, large numbers of Arabs in urban areas enjoyed color television as well as magazines and newspapers printed according to high standards.

Observers of political and other trends in the Arab world follow the Arab media closely. Foreign correspondents reporting on the area use Arab media as a resource for their stories. Foreign embassies in Arab countries depend heavily on the local press for their reporting back to their home governments. The United States government spends millions of dollars annually monitoring Arab radio broadcasts twenty-four hours each day, a service that Washington officials and analysts cull for useful information on Arab policies, ideas, and perceptions. Merely looking at headlines of the daily newspaper, in fact, can often give some indication of local concerns and preoccupations; to cite one example, the Arab press on May 28, 1973, reported on the same meeting of the Organization of African Unity chiefs of state under the following different headlines: "General Gowan Elected President of African Summit Session" (*al Sabah*, Tunisia); "Gowan: We Must Control Our Own Resources to Liberate Africa Economically" (*l'Opinion*, Morocco); "Arab-African Split Within OAU Because of Somalia and Ethiopia" (*al Madinah*, Saudi Arabia); "Soviets Congratulate Sudan on 10th Anniversary of OAU" (*al Sahafah*, the Sudan); "Africa Concern for Mideast Problem" (*al Dustur*, Jordan); "New Step to Liberate Palestine" (*al Sha'b*, Algeria); "Results of Sadat's Contacts Appear in Strengthened African Decision Exposing the Position of Israel" (*al Akhbar*, Egypt).

There is, of course, much more in the press than headlines. Readers look for information, but they also seek nuances in language and even omissions in reporting, which they may detect if they listen to foreign radio broadcasts. In an area of the world where public opinion polls and open parliamentary debates are rare, observers look at media

content for indicators of political trends and probable future developments.[4]

   This study does not focus on media content, however. It examines
the organization of Arab media institutions which shape that content,
and it analyzes the influences that are brought to bear on Arab journalists in writing their news copy, editorials, and other material. The Arab
journalist, in order to succeed, must be highly sensitive to the political
realities prevailing in his country, which constitute real constraints and
incentives on his work. The organization he works for fits into his country's prevailing political system, and he must take that into account, as
he must be aware of the ways in which his organization is linked with
the government and/or the political system.

   In other parts of the world, the relationship of the press to the government has been analyzed in detail, and several different types of press
system have been described.[5] Does the Arab press fall into any of these
categories? The first chapter of this book answers that question in the
negative, although there are some characteristics of the so-called authoritarian system which are found in most of the Arab countries. The
Arab press, however, has some characteristics which set it apart from
systems elsewhere, so we have had to describe these with specific reference to the manifestations in the various Arab countries. The first chapter presents those characteristics of the Arab news media which are
present in all eighteen Arab countries and which seem to be typical of
the Arab press as a whole. The book then presents an analysis of the
Arab daily newspapers which shows that they can be divided into three
fundamental sub-types which have appeared and survived after independence. The Arab countries have organized their daily newspapers
according to one or another of these three systems, but the organization
is not necessarily static: some countries have gone from one system into
another, depending on conditions which are described in Chapters 2
through 5 that discuss these sub-types.

   Chapter 6 describes and analyzes the organization and function of
radio and television institutions in the Arab world. These systems can
be dealt with together because they are simpler organizationally and
have much more in common than do the newspaper organizations.

   Chapter 7 discusses the various sources of foreign news available
to Arab editors and — directly or indirectly — to the Arab public. Finally, Chapter 8 brings together the conclusions of the analyses and offers some generalizations about the conditions under which the various
organizational forms have appeared and will probably continue to appear in the Arab world.

Arab Information Media: Function and Structure

THE ARAB WORLD in the 1970s includes eighteen sovereign, independent states stretching across an area from the Atlantic Ocean to the Persian Gulf, with a total population of more than 140 million people. In some respects, these countries are quite diverse. Economic prosperity measured by annual per capita income ranged in 1978 from below $300 in the Yemen Arab Republic to a worldwide high of over $22,000 in the United Arab Emirates. The level of education runs from Oman, where secondary schools were first opened in the 1970s, to Lebanon, which has several long-established institutions of higher learning and a literacy rate of nearly 90 percent. There are different types of government, too—absolute and constitutional monarchies, presidential and one-party regimes, and some representational institutions. Even their pre-independence political histories varied considerably. To cite two examples, Algeria, for more than a century considered to be an integral part of France, liberated itself in 1962 after a traumatic war, while Saudi Arabia had only minimal experience with colonial rule and achieved full independence and unity well before World War II.

Nevertheless, the peoples of the eighteen Arab states feel bound together by strong cultural and psychological ties. The vast majority of them regard Arabic as their mother tongue; most of them share a single culture, language, and religion, and their sense of a common destiny is very strong.[1] Nationalism, both in the pan-Arab sense and as felt toward the newer individual nation-states, separate and distinct from Western or any other identity, is a powerful force. And despite the differences in wealth, the Arabs are all living in a developing world environment of rapid economic and political change in which a high priority is given to modernization.

What role do mass communication media play in these Arab societies? A basic assumption of this study is that a media system necessarily responds to and reflects its environment, particularly the existing political realities, but also economic, cultural, and other factors. Mass media facilities—radio, television, and the press—of course serve the function everywhere of disseminating messages from single originators to mass audiences, and their roles are circumscribed to that degree. But the precise function and structure of the media in a particular country can only be understood within the context of existing political and other factors in that country. Therefore, as there are some common cultural and other elements throughout the Arab world, there are some similarities in Arab media systems; and as there are political, economic, and other differences there are naturally differences among their media systems.

In this chapter we will look at some of the general characteristics of Arab mass media, and then in the next five chapters we will look at factors that make them different. First, how widespread are the mass media in the Arab world?

MASS MEDIA DENSITY IN THE ARAB WORLD

Newspapers and magazines are published in every one of the eighteen Arab countries, some of which have press traditions going back more than a century. The first Arab newspaper—the first periodical publication carrying news written by and for Arabs—was apparently *Jurnal al Iraq* that began appearing in Arabic and Turkish in Baghdad in 1816. Two Arab newspapers were published in Cairo in the 1820s; Algeria followed in 1847, Beirut in 1858, Tunis 1861, Damascus 1865, Tripoli (Libya) in 1866, San'a 1879, Casablanca 1889, Khartoum 1899, and Mecca 1908.[2] The first Arabic daily was published in Beirut in 1873.

Radio listening began in the 1920s, but the size of the audience was small until later decades and only some of the Arab states began their own radio broadcasting in the period before World War II. Television viewing began on a small scale in the late 1950s in Iraq and Lebanon, when those countries established TV transmitters in their capital cities. The only other Arabs who could watch television in the 1950s were those few who happened to be able to see non-Arab television: French TV could be seen by some Arabs in the Maghreb states of North Africa, U.S. military-operated TV could be seen by Libyans living near

Wheelus Air Force Base, and telecasts by the Arabian-American Oil Company could be seen by Saudis living near ARAMCO headquarters in Dhahran. Not until 1970, when Oman opened its radio transmitter, has every Arab state had indigenous radio broadcasting, and not until the fall of 1975 when Yemeni TV went on the air has every Arab state had its own indigenous television capability.[3]

Despite the long head start by the print media, the electronic media in the Arab world have by the 1970s spread much farther among the population, as Table 1 shows.

TABLE 1
Media Density
(1974–75 figures)

	population (millions)	radio receivers (1000s)	radio/1000 people	TV receivers (1000s)	TV/1000 people	literacy rate (%)	daily newspapers (no.)	total daily newspaper circ. (1000s)	copies of daily papers per 1000 people	weekly papers (no.)	GNP ($ billions)	per capita GNP ($)
Algeria	17	1,350	79	355	21	30	4	265	16	8	12.1	719
Bahrain	0.2	35	175	15	75	35	0	0	0	19	0.4	1,650
Egypt	38	7,000	184	960	25	30	7	833	22	7	9	240
Iraq	11	1,700	155	350	32	30	5	84	8	10	13	1,180
Jordan	2.7	1,700	56	225	83	38	0	40	15	7	0.8	328
Kuwait	0.9	500	500	200	200	60	6	65	77	29	9.6	10,060
Lebanon	3.1	1,500	520	410	150	86	30	222	72	198	1.5	500
Libya	2.5	200	80	6	2	27	3	21	8	0	6.5	3,010
Morocco	17.6	1,500	85	350	21	20	8	206	13	10	6	350
Oman	0.7	30	43	1	1.4	10	0	0	0	0	1.0	1,400
Qatar	0.2	20	100	32	160	15	1	2	10	3	2.1	110
Saudi Arabia	6	1,000	166	600	100	20	8	107	7	3	28	4,667
Sudan	18	780	43	74	4	10	2	170	9	6	1.6	100
Syria	7.5	1,370	183	425	61	50	6	134	18	7	2.1	300
Tunisia	5.8	400	69	200	34	35	5	139	24	2	3	530
UAE	0.3	50	167	17	57	20	2	8	27	8	4	16,600
Yemen AR	6.6	90	14	1	0.2	15	2	3.5	0.5	3	0.3	50
Yemen PDR	1.6	25	16	21	13	10	2	16	10	4	0.1	60
Total Arab	139	19,250	—	3,931	—	—	95	2,315.5	—	330	101.1	—

Sources: USIA Country Data Sheets, 1975; U.S. Department of State Background Notes; interviews with editors, information ministry officials, and independent observers in the Arab countries; data may be considered valid for purposes of general comparison.

In most Arab countries the people have relatively good access to radio and television, while the press remains primarily a medium reaching elite groups. This can be seen, for example, if we match the statistics against the minimum standards used by UNESCO, which suggested that every country should provide at least the following media facilities per thousand people: fifty radio receivers, twenty television receivers, and a hundred copies of daily newspapers.[4]

Most of the Arab countries have surpassed those minimum standards for both radio and television. Only the Sudan, the two Yemens, and Oman have not. They have been held back essentially by economic constraints, since they are all relatively poor countries which have had to devote their scarce resources to more urgent projects. In addition, the mountainous terrain in the southern part of the Arabian Peninsula has imposed special technical difficulties on the attempts by the Yemens and Oman to establish radio and television systems that reach mass audiences.

Radio listening is nearly universal in most Arab states (assuming 5–10 listeners per receiver) because of the availability of inexpensive transistorized receivers, the prevalence of group listening, and the great amount of international medium-wave broadcasting of interest to Arab audiences that takes place especially in the Mediterranean–Fertile Crescent area. Television, too, reaches a remarkable number of Arabs —probably more than 40 million—and has grown very rapidly in recent years. By comparison to other developing areas of the world, the Arabs have kept pace in radio listening but seem to be on the whole ahead in the extent of their television viewing.[5] The wealthy petroleum-exporting states especially have achieved relatively high radio and TV audience densities as their citizens have spent more and more money on receivers to tune in to their own national and some foreign stations (see Chapter 6).

The Arab press, on the other hand, still reaches only a highly select audience. Lebanon is the one Arab country which has surpassed the UNESCO minimum standard of daily newspaper circulation. Low literacy rates are the main inhibiting factor in newspaper circulation; Lebanon's 86 percent literacy rate is far ahead of that in most Arab countries, and newspaper circulation is quite low elsewhere. It is probably as high as it is in Kuwait and the UAE because these are small wealthy states with small populations which are largely urbanized and have many literate, newspaper-reading expatriate Arabs working and living there. Egypt and Syria are not as low as some others in circulation because they, like Lebanon, have a long tradition of newspaper publishing and reading.

The Arab press has always been written for an elite audience. Twenty-five years ago an Egyptian newspaper had the highest circulation of any Arab daily with 7,000 copies, and most dailies did not surpass 2,000.[6] The total number of Arab newspaper readers in the 1970s is still relatively small; each copy may be read by an average of two to six people, depending on the paper and location, but many readers see more than one paper. Therefore there are probably not many more than six or seven million regular newspaper readers in the Arab world, or under 5 percent of the population. Not all of the Arab states have had enough newspaper readers to sustain indigenous daily papers; Qatar and Bahrain did not have successful dailies until 1975 and 1976, respectively, and Oman still did not as of 1979. Half of the Arab countries have daily newspapers which distribute between ten and fifty thousand copies and five countries have dailies only in the 1–10,000 range. Only Egypt has dailies which distribute more than a quarter million copies.

CONDITIONS AFFECTING ARAB MASS MEDIA

What special circumstances and conditions have affected the mass media generally in the Arab world?

Weak Economic Base

Arab information media have by and large been established on a weak economic base. Newspapers developed when the national incomes and populations were small, and the literacy rates were low. Thus both advertising revenues and mass-circulation sales, the two main sources of commercial newspaper income, were precluded. Even after World War II, as the Arab economies developed, advertising did not become important enough to Arab businessmen, or promising enough in the modest-circulation press, to help newspaper publishers very much. A few publishers, like Cairo's al Ahram Publishing House, have been able to expand their operations into printing periodicals and books in their own plants, advertising, and distributing foreign publications, but the majority of daily newspapers has a far more modest financial base. The short supply of newsprint, other printing costs, plus the various limitations on distribution such as political differences and poor domestic and international transport facilities work against the publisher who is trying to make a profit from his newspaper. The daily paper is no longer an expensive luxury for the middle class throughout the area, as it was in the early 1950s,[7] but price and illiteracy are still keeping circulation figures and income down.

High costs are even more restrictive in the case of the electronic media, which are considerably more expensive to operate, and in most cases private Arab entrepreneurs have not been able to afford such an undertaking. This is a major reason why most radio and television stations are monopolies owned by the government.

Politicization

Arab information media have always been closely tied to politics. The first newspapers that appeared in the Arab world were not private but official government publications intended to tell government bureaucrats and the people what the government wanted them to hear. The newspaper Napoleon printed in Egypt on his own presses starting in 1798, *Courier de l'Egypte,* was intended to inform and instruct French expeditionary forces and improve their morale.[8] The first indigenous Egyptian papers, *Jurnal al Khadyu* and *al Waqa'i' al Masriyah,* which began in 1827 and 1828, were published by the Egyptian government. They contained news and entertainment, such as stories from "A Thousand and One Nights", but they also contained official government guidance and authorized editorials. Similarly, the first newspapers that appeared elsewhere in the Arab world at that time also were official organs of the authorities. *Jurnal al Iraq,* which began in 1816 in Baghdad, was issued by the government for the army, the bureaucracy, and the literate population. *Al Mubashir* which started in Algeria in 1847 was an official bi-weekly; *al Ra'id al Tunisi* was begun by the Tunisian authorities in 1861, *Suriya* by the authorities in Damascus in 1865, *Trablus al Maghrib* by the authorities in Tripoli in 1866, *al Zura* by the government in Baghdad in 1869, *San'a* by the government in Yemen in 1879, *al Sudaniyah,* by the government in the Sudan in 1899, and *al Hijaz,* by the Ottoman representatives in Mecca in 1908.[9]

A very few newspapers were published by private individuals or families in the nineteenth century but these appeared only in Egypt, Syria, Lebanon, and Morocco. Khalil Khuri printed *Hadiqat al Akhbar* in Beirut in 1858; *Wadi al Nil* and *al Ahram* appeared in Egypt in 1867 and 1876, respectively, and *al Maghrib* started in Morocco in 1889. As one student of the press has observed: "We can say that the Arab press [in the nineteenth century] was published officially except for a few places like Lebanon and Morocco, and the press was influenced by this official character in that from the point of view of the reader it expressed the opinion and biases of the government. . . . Arab journalists working under Ottoman rule realized it was a tool for battle and revolution."[10]

Arab governments tended to control the early newspapers and colonial administrations in the Arab world sought to do the same, also for political reasons. With the growth of Arab nationalism in the twentieth century, Arab newspapers were attracted to this cause in opposition to colonial rule; they were thus drawn into political issues, and the nationalism/anti-imperialism theme has remained strong in Arab media to this day. The fact that the British and French had a tradition of free press at home made, in most cases, less of an impact on media development on Arab areas under their control than did the overriding issue of nationalism and politicization of institutions. As radio became technologically feasible for mass broadcasting, most of the governments recognized its importance also, and controlled it as well.

In recent years, changing political conditions, differences over policy, changes of regime, and changes of political system have helped to focus attention on the value of the media for political purposes. Periods of tension and instability have made governments especially concerned about the influence of the media and their control. Radio stations —and today also television facilities—are prime targets of revolutionaries, who typically seize them first in any move to take power. Consequently, Arab regimes take special care to protect them carefully with military guards against such politically significant eventualities.

Arab governments since World War II have increased their influence and control over the mass media in part with the justification that their newly independent nations face overwhelming external and internal problems requiring unity and purposefulness and a minimum of dissent in the public debate. The country cannot afford, so the argument goes, the luxury of partisan conflict, and the media must further the national interest by supporting governmental policies.

This argument is used in connection with economic development and other domestic problems, but the most common focus of such reasoning has been the Arab-Israeli conflict. This conflict has been the single major political preoccupation for the Arab world since the late 1940s. Every Arab government has had to deal with it and has felt compelled to declare its support for the "struggle" against the Israeli enemy, calling upon citizens to sacrifice for the sake of this vital national cause. In this context, Arab governments have been able to justify explicitly and implicitly their influence over the mass media as necessary "while the country is at war" with Israel. Because of the degree to which the Arab-Israeli dispute has become the central issue and a matter of Arab patriotism, this justification is difficult to oppose.

Cultural Influence

Historically, the Arab press has had a strong tie to Arab culture. Arab literature—poetry, tales, and stories—predated mass media by more than a millennium and had developed a very rich tradition by the time the first newspapers appeared. The publishers of these papers, influenced to some extent by the example of the contemporary French newspapers which were heavily cultural in content, quite naturally regarded the Arab press as a proper vehicle for Arab literature.

CONSEQUENCES FOR ARAB MEDIA

Economic, political, and cultural factors have influenced the character and shape of the Arab mass media in several ways.

Political Patronization

The weak economic base of the newspapers has led many of them to seek financial support from a variety of government and private sources, and recognition of the political importance of the press has encouraged patronization. Many private newspapers throughout the Arab world have been able to survive only because they have been subsidized, openly or otherwise, by outside elements. Subsidization may take the form of across-the-board payments by the government to all media, government ads, or material benefits such as low postage rates, contributions from political parties, businessmen, or individuals, or secret payments from local or even foreign groups. Because some of this subsidization is kept secret, it is difficult to know the exact magnitude and nature of it, although attempts have been made to get some idea by calculating the budgets of individual newspapers and assuming that those in the red must receive hidden revenues.[11]

Subsidization may, of course, be directly related to media content. Many of the first Arab newspapers in the nineteenth century were financed by government and then political party interests, in order to promote the views of that particular interest. Even private newspaper owners, finding themselves in need of additional financial resources to keep their journal going, "shopped around among elements" in this community with which it agreed politically and philosophically, in order to find backers. Usually like-minded patrons were found, so the newspaper owner did not have to give up his principles and alter editorial policy to obtain funds, but occasionally that happened as well.[12]

Many newspapers were able to survive without patronage, and still others were party newspapers and openly labeled as such. The latter tended not only to follow party guidance in editorial policies, but to staff the paper with loyal party types also. Right after World War II the Arab press had many more truly "party" newspapers than it does today, and at that time observers compared it to the American press before 1860.[13] The numerous, small enterprise, highly partisan newspapers that dominated American journalism in the years after the American Revolution were quite similar to those that appeared in the Arab world as the Arab states emerged from colonial domination and wrestled with the basic questions of national political organization. Partisan journalism in the United States, which emerged after the American Revolution, increased during the thirty years before the Civil War so that every party schism or prominent new political leader brought with it a new newspaper: "politicians arranged such newspaper affiliations with care, and considered them essential to success."[14] The Arab world has seen such arrangements also.

The proportion of party-affiliated newspapers has decreased in the last twenty years, and there has been some increase in the information function of the press, aimed at a mass audience. But the press as a whole, and even more so the electronic media, have not developed in the direction of American big business, mass-oriented media as some observers thought they might. It is still true that "all Arab daily papers are partly business and party politics, but the politics is dominant."[15]

Patronization is still a major feature of the Arab press, but it has become primarily a function of governments. As we will see in subsequent chapters in many countries the regime and its agents have taken over the exclusive right to patronize the politically important newspapers, excluding political parties and other private groups from patronizing them. Radio and television, too, have been sponsored almost without exception by governments, because of their considerably higher cost, the limited number of broadcast frequencies, and broader (mass) political importance they are assumed to have.

In short, all of the media have been susceptible to political influence of one kind or another, particularly, in recent years, by strong national governments. It must be remembered, however, that not all of the content of a newspaper or broadcast can be politicized; a large proportion of it, as we shall see below, is cultural and otherwise nonpolitical.

Fragmentation

Secondly, the factors mentioned above have led to considerable fragmentation in the Arab media. The development of the press in various periods of political conflict and competition, with the support of various political and individual factions, has led to a proliferation of newspapers in most Arab countries beyond the number warranted by literacy rates. Although the overabundance of newspapers was more of a problem in the earlier decades of the twentieth century when political parties and factions were emerging more rapidly, it is still a problem in Lebanon, for example, and the tendency affects other Arab states as well. There are more newspaper conglomerates than there used to be (Cairo's al Ahram Publishing House is the largest), but these are exceptional still, and many governments have attempted to consolidate the press in recent years. Moreover, looking at the Arab world as a whole, most daily newspapers are limited in circulation to one country because of restrictions on importation of papers frequently imposed by governments seeking to keep out hostile ideas, and because of the weakness of transportation/distribution systems throughout the area. Radio and television are less hampered by these barriers, but they too are fragmented along state lines because no Arab government wants these media to be controlled in any way by other countries, so that even two small adjacent states like Bahrain and Qatar have completely separate radio and TV systems. There is no pan-Arab broadcasting station, and attempts at cooperation among national systems have not met with much success.

In addition, there have in the past been relatively high birth and death rates for Arab newspapers, although the situation has stabilized somewhat in recent years. It is no longer possible to "start an Egyptian paper on a shoestring"[16] as it was in the late 1940s, but political change in the Arab countries has and still does bring with it turnovers in newspapers. The Arab states that went through the most political change after World War II experienced the rise and fall of so many newspapers that it would be difficult to chronicle them all. With greater political stability in the 1960s and 1970s has come a much greater longevity in newspapers. Radio and television, which grew up in this latter period and which require much greater financial resources, have changed hands very little once established.

Geographic Concentration

A third consequence of the abovementioned factors is the tendency of the media to concentrate in the more densely populated urban centers of the Arab world. Close ties with both politics and cultural expression, plus such economic factors as low literacy rates, little advertising, and weaknesses in distribution systems, have encouraged Arab newspapers to grow in the cities but not so well in the provincial areas. In most Arab countries, one city serves as the political, economic, and commercial center, and all daily newspapers plus all radio and television broadcasting emanate from that city. The Arab world has no equivalent of New York City, where economic and commercial activity attracted the most press and information facilities from the start, despite the growth of the central government elsewhere, and they stayed in New York. Jidda and Alexandria began that way, but later the national political capitals in Riyadh and Cairo caught up in media development. In these countries and in a few others (Syria, Morocco, Algeria, and Yemen) a second city is economically important, and they have important daily newspapers, too, but there are no dailies or broadcast programming of national significance outside these two cities. Radio listening of course extends throughout the country but newspaper reading and television viewing tends to be concentrated in a few urban areas.

Media Credibility and Low Prestige of Journalism

As a result of many of these factors, news journalism as a profession has been slow to develop and has not achieved the high status that it has in the West, for example. Political influences on the media, their relative economic weakness, and the absence of an independent "Fourth Estate" concept of the profession have made journalism a less attractive profession than many others in the Arab world. Although there are today many competent Arab professional journalists, the economic and sometimes political risk in entering the profession has to some extent kept talented people away from it. A shortage of trained personnel is a basic problem for all Arab countries, and the economic and political pressures on journalism merely make the situation worse for the media. Schools of journalism are few and recently established, so most media staff have learned their trade on the job. Many media personnel, especially in the smaller newspapers, must supplement their incomes by working concurrently at other jobs, and their professionalism suffers. Although media units are generally on a larger scale and more prosperous than they were in the late forties[17] and professionalism has increased, still it remains a problem in many places.

Only a handful of news journalists in the entire Arab world have become famous and respected throughout the area, partly because of the limited distribution of the media, but also because so many journalists are suspected of being merely spokesmen, mouthpieces, or "hired pens" of one political group or another. Muhammad Hassanain Haykal, the most widely read journalist in the Arab world in modern times, gained his popularity not only by his facility with the Arabic language —which is conceded even by his critics—but also because his readers were convinced that he was such a close friend of Egypt's President Nasser that he was in effect speaking for Nasser, the most important leader in the Arab world. Thousands of Arabs read his weekly column and followed the news in the daily paper he edited, not as much for factual reporting and objective analysis as for clues about what the Egyptian regime was thinking and doing.

There are newspapers, such as Beirut's *al Nahar*, which have achieved reputations for relative objectivity in news reporting, although their columnists are known for their various political biases.[18] But typically the news treatment as well as the commentaries of a newspaper or broadcasting station will be regarded by the audience with a large measure of defensive skepticism, akin to that of an American toward a commercial advertisement. Certainly the most sophisticated groups, and to a large extent other people as well, do not accept the news in the mass media entirely at face value, but assume that it may not be completely objective or reliable. They read between the lines, looking for significant omissions and implied meanings. The credibility for the news writers and political columnists in the media tends to be lower than in the West. They are frequently suspected of being politically motivated rather than professionals dedicated solely to accurate, factual reporting and enlightenment of the public. Journalism ranks relatively low in prestige except for the handful of prominent columnists in each country—usually fewer than a half dozen—who write the signed political analyses that appear in the daily press. Most of them are chief editors as well, and their relationship to the regime in power is a very important political factor, as we shall see in subsequent chapters.

In the electronic media, the professionals who read the news regularly gain some prominence and prestige, but reporters and commentators are generally unknown.

The rank and file of Arab reporters, writers, and copy editors in all the media tend to be unknown to the public, and their profession is not one to which large numbers aspire. In addition to their relatively low prestige (compared to the profession in the United States, for example), Arab journalism suffers from low pay and a shortage of trained personnel prevalent in most Arab societies in this period of rapid economic growth. Moonlighting and part-time journalism is common. Mastery of the Arabic language as such seems to be a sufficient prerequisite for entering the profession, and other necessary skills are learned on the job. In the 1960s and 1970s the profession did gain some prestige, especially with the spread of the newer electronic media, but it still has not achieved the status that it has in the West.

The quality of journalism varies considerably throughout the Arab world, and local characteristics will be discussed in subsequent chapters. Suffice it to say here that the areas where the mass media developed more recently and which are today expanding most quickly— particularly the small states along the Persian Gulf—have attracted many Palestinians, Egyptians, and others who have been trained as professional journalists in areas with long press traditions; some surplus of talent is available. They are attracted by the high salaries paid by the oil-rich states which are promoting mass media expansion as fast as possible. Thus the radio and television stations as well as the newspaper offices in Bahrain, Qatar, Abu Dhabi, Dubai—and to some extent still in Kuwait—are in the 1970s full of non-Gulf Arab media professionals, including some of the most qualified in the Arab world. They have in a very short time raised the standards of journalism, at least technically, to compete with the much older media in other parts of the Arab world. The movement of journalists around the Arab world is not new; Egypt's famous *al Ahram* newspaper was founded, for example, by two Lebanese in 1875. But the direction of movement is primarily toward the newly rich states on the Persian Gulf. Standards of journalism on those areas are consequently rising rapidly.

Continued Importance of Oral Communication

A fifth consequence of the circumstances mentioned above is that despite the widespread and recently quite rapid growth of mass communications media in the Arab world, oral communication channels remain extremely important throughout the area.

Arabs seek information through oral communication in a number of forums. First of all, families tend to be close, stay in contact, and discuss a variety of matters among themselves on a regular basis. Secondly, trusted friends supplement the family as a group of people who can also be relied upon to supply useful information. It is common in contemporary Arab society to find informal circles of friends—usually not more than a dozen—who meet regularly and talk frankly about public affairs as well as private concerns. Opinions are formed and information is exchanged in these sessions in ways that the mass media do not and cannot duplicate. In these groups, known as *shillas* or by various other names,[19] trusted friends talk openly about matters that are politically or otherwise too sensitive to appear in any detail in the press or on the radio, and they depend on these informal gatherings to supplement the mass media. Thirdly, face-to-face oral communication takes place more broadly in Arab society among acquaintances meeting privately, and among people meeting in semi-public places, such as at work and in the bazaar, the coffeehouse, or the mosque. Information and opinion of a political and non-political nature is exchanged in these forums as well.[20]

Face-to-face spoken communication has always been very important in Arab society, and the traditional reliance on information from friends and personally known individuals has continued as a strong preference among Arabs. Information from the impersonal mass media is not necessarily trusted more just because it is printed or broadcast, in fact its credibility is in some cases lower because the source is remote. Trusted friends are believed; they do not have the credibility problems the mass media suffer from. In addition, of course, the mass media do not reach Arabs uniformly, so many must depend quite heavily on oral communication. Literate, urban Arabs who can afford television and radio have access to all mass media channels, but illiteracy, rural residence, and poverty reduce these opportunities for many other Arabs, who consequently must depend more on word of mouth for their information. For these reasons, direct oral communication continues to be important throughout the Arab world as a channel for information which coexists with and supplements the mass media.

Variations among Countries

It must be emphasized that although some characteristics are shared by media throughout the Arab world, there are of course many

ARAB INFORMATION MEDIA   15

differences between countries and some within each country. As we
shall see in subsequent chapters, the mass communications media have
emerged in different ways depending on a variety of factors. The press
went through different historical evolutionary patterns; the early development of the press in Lebanon, Egypt, and elsewhere was not, for
example, followed until much later in the Arabian Peninsula. For economic reasons, such as the sudden rise of petroleum wealth after World
War II in some Arab states, those states accelerated their media expansion, particularly in radio and television which were concurrently coming into use, so that the oil-producing states have acquired some of the
most modern equipment and some of the best personnel in the area.
Connections and ties with other countries have also affected media development. North Africa's long French connection has, for example,
left behind media systems which are still nearly half in French and only
slowly being Arabized. And political conditions profoundly affect the
functioning of the media, so that the latter vary in their operation as do
the former.

MEDIA FUNCTIONS

The Arab mass media perform generally the same basic functions as media elsewhere, but in different ways. The basic functions of media can
be defined as follows: (1) conveying news and information of general
interest; (2) interpreting and commenting on events, providing opinion
and perspectives; (3) reinforcing social norms and cultural awareness
by transmitting information about the society and its culture; (4) providing specialized information for commercial promotion (advertising)
or available services; and (5) entertaining. [21] How do Arab media carry
out these functions?

By and large, the Arab media follow the same format as media
elsewhere in the world, and there are superficial similarities. Arab radio stations typically broadcast 18 or 20 hours per day, of which less
than 20 percent is devoted to news and commentary, either in two or
three long newscasts or in shorter ones throughout the day. The Arab
radio listener can hear his own country's single national network
throughout the day, and after sundown (because signal propagation
improves then), the listener usually has a choice of several regional stations from neighboring countries. Most Arab television stations are on
the air from about 6 P.M. until midnight, with an additional afternoon
program on weekends. News is typically confined to two 20-minute

bulletins, sometimes followed by a comment, but a few stations devote more attention to these topics.

Arab daily newspapers average eight to ten pages in length, which is somewhat more than the four to six pages of the 1940s[22] but nowhere near the bulk of a successful Western daily. Their size and printing are similar to Western papers everywhere except in the poorly developed countries like Yemen where smaller, badly printed sheets without photographs are the only ones available. Page one is usually devoted to major national, government, regional, and international news and to the lead editorial. Headlines tend to be bolder and longer than in the Western press, and news stories tend to be shorter, with less detail and background. Inside, the Arab newspaper usually has another page of international news and one or two more of local news, plus additional editorials—there is typically no editorial page—a page or two of features on sports, science, women's affairs, and culture. Larger papers carry classified ads. Personal notes on comings and goings of prominent citizens generally appear in a special column with stock photos and are popular with readers in this highly personalized society. Some of the more successful dailies, for example in Lebanon and Egypt, have weekly supplements containing features on the arts, cinema, literature, and history. Most dailies actually publish six times per week and do not appear on either Friday, Saturday, or Sunday; the weekly supplement, if there is one, usually appears on that off day.

It is not in format, however, that Arab media differ most from other media elsewhere, but in content. How are each of the five functions mentioned above handled?

News and Commentary Functions

We shall examine the first and second functions, news and commentary, together. Newshandling and the role of commentaries will be a major theme in all subsequent chapters because they are key manifestations of the relationship between the media and the political environment. Here we will make a few generalizations that seem to apply throughout the Arab world. Since very few systematic content analyses have been made of Arab media, these generalizations are based primarily on the conclusions of qualified observers who have extensive familiarity with the media themselves.

Arab newspapers and radio stations tend to be more obvious in their editorial comment than American papers and radio broadcasts do;

Arab television generally carries somewhat less commentary, but total air time is much shorter than in the United States.[23]

In their interpretive, or opinion function, Arab media are very active but they perform it somewhat differently from Western media. Much more rarely do the Arab media meet the ideal expressed for American journalism in this regard, of providing "a forum for the exchange of comment and criticism."[24] Specific opinions, attitudes and articulation of goals which are expressed in Arab media are usually those of a small elite group, but there is not much two-way exchange. Letters to the editor are rarely published. Non-governmental sentiment is sometimes expressed, but it is filtered through a few editors, so the flow of opinions is rather restricted.

The concept of the watchdog function of the media acting for the public against the government is manifest only in limited ways in the Arab world. However, looking at the Arab world as a whole, an exchange of opinion between groups does take place between Arab countries, whose elites speak to each other, in effect, via radio and to some extent via press and television. These elites have differing views, and they are not uncritical of each other.

The content of the news is a complex subject. One professional American journalist, in writing about the media in an Arab country, concluded that there was "scarcely any distinction between news and editorial matter,"[25] by which he implied that Arab editors do not follow the ideal of contemporary American journalism which is to strictly separate news and commentary. This judgment is a broad generalization that must be qualified and made more specific. It is true that the Arab editor in performing his function of selecting news items, and positioning them in a newspaper or in a broadcast, may from time to time do so in a way that reflects opinions which are also expressed in that medium's commentaries. The editor can do this in many ways—by omitting parts of the story, by emphasizing other parts by putting them in the lead paragraph or headline, by juxtaposing elements of the story to create a certain impression, by printing as unattributed fact information from only one source on a controversial issue, by uncritically publishing information from a doubtful source, or by outright fabricating. Arab editors have at one time or another done all of these. Their reasons vary.

The most common reason is that the editor's perceptions of events, which are determined by his own experience and his cultural, economic, and political environment, cause him to make certain choices in the presentation of news. This cultural bias is the major reason for a given medium's particular slant on the news. It leads to similarities within a given Arab country and also on another level within the Arab world, in the news-handling function of the media.

The second most important important factor influencing Arab editors in their news presentation is political bias. That is, in presenting the news they sometimes make choices because of prevailing political factors, such as the policies and preferences of the government. The editor may do this in order to support a government he favors or simply to avoid trouble with a government he fears. Political bias is usually a conscious act in which the editor has deliberately compromised the truth as he saw it because of the consequences of presenting the truth. Cultural bias, by contrast, is usually unconscious conformity with accepted norms. The extent of political bias varies greatly in the Arab world; in some places it affects very little of the newspaper or broadcast, in others it permeates all parts of them.

Distortions in news-handling also occur, of course, because of error or sloppy journalism, when the reporter or editor fails to do his job properly and does not obtain all the facts or present them strictly according to their merits. Such distortions occur throughout the area, but they are relatively rare in those countries which have had time to develop the profession.

How truthful is the news in the Arab media? The answer depends partly on the definition of truthfulness. As we have seen, there may be some inadvertent misstatement of fact resulting from poor journalism, which is not deliberate untruthfulness; and there is cultural bias, which leads Arab editors to make choices different from editors elsewhere simply because of the way they see the world. They are not being deliberately untruthful but rather honestly expressing their different perceptions. If these two types of influence over news selection are put aside, leaving deliberate political bias as the only real type of untruthful news distortion, we see that the majority of the news in Arab media is basically unaffected by it, and straight.

It is true that many of the major *political* news stories in many of the Arab countries are affected in some way by political bias, and that Arab readers can in some cases detect that bias by reading the front page of the newspaper or listening to a newscast, provided they have other sources of news for comparison.[26] It is also true that many news stories in Arab media do not entirely measure up to the ideal that some have set for the American press, for example, of a "truthful, comprehensive, and intelligent account of the day's events in a context which gives them meaning."[27] However, the bulk of the material in a given newspaper or on a given broadcast day is factual. The Arab media perform the function of presenting facts about events in order to inform their audiences, and it is probably fair to say that most of these facts conform to reality. The facts are accepted with a degree of skepticism, as noted above, and supplemented by oral communication, but they provide the basis for information exchange for most of the community on a wide range of subjects.

Cultural Reinforcement Function

Arab media also perform the function of reinforcing Arab cultural values, defined broadly as those values learned by an individual because he is an Arab. As noted above, the media present information in ways that are understandable only by reference to local social, political, and other factors. Thus they help reinforce the attitudes and perceptions of the society, or more precisely of its majority.[28] In addition, although some believe the mass media today are destroying classical Arabic culture by trying to popularize it or by promoting colloquial forms, it can be argued that the media transmit some of those values of Arab culture more narrowly defined as a heritage in creative endeavor and thought. A sophisticated and complex Arab culture developed hundreds of years before the advent of the mass media. It was logical that the media would be influenced from the beginning by the rich Arab intellectual tradition in literature, religion, philosophy, and music. Communicators in those fields were well established in Arab society, so naturally many of the earliest Arab newspapers in the nineteenth century resembled the political-literary journals being published at the time in Europe. The latter were being imitated in form if not in content, and in this way the Arab writers and poets found outlets in the press for their creativity.[29]

Even today, much of the content of the Arab media is created not by professional journalists in the modern sense but by educated Arabs who have careers outside the mass media. Non-political authors have gained wide prominence and respect by writing poetry and stories for the press and plays for television and radio. Arab newspapers generally carry more literature than do Western ones, and it is not uncommon for prominent local literary figures to write for the newspapers and the electronic media. In Egypt, for example, the noted writer and theological reformer Shaikh Muhammad Abduh first became known through his columns in *al Ahram* newspaper, and more recently the press has given considerable space to the fiction—and to the current affairs comments —of literati who are well known throughout the Arab world (see Chapter 2). Several of these writers are on regular newspaper staff payrolls, and a few have even become chief editors.[30]

By giving considerable time and space to literature, Arab media help to reinforce Arab cultural identity. The same function is performed by the electronic media in carrying a great deal of Arab music as well as dramas on traditional themes. The music is both traditional and modern, and is performed by local artists and artists known throughout the area, such as Um Kalthoum. In many Arab countries such programs take up hours of prime time on television as well as on radio. Similarly, readings from the Koran are broadcast regularly by stations all over the Arab world, and in some places religious commentaries or advice on proper moral and ethical behavior are featured on radio and TV.[31]

The Arabic Language

The language used in the media also serves the function of communicating cultural identity. Indeed, the Arabic language is an especially crucial element linking the Arabs with each other and with their culture; it is inseparable from Arab culture, history, tradition, and Islam, the religion of the vast majority of Arabs. The best definition of who is an Arab is not in terms of religion or geography but of language and consciousness—that is, one who speaks Arabic and considers himself an Arab. Arabic is extremely important to Arabs; they pay considerable attention to the language, and it shapes their thinking in many ways. There is an "intimate interdependence" between Arabic and the Arab psychology and culture, and, thus, as carriers of the language, the mass media are very important in the communication of Arab cultural commonality. As the historian Philip Hitti says, "no people in the world has such enthusiastic admiration for literary expression and is so moved by the word, spoken or written, as the Arabs."[32]

There are several reasons for the fact that language carries special meaning for Arabs. First, Arabic is intimately connected with Islam; the Koran is accepted as the highest linguistic achievement in the language and remains after more than thirteen centuries the standard for good usage today. Secondly, there is a close association between Arabic and an historic past in which Arabs take pride; they are proud to use the language of their illustrious ancestors. Thirdly, Arabic is an essential element today in their very strong concept of an "Arab nation," that is, pan-Arabism to which leaders continuously vow their allegiance. Even the Arabic word for *foreigner (ajnabi)* is usually used today to mean *non-Arab* foreigner only. And finally, Arabs love their language because of its intrinsic beauty quite apart from the meaning it conveys. Arabic is filled with what speakers of English would consider exaggeration and repetition. Observers have noted a kind of "magical power ascribed consciously and/or unconsciously to words" in Arabic and so much attention to the language itself that there is a "tendency to fit the thought to the word" rather than the reverse.[33]

For all of these reasons, the mass media which use Arabic have a particular impact on their audience, which a literal translation into English cannot convey. The importance of the language itself helps shape the content of the media. Whereas the American journalist seems to have a passion for factual details and statistics, the Arab journalist by contrast seems to give more attention to the correct words, phrasing, and grammar he should use in describing an event. It would be oversimplifying to say that "It is a characteristic of the Arab mind to be swayed more by words than by ideas and more by ideas than by facts,"[34] but a tendency in that direction can be seen in the style of the mass media.

Two Levels of Cultural Reinforcement

Arab media may be unique in that they convey sociocultural values on two levels, namely to the large pan-Arab audience and to the smaller nation-state one. A great deal that is of cultural value to an individual Arab is commonly shared with other Arabs throughout the area. Arab media convey such cultural messages. On the other hand, other cultural aspects are strictly local and are shared only with others who live within the borders of a country or region. Arab media also convey effectively these local Arab values. For example, the media in Saudi Arabia do not carry pictures of adult Saudi women because they are still required to wear the veil in public, but they do carry pictures of women from other Arab countries. Thus all Arab newspapers and radio or TV broadcasts carry sociocultural characteristics of their country of origin, and they also carry sufficient pan-Arab "flavor" to make them familiar to Arabs everywhere.

The duality of this cultural identification function can be seen clearly in the language used by the media. The Arabic language used in newspapers throughout the Arab world is a modified and somewhat modernized form of "classical" or literary Arabic which is universally understood by educated Arabs. Moroccans and Saudis and Lebanese who can read Arabic are able to read each others' newspapers just as they can all read the Koran, the highest authority for classical Arabic. Similarly radio and television throughout the area use the same slightly modified classical Arabic for all news and other serious programming. There are some minor differences in the accents of professional radio and TV people from country to country, but these are little more than exist in the United States, and they are all understood.

Simultaneously the media use colloquial Arabic for special purposes. Each local dialect, derived originally from the classical, has been modified so much over the years that it is only understood well by the local group that uses it. This colloquial Arabic appears only to a very limited extent in the printed media—for example in some cartoon captions, short stories, and quotations of spoken Arabic—because it is not generally considered appropriate to write it down. However, it is used extensively in radio and television, particularly when dealing with less serious subjects. Some interviews and discussions about local matters, vernacular plays and soap operas, comedy routines, and other programs which are intended for the local audience are usually in colloquial Arabic. And it is not uncommon for a national leader, when making a political speech broadcast on radio and television, to sprinkle his rhetoric with colloquial phrases designed to develop rapport with his audience, although it is considered more correct for the main body of the speech to be in classical Arabic. President Nasser, for example, often began formally in classical Arabic but increased his use of Egyptian colloquialisms as he warmed up to his listeners; however, the printed version of his text that appeared in the newspapers the following day did not give that localized flavor.

Thus the media communicate in modified classical Arabic horizontally to educated elite groups throughout the Arab world, and at the same time they communicate vertically to literate and illiterate members of their respective nations. It is also a characteristic of the language that the colloquial varieties, while differing from each other, use words that are quite concrete and tangible in their meaning. The classical, on the other hand, has a great capacity for vagueness, ambiguity, and exaggeration. As a result, newspaper editorials dealing with more abstract subjects are especially difficult to pin down as to their precise meaning. They convey a sense of what the writer is thinking but with far less economy than an editorial by a native English speaker.[35] Such ambiguity and vagueness in the interpretive function is a characteristic of Arab media. One important complicating factor in Morocco, Algeria, and Tunisia is the extensive use of French due to earlier colonial ties and continued cultural connections with France. In the early years of independence, roughly half or more of the press and the radio and television air time in these countries was in French because so many people especially in the elite groups had learned French in school and used it in their work. The three governments have deliberately promoted Arabization policies, and the balance has shifted in favor of Arabic, but still a large segment of the media uses French. In Algeria, for example, where half of the 30 percent literate population are literate only in French and another third are literate in French and Arabic, it is understandable that *el Moudjahid,* politically the most important daily, is still written primarily in French (it began as an all-French paper[36]).

Those Arab media which convey their message in French perform a somewhat different function, because of the added filter of French. The effect is complex, but in general Arabs who communicate in French tend to convey ideas and values that are part Arab and part French, thereby keeping French perceptions alive in the society. To a limited extent this occurs in Lebanon also, where some radio and television broadcasts and an important newspaper are presented in French. In the rest of the Arab world, however, all major mass media are essentially in the Arabic language.[37]

Advertising and Entertainment Functions

The two functions just discussed—interpretation and socialization—tend to overlap with and permeate all other functions, even the entertainment and advertising. Thus the type and amounts of entertainment and advertising presented are governed by local social and cultural norms and even by political conditions, so their presentation helps reinforce those norms and conditions.

Entertainment per se plays a relatively small role in the Arab press. The few cartoons that appear are usually political, and the only comic strips are the few translated from English that a handful of papers publish; puzzles and quizzes are rare. The newspapers do print fiction and even poetry, but this can be considered as much cultural as entertaining. The press is regarded primarily as a serious vehicle for news, information, and opinion intended to be read by the literate elites, not as entertainment.[38]

Because radio and television are mass-oriented media, they generally devote a majority of their time to entertainment, but the entertainment programs usually do more than just entertain. Popular radio and TV dramas not only convey ideas about Arab society, but often they are frankly political, communicating themes that relate directly to current political questions such as the Arab-Israeli conflict, anti-imperialism, etc. Popular songs do the same; for example Egypt's famous singer Um Kalthoum broadcast some patriotic songs at the time of the 1967 Middle East war which were especially written to exhort Arab soldiers to greater efforts.

As for the advertising function, it, too, is affected by other factors. Commercial advertising plays a relatively small role in the Arab press, as contrasted, for example, with the American press. Whereas the latter is run as a business enterprise in a consumer-oriented advertising-dependent system, the Arab press is regarded as having primarily other purposes such as information and interpretation, with advertising clearly a subordinate or even marginal function. Commercial advertising revenues make up only a minor part of a typical newspaper's budget, although government ads are important in some places. Arab radio and television take this even further, and nearly all stations exclude commercial ads entirely because they are government-owned stations which receive all of their income from the government. Aside from commercial advertising of consumer goods, the Arab daily press generally serves as what has been called "bulletin board for the modern sector,"[39] announcing filmshows and other local public events, but this function is limited.

MEDIA SYSTEMS

How should we classify Arab media systems? How are the media structured? Who controls them and for what purpose? What is the theory, or theories, behind Arab media?

To answer those questions it is not enough to look at the legal status of the press and the electronic media. In the Arab world, press and broadcasting laws do not reveal all the details of who decides the content of a newspaper editorial and why. In fact, looking at the laws alone may obscure the real dynamics of the system, because the laws tend to imply that the media are freer than they really are, and they do not mention some essential extralegal influences. In the Arab world, that system cannot be understood without specific reference to political and other conditions prevailing at the time in the country. Such factors as the existence of open political opposition groups and/or parties, the strength and legitimacy of the ruling group, its character (revolution-ary or traditional, for example), the stability of the political system, the perception of an external threat, the existence of a tradition of journal-ism and a Fourth Estate, and the economic strength of the media are all very important influences on the structure of the media.

The Arab media system and the "theory" under which it operates tend to grow out of such political, economic, and other realities that prevail in that country. We must therefore look more closely at the indi-vidual countries to see how their media systems operate, and we will do that in Chapters 2–6.

Can we make *any* generalizations about Arab media systems? Can we classify them under any of the categories used by students of other mass media? One standard classification is the four-fold one of (1) au-thoritarian, (2) libertarian, (3) social responsibility, and (4) totalitar-ian.[40] The Arab media do not fit neatly and completely into any one of those categories, and there are some elements of all four present in the Arab world. However in most—but not all—of the Arab countries the media operate under variations of the authoritarian theory, and of the four theories, this one comes closest to explaining what is taking place. (These countries tend to have authoritarian governments also, based on the same general theory.)

In the authoritarian system, the media support and advance the policies of the government, which controls the media either directly or indirectly through licensing, legal action, or perhaps financial means. The regime allows the media some discussion of society and the ma-chinery of government, but not of the people in power. This system is based on the theory that truth is "not the product of a great mass of peo-ple, but of a few wise men . . . in a position to guide and direct their fellows."[41] Comment and criticism are carefully guided, and articu-lated goals for the community conform with goals of the regime itself. There are authoritarian features in many of the Arab media systems, even in places where the press is not under government ownership—a common element in authoritarian systems elsewhere.

A leading Lebanese chief editor and sometime Minister of Infor-mation described the philosophy prevalent in the Arab world, attribut-ing it to all developing countries:

> In developing societies, truth has always been considered divine in form as well as in content, to whatever god or prophet it is attributed. The

knowledge of this truth is therefore considered a privilege, the privilege of one man or of a few men, who henceforth necessarily claim a monopoly of freedom—the freedom of those who know and have alone the right to tell the others what they must know and believe. A phenomenon accentuated by the sacred character of the written word, to be written in the most perishable fashion: in newspapers. . . . In such a context, it is natural and logical that the press should assume a very particular role. Instead of being a "mass medium" in the sense commonly held, it becomes the instrument of transmission of the official truth, the media by which this truth is authoritatively communicated to the masses.[42]

The libertarian theory, by contrast, holds that the media must be completely free of government controls and provide the consumer with sufficient objective information and variety of opinion so that that consumer can make up his or her own mind. The libertarian media are both an outside check on government—the watchdog function—and a vehicle for what Milton called a "free and open encounter" of ideas which should help reasoning people to distinguish truth from error. The social responsibility theory seems to be a modification of this, developed in recent times when it appeared that a laissez faire approach to media control did not guarantee freedom. The libertarian theorists did not deal with the problems of economic independence or of a party's political influence, both of which are crucial for Arab media, as they were important to the history of the American press: "It was easy [in the nineteenth century in America] to enter publishing, and so practically every party found a voice. Unfortunately the party press was a severe strain on the vaunted ability of man's reason to discriminate between truth and falsehood, because its news was just as slanted as its editorial opinion."[43]

In America the response was development of a social responsibility theory. This does not have complete faith in a "self-righting process" through free competition of information and ideas, but instead it refines the libertarian theory and calls for financial self-sufficiency of the media, government promotion of press freedom, and a commitment by journalists not to publish just anything they please but to elevate social conflict to the "plane of discussion."[44]

The Arab response has been different. To be sure, there are examples of such journalistic responsibility in the Arab world, and evidence that some of the Arab media reflect a few features of both the libertarian and social responsibility theories. But these features tend to be in the effects of the system rather than in the underlying philosophy or purpose. The prevailing Arab attitude toward mass communications seems to be more akin to the authoritarian view than to Milton's, and the efforts to publish or broadcast the truth have come under strain from a variety of sources—cultural, social, and especially political. This is, in fact, from a worldwide perspective, more the norm than unique; as one scholar has noted: "A greater concern for the consequences of statements than for their correspondence to some criterion of objective truth has characterized . . . most human societies. The democratic liberal tradition is the unusual one in this respect."[45]

The pressures on an Arab newspaper or broadcast editor from his society, which is simultaneously going through the trials of economic development and national self-fulfillment, are enormous. Regional tension and the perception of an external threat tend to exacerbate the situation, and the editor is caught in the middle because of his very public role. A comment by one observer of journalists in other societies applies quite well to the Arab world: "Where the political temperature is high, the journalist usually considers 'objectivity' and 'commitment' to be the same thing, because both are identified with 'truth'."[46]

On the other hand, looking at the Arab media area as a whole, it seems that a Miltonian clash of views does take place. There is a variety of partisan voices in the Middle East and North Africa, particularly on radio broadcasts which can not be contained within national frontiers, which has provided Arab audiences with an open encounter of ideas from which to choose. It is within each country that restrictions are more effective.

Are any Arab media totalitarian? While a few elements of the totalitarian system have appeared at times, none of the Arab media systems can really be classified in this fourth category. Under the totalitarian system,[47] all information media are centrally controlled by the government, whether they are in private or public hands, and unapproved foreign or other competing media may not be distributed at all in the country. Unlike the negative controls of an authoritarian media system, which merely restricts anti-regime content in available media, totalitarian controls are intended to force the media into a positive, active role of agitation and propaganda within an overall scheme to mobilize the population. Most important, while the authoritarian system generally is concerned only about mass media and outward obedience, and allows free speech in private, in the totalitarian system the rulers attempt to control all aspects of a person's life, demanding an individual's positive, active commitment in public and private to their goals.

In the Arab world, there are some restrictions on the importation of foreign print media, and even a few cases of jamming of foreign radio broadcasts. But these restrictions are by no means comprehensive. The media have not been forced, even under one-party regimes, into the single-minded agitation and propaganda effort of the kind found in the Soviet or other totalitarian systems. The most restrictive Arab regimes have, in general, been satisfied with outward compliance by press, radio, and television, and they have not invaded the sphere of private, face-to-face oral communication which is still so important in the Arab societies. Thus while there are a few elements of totalitarian thinking behind the controls on Arab media, the systems themselves cannot be put in this overall category.

However, with these four categories—authoritarian, libertarian, social responsibility, and totalitarian—we can do no more than put the Arab media systems rather roughly into a worldwide context. These generalizations are not at all sufficient to make the Arab media systems and their dynamics fully comprehensible. Indeed, none of the existing analytical theories helps much in going beneath the surface of the Arab media systems, and in order to explain their real functioning we must devise new theories designed to fit the cases at hand.

Beyond the generalizations in this chapter, which apply to media in all eighteen Arab countries, we have found three major sub-types which we shall examine later. One group includes the Arab republics which call themselves socialist and have undergone the most political change in recent years—Egypt, Syria, Iraq, Libya, Algeria, the Sudan, and South Yemen. Each of these states has experienced European colonialism, and their media systems have developed during periods of political turbulence, rising nationalist and anti-imperialist sentiment, and episodes when political parties participated in national life. They have all gone through four identifiable stages in media development, ending in a kind of nationalization by the regime. The regime attempts to mobilize the media, giving them considerable guidance on goals which should be emphasized, on how to interpret events, and even on news presentation.

Media systems in a second group of states—Saudi Arabia, Jordan, Tunisia, Qatar, the United Arab Emirates, and Bahrain—have experienced a more even, linear development along traditional authoritarian lines, although there have been ups and downs in the degree of freedom. Political parties have played little or no role in media development in these states, and ownership of the press remains largely in private hands, though radio and TV are owned by the governments. Like the first group the tenor of the theory behind the media is authoritarian, and the degree of government influence is high, but the system and the style are quite different. Influences and controls over the press, particularly, are quite indirect and subtle, not discernible so much by reading the press laws in search of legal restrictions as by reading the newspapers themselves. In practice they tend to be loyal to the regime in presenting news and commentary on important issues.

The third main category of media systems is considerably less authoritarian in nature than the others, and it exhibits a clear degree of diversity and freedom of expression not found elsewhere in the Arab world. The archetype of this group, the Lebanese system, has the freest journalism in the Arab world and is practically a case by itself. However, the press in Kuwait and Morocco have a degree of diversity and independence which puts them, too, in this special category—and for some of the same reasons as exist in Lebanon.

These three categories account for all but two of the eighteen Arab states. The Yemen Arab Republic and Oman have been omitted because their media are still relatively underdeveloped and also because their media are organized in a way that distinguishes them from the other Arab systems. As of 1979, these two countries had less than five years of experience with television, the last of the Arab world to acquire it, so the medium was less sophisticated than elsewhere. Radio broadcasting there was somewhat older but, like television, lacked strong local talent sufficient to maintain high standards.

The press in both countries also played a relatively marginal role. Oman as of 1979 still had no daily newspaper, the last Arab country in that category. Since 1972 it has had a weekly paper in Arabic, 'Uman, and several other non-daily publications do appear—al Watan, al Nahdah, al 'Aqidah and the Times of Oman. But all of these are issued by the Omani government and much of the content is government-generated news. In (North) Yemen, there are two daily newspapers, al Thawrah of Sana'a and al Jumhuriyah of Taiz, but these also are government publications which specialize in official announcements and government-approved news. Foreign news rarely takes up more than half a page. The editorial staffs of these Yemeni dailies tend to be slightly more leftist in outlook than the government, especially at al Thawrah, but they do not challenge the government's basic policy and readers generally see them as reflecting the official line. Yemen's weeklies al Salam, al Sabah, and al Yaman are only slightly more interesting.

The following five chapters will therefore omit Oman and North Yemen and concentrate on analyzing the three major media types mentioned above.

IMPORTANT MAGAZINES

A word must be said about non-daily periodical publications in the Arab world, since they are important but are not discussed in detail in the next five chapters, which are limited to the daily press plus radio and television.

Every Arab country has some non-daily publications. Many of them have a variety of different types. The most common are the weekly pictorial current-events magazines such as Egypt's *al Musawwar* or Lebanon's *al Hawadith*, and the radio-television magazines. But also there are scholarly journals such as Egypt's *al Siyasah al Dawliyah* (International Politics), religious magazines such as Saudi Arabia's *al Da'wah* (The Call), and another in Egypt by the same name, literary quarterlies, and special publications for women, youth, and the military. Each of these publications reflects, in one way or another, its country of origin and most are unknown outside their borders. But some, particularly a few Lebanese and Egyptian weeklies, and one Kuwaiti monthly, *al 'Arabi*, have been successful in developing readerships outside (see Chapter 7).

We must now look more closely at the individual Arab states. In many ways, each state is unique in the way its media function. But for purposes of analysis we shall examine them grouped into three subtypes, starting with what we shall call the mobilization press.

2

The Mobilization Press

IN THE 1970s the daily newspapers in seven Arab countries—Algeria, Egypt, Iraq, Syria, Libya, South Yemen (the People's Democratic Republic of Yemen), and the Sudan—play generally a similar type of role in the political process despite the fact that they vary greatly in age, origin, and history (see Table 2). On superficial examination the press appears to have been nationalized in these countries, but this would be an inaccurate and oversimplified term to use. The state does not itself own the newspapers, and the relationship between the government and the journalists is a subtle, complex one which will be dealt with in this chapter. We shall briefly describe journalists' behavior, then analyze the underlying factors, the structure of the press, and the channels of political influence.

PRESS BEHAVIOR

No Criticism of Policy

The mobilization press does not criticize the basic policies of the national government. The government's foreign policies are particularly unassailable, but the major lines of domestic policy, too, are never attacked. The newspapers may carry stories and editorials critical of government services on the local level, such as the shortage of electricity or shortcomings of the public sanitation department. In these cases, how-

TABLE 2
Daily Newspapers in Seven Countries
(1976)

	Est. circ.	Location	First pub.
EGYPT			
Al Ahram (The Pyramids)	520,000	Cairo	1875
Al Akhbar (The News)	650,000	"	1952
Al Gumhuriyah (The Republic)	60,000	"	1953
Al Masa' (The Evening)	55,000	"	1956
The Egyptian Gazette*	35,000	"	1879
Le Progres Egyptien†	10,000	"	1897
Le Journal d'Egypte†	3,000	"	1936
IRAQ			
Al Jumhuriyah (The Republic)	35,000	Baghdad	1958
Al Thawrah (The Revolution)	35,000	"	1968
The Baghdad Observer*	3,500	"	1967
Taakhi (Brotherhood)	6,500	"	1969
Tariq al Sha'b (The Path of the People)	5,500	"	1973
SYRIA			
Al Thawrah (The Revolution)	50,000	Damascus	1964
Al Ba'th (The Renaissance)	50,000	"	1964
Al Fida' (The Sacrifice)	8,000	Hama	1963
Al 'Urubah (Arabism)	10,000	Homs	1965
Al Jamahir (The Masses)	11,000	Aleppo	1966
Tishrin (October)	4,500	Damascus	1974
THE SUDAN			
Al Ayyam (The Days)	80,000	Khartoum	1953
Al Sahafah (The Press)	90,000	"	1961
ALGERIA			
El Moudjahid (The Warrior)†	150,000	Algiers	1956‡
Al Sha'b (The People)	40,000	"	1962
Al Nasr (The Victory)	35,000	Constantine	1963
La Republique†	40,000	Oran	1963
LIBYA			
Al Fajr al Jadid (The New Dawn)	10,000	Tripoli	1972
Al Ra'y (The Opinion)	6,000	"	1973
Al Jihad (The Holy War)	5,000	Benghazi	1973
SOUTH YEMEN (PDRY)			
14 October	9,000	Aden	1967
Al Thawri (The Revolutionary)	7,000	"	1968

Note: Iraq's Taakhi was replaced after 1976 by al Iraq.
*Published in English.
†Published in French.
‡First published sporadically, then weekly, then in 1965 daily; in 1962 it moved from exile in Tunis to Algiers.

ever, the lower-level bureaucrat rather than the national leadership is held responsible, and the criticism serves a pedagogical purpose for the leadership as well as providing an outlet for very limited debate. This airing of the views of the "public," dissatisfied with the service and with the bureaucrat who is supposed to provide it, is the only internal political discussion that appears in the press. Otherwise, politically important issues are not treated from various angles but are presented from the one point of view which is acceptable to the government.[1]

Sanctity of Leaders

The mobilization press never criticizes the personalities heading the national government, either in editorials or by unfavorable newsplay. Negative information about the character, behavior, or personal lives of the top rulers does not find its way into print, no matter how well known by the newsmen or even the public.

Non-Diverse

It follows that there is no significant diversity on important political issues among newspapers in any one of these countries. Since they are all highly respectful of the national leadership and its fundamental policies, their editorials and news stories on these matters tend to be strikingly similar.[2]

These three newspaper characteristics can be found not only in the seven countries we are dealing with here, but elsewhere in the Arab world as well (see below). What sets the seven apart as a group are the following special traits.

Mobilization Tool

The regimes in these seven countries regard the press as a very important tool for the mobilization of popular support for its political programs. These regimes tend to adhere to activist domestic and foreign policies which advocate social, economic, and political change, and their ideologies usually include elements of intense struggle against alleged hostile forces ranged against the national welfare. The ruling group seeks to use the press to advance its causes and help fight these battles.

The term "mobilization" has been used in the phrase "social mobilization," which is "an overall process of change, which happens to substantial parts of the population in countries which are moving from traditional to modern ways of life, . . . where advanced, non-traditional practices in culture, technology, and economic life are accepted on a considerable scale. . . . The process in which major clusters of old social, economic and psychological commitments are eroded or broken and people become available for new patterns of socialization and for behavior."[3]

The term "mobilization" has also been applied to political systems in which new values are being created and "political leaders are trying to work out a moral system of authority" in order to "establish, as much as possible, different solidarities and identities," so that society will rapidly modernize and industrialize, and the new leadership will acquire legitimacy.[4] This is essentially what was happening in these seven Arab states in the third quarter of the twentieth century. It is appropriate to apply the same term to the press in these seven states because the mass media are seen by these regimes as crucial to the mobilization process. Some outside observers have recognized that "the mass media can be used to mobilize the energies of living persons . . . by the rational articulation of new interests. . . . The mass media can simultaneously induce a new process of socialization among the rising generation that will, among other effects, recruit new participants into political life."[5]

This power of the mass media is fully appreciated—perhaps even over-valued—in the seven Arab states. The regimes there, seeking revolutionary change and active popular support against obstacles to development and perceived enemies, look to the media for support. As the Iraqi press law puts it, the "current battle the Arab nation is waging against imperialism, Zionism, and reaction requires that the Iraqi press be guided on sound national lines . . . to disseminate sound ideas, provide true guidelines, and carry out constructive criticism that would preserve the state."[6]

Constructive criticism is not free speech but part of the mobilization process. As the ruling Ba'th Party has declared: "The masses [have] the right of constructive criticism within the limits of the nation's progressive line of destiny. Naturally, criticism under the socialist revolutionary regime cannot be an end in itself, nor can it be allowed to proceed unchecked to the limit of undermining the nationalist socialist line itself."[7]

The Sudanese regime has basically the same attitude toward the press, which it expresses in slightly less vigorous terms: "The information media play an important role in the national, political, economic, and social revolution and share in an important strategic line of revolution and change by clarifying the path before the masses."[8]

Similar revolutionary socialist language is used in each of these seven Arab countries. South Yemen's ruling National Front makes such declarations as: "The spread of the scientific socialist ideas among the revolution's workers and toilers . . . constituted a prominent ideological transformation . . . [which] has made it possible to lay the correct scientific bases for connecting political action with productive work for the sake of the progress of the society and the masses."[9]

A Seminar on Information and Indoctrination held by Algeria's ruling party stressed the "need to heighten political sensitivities and to improve methods of action to achieve more effective mobilization behind the goals of the Revolution"—primarily the elimination of inequality, underdevelopment, and "the after-effects of colonialism."[10]

Similar social, economic, political, and even cultural goals are enunciated by the leadership in all seven countries, and it is toward these objectives that the press is supposed to help mobilize public support. The newspapers are expected to help publicize great campaigns launched by the regime against some obstacle to economic development or against a foreign enemy, for example. They are supposed to help announce and explain, loudly and clearly, any new government policies. And they are, in the process, expected to convey the idea that all right-thinking people are united behind such policies, and that the regime has chosen the goals wisely.[11]

The tone of editorials and headlines is often stridently aggressive, combative, hyperbolic, quick to react to events and to paint black-and-white pictures. The mobilization messages, implied as well as explicit, are intended to generate support for the regime's programs on several levels, mainly philosophical and institutional but also personal. They are addressed primarily to the domestic audience, but occasionally also directed at a foreign target, for example to persuade a foreign government to change its policy while persuading people at home that the foreign government should change its policy.[12]

Many of these characteristics would apply to the press in a totalitarian system. The system in these seven countries is not, however, totalitarian. It seeks active support for programs rather than just passive compliance, but it does tolerate some passivity and it does not go so far as to invade the sphere of personal privacy. In the totalitarian system, "the atmosphere of mobilization is one of crisis and attack"—an atmosphere which is developed on some occasions in the press in those Arab countries but tends not to be sustained over long periods of time or on many issues.[13] And the newspapers in these seven Arab countries have generally not become so "highly rigid, formalized and bureaucratic," and dull as the totalitarian ones which "adhere to rigid connections both of format and content,"[14] although a few of these newspapers have moved in that direction in the sections that deal with politically sensitive news.

How does the government obtain this kind of support from the press? The answer is that a certain type of press structure and journalistic behavior has been established under political conditions particularly conducive to the emergence of this system. Let us look at those factors, starting with the political environment.

POLITICAL CONDITIONS

There are several characteristics common to the political environments of Algeria, Iraq, Syria, Egypt, Libya, South Yemen, and the Sudan which seem to be important to the development of the mobilization newspaper. Aside from other political factors which may be important for other purposes, we find four factors which are directly related to the press system. First of all, a small, aggressive ruling group is in authority, effectively in control of all important levers of power. It faces no genuine organized opposition and allows no challenger to its authority to speak out publicly on the domestic scene.

Secondly, this ruling group tends to regard itself as a revolutionary vanguard of the people, engaged in a struggle for social change domestically and representing strong nationalistic sentiment in fighting alleged foreign and domestic enemies of the people. It claims to represent the true interests of "the masses" and typically uses revolutionary socialist language to rally support and warn of enemies.

Thirdly, this ruling group is not content with passive acquiescence from the population, but is instead highly conscious of a need to appeal for active support of the people, and it recognizes that this must be done through the mass media.

Finally, the ruling group usually has behind it a single political party which is the only really powerful political organization allowed to function in the country. It is a monopoly "party of solidarity" rather than a representative party of the type found in Western democratic systems which must compete for power against other parties on an equal basis.[15]

Such a political organization is called by different names in the seven countries—Arab Socialist Union or National Liberation Front for example. In three of the countries no other legal political organizations exist; in the other four—Egypt, Syria, Iraq, and South Yemen—the additional political organizations that are allowed to function do not espouse policies which are basically different from those of the regime and its party. The regime maintains this party in order to help mobilize popular support, since the style of the leadership is to confront what it perceives to be its enemies in a highly partisan manner, despite the fact that there are no real opposition parties and no real party system exists.

Political Agents and the Structure of the Press

In such an environment, there are strong incentives for journalists to support the regime and its policies, at least on issues about which the regime is sensitive. Without an organized opposition party or group, there is no public criticism of the regime to report in the newspaper columns, and the psychological atmosphere makes it very difficult for the newspaper columnist independently to voice criticism of the government.

In addition to this psychological pressure on journalists, the ruling group in each of these countries had structured the press in such a way that it has clear and legitimate mechanisms to influence journalists' behavior. This has been achieved primarily by taking all newspapers of any consequence out of the hands of private owners and making them the property of political agents and supporters of the regime, most commonly its own party. In all of these countries, the ruling party derives its importance solely from the fact that its leaders hold political power. These parties are fundamentally quite weak institutions, but the ruling groups have built them up as instruments of rule and mass mobilization. It is natural, then, that these parties would be used to control the press. Control is ultimately assured because the head of the ruling group is also leader of the ruling party.[16]

In Algeria, Libya, and the Sudan, and until 1976 in Egypt, the ruling group's party has been the only legal party in the country and at the same time the owner of all politically significant newspapers.

Egypt was the first Arab country to adopt this system. Egypt's Law no. 156 of May 24, 1960, stipulated that no newspapers could be published without the permission of the country's only political organization, the National Union (later renamed Arab Socialist Union). The law also transferred ownership of the four large private publishing houses—Dar al Ahram, Dar Akhbar al Yawm, Dar al Hilal, and Dar Rose al Yusif—to the National Union, which already owned Dar al Tahrir publishing house. And thirdly, the law required that the National Union appoint the boards of directors for the newspapers it owned. This political organization, therefore, was given wide licensing, financial, and personnel powers over the press. Since the organization was controlled by the regime, the latter in effect controlled the press by these means.[17] The system was modified only slightly in March 1975, when a Higher Press Council was created which was given 49 percent ownership of the press and the power to issue publishing licenses. Since the key members of the Higher Council were the Minister of Information, ASU officials, and media officials, and since the latter were still appointed by the regime, the government did not lose its *de facto* control.[18]

Egyptians argue that what happened in 1960 was not really nationalization of the press, because it was not the state or the government which took over ownership of the newspapers. The 1960 law deliberately uses the phrase "organization of the press" (*tanzim al sahafah*) rather than "nationalization" (*ta'mim*), and Egyptian law does not regard the National Union or ASU as an organ of the state. One legal expert adds that the publishing houses have "no connection with the authority of the state" (*sultah al dawlah*).[19] There is no regular government financial connection with the press. *Al Gumhuriyah* chronically lost money until the late 1970s and received government subsidies, but the other dailies usually operate in the black and manage their budgets without any government involvement.[20]

Starting in 1976, President Sadat laid the groundwork for possible changes in the press structure, by allowing political parties to emerge and by permitting parties to publish newspapers, but no substantial changes had resulted by 1979.

Following the parliamentary elections of 1976, Sadat declared that the three so-called platforms (*manabir*) of the Arab Socialist Union which had competed in the election campaign, were henceforth to be separate political parties. Law no. 4 of 1977 endorsed this change and made it possible for new parties to be formed by members of parliament. The ASU was thus made obsolete, and in June 1977 Sadat abolished all strata of the ASU except for the Central Committee, which remained pending a constitutional amendment and a political decision on what to do with such matters as ownership of the existing newspapers, still legally in the hands of the ASU. Discussions of the latter issue in governmental, parliamentary and press circles were prolonged, extending into 1979, as the government searched for an institutional formula to ensure that the right people remained in charge of the politically important publications. At the same time, the political parties tried to take advantage of their right, under the 1977 parties law, to issue their own newspapers. However, their initial efforts did not amount to much (see below), so in 1979 the basic press structure was still intact.

In Algeria, the ruling group under Ahmad Ben Bella followed a course similar to Egypt's in 1960. In September 1963, the Algerian regime put all of the newspapers except one under the control of the country's only legal party, Ben Bella's National Liberation Front.[21] The one remaining paper, *Alger Republicain*, was already at that time a supporter of the government, and in June 1965 it was merged into the FLN daily *Le Peuple*. Since then this paper has appeared under the name *El Moudjahid*, and all Algerian newspapers are owned by the FLN. Like the Egyptians, the Algerians maintain that the press is not under control of the government, but speaks for the party.[22]

In the Sudan, too, the press is owned by the country's only political party, President Ja'far Numeiry's Sudanese Socialist Union. However, Sudanese law also gives the ministries of the government joint control with the SSU. The press law of August 1970 took all publishing out of private hands and turned it over to a public corporation. The successful private dailies *al Sahafah* and *al Ayyam* were continued but under separate publicly owned publishing houses, which also issued other periodicals.[23]

The following year, a republican decree made all newspaper and magazine publishing houses property of the SSU, and the 1973 press law clarified the dual party-ministry control system: "Newspapers shall be the property of the people in whose name and on whose behalf they shall be run by the Sudanese Socialist Union . . . [which has the exclusive right to license publications, while] the Minister [of Culture and Information] shall be responsible for the daily direct control of newspapers in order to ensure harmony with the general information line and commitment to the political plan of the Sudanese Socialist Union."[24]

In practice, there are personal connections which make control easier, such as the fact that the Minister of Information is usually a member of the SSU executive committee and chairman of its information committee.[25]

In Iraq, South Yemen, and Syria, other parties exist alongside the ruling one; ownership of the press is not exclusively in the hands of the ruling party, but the effect is the same as if it were.

In Iraq, law no. 155 announced over Baghdad Radio on December 3, 1967, abolished all private newspapers and stipulated that no papers could be published subsequently without a license issued by the "General Establishment for Press and Printing" of the Ministry of Information. Since then it has been practice that the Ministry licenses only those papers which conform to the basic policy line of the ruling group. In the late 1970s the Iraqi ruling group controls the largest daily, *al Thawrah*, through its Ba'th Party organization which owns the paper, and it controls two other dailies, *al Jumhuriyah* and the *Baghdad Observer*, through the Ministry of Information which publishes them.

In recent years, two small dailies, *Tariq al Sha'b* and *Taakhi* have been permitted to appear because they are under the auspices of two National Front member parties which are loyal to and do not substantially differ in policy from the Bath, namely the Iraqi Communist Party and the Kurdish Democratic Party, respectively.[26]

Syria since 1963 has been ruled by one or another wing of the Ba'th Party, whose leadership controls the press either through the party or through the governmental machinery. Currently the party itself publishes the largest-circulation daily, *al Ba'th*, while the Ministry of Information publishes the other major daily, *al Thawrah*. Similarly, in South Yemen, the ruling National Front controls all the newspapers and the other parties control none.[27]

Control Mechanisms

The regime influences the press under this system primarily through its control over personnel. Even though the state does not own the press, the regime is able to assure itself of basic press loyalty because of the people who run it.

First, the head of the national ruling group is usually head of the political party or other agency which owns the press. Journalists working for such newspapers are aware, without being told so explicitly, that they are expected to promote these policies to the extent that they can.

Beyond that, the ruling group can also control the content of the press through its influence over press personnel assignments. It can, and does, see that right-thinking people are appointed to key editorial positions. In addition, it can cause its political party or other owning agent to dismiss a recalcitrant journalist from the newspaper or suspend him from work. Just the threat of being barred from one's profession is a strong incentive to conform. Dismissals or suspensions usually occur on an individual basis, but in Egypt in 1973 the ruling group caused its party, the Arab Socialist Union, to withdraw the professional licenses of more than one hundred journalists so that they had to leave the newspapers. After six months, their licenses were restored and they returned to their jobs, reminded effectively of their dependence on the regime for their livelihood. For the most part they were paid salaries anyway during this period, as a humanitarian gesture; but the threat of being prevented from exercising their profession on a long-term basis hung over their heads as an effective incentive.

The ruling group under this system can also use the powers of the state, such as arrest and detention of journalists, to help enforce conformity with the regime's basic policies. This weapon may be available in other countries as well, but it is especially easy to use where the law has put ownership of the press in the hands of an agent which is known to have primarily a political purpose. Serious deviation from basic policy can readily be used as a reason for arrest and punishment of the offender.

By the same token, the rewarding of "helpful" newspapermen by providing them with inside information which enhances their role as journalists is a technique used by regimes in many countries, but it is especially common under this system because of the political affinity between the ruling group and most of the leading journalists. The most famous example of the symbiotic relationship between an Arab leader and a journalist is that of Nasser and Haykal in Egypt from the early 1950s until Nasser's death in 1970. Their thinking was similar; Nasser found him a useful sounding board for ideas while Haykal gained insights into the Egyptian leader's planning which made his columns more interesting.[28]

Finally, the regime usually is able to exercise direct censorship over these newspapers more easily because of the fact that their political agent owns the press, and because of the general political climate— especially in a crisis situation.[29] But most of the time a kind of gentleman's agreement is in operation, and the ruling group ordinarily does not have to resort to censorship because of the self-censorship by the newspapermen.[30] Thus the political climate, personnel considerations including both assignments and dismissals or suspensions, plus the stick of legal sanctions and the carrot of access to inside information all are powerful inducements to make the journalist in this system conform to the regime's basic policy line. Whether motivated by true sympathy, loyalty, conformity to the constraints of the environment, fear, or opportunism, the newspaperman supports and actively promotes this line. He will write independent news stories and editorials where he can, but when he touches areas that are sensitive to the regime he will support the official policy.[31]

Guidance Channels

How does the journalist know the policy line on a regular basis? What are the channels for guidance under this system?

Censorship is one of the means used to convey the regime's specific views on what should or should not be published. But instructions by the censor generally play an important role only during a period of real crisis, such as wartime.[32] In normal circumstances, and on a daily basis, guidance is transmitted to the press in more subtle ways, and prepublication censorship is not necessary because the editors know their paper will be read carefully and they will hear if they make a mistake.

Most of the guidance used by editors and other journalists under this system is not labeled as such, but derives from two open sources. First, they closely watch all of the public statements of policy made by the ruling group and its representatives, in order to keep abreast of current policy initiatives and the regime's official view of events. Whether they are formal declarations, press conference remarks, or explanations of policy in a national assembly, these statements are taken as guidance by the newspapermen.[33]

Secondly, in all of these countries the government controls and operates a national news service which is used as an important source of policy guidance. The Iraqi News Agency, the Syrian News Agency, the Sudanese News Agency, the Aden News Agency, Libya's "Arab Revolutionary News Agency," the Algerian Press Service, and Egypt's Middle East News Agency are all controlled by the respective governments, usually through ministries of information. They not only convey news of the regime's activities, which the press is expected to carry, but also provide occasional commentaries or backgrounders which contain the regime's interpretation of events. Transmitted daily by teletype to all major newspapers in the country, this regular supply of material is published and is also taken by newspapermen as guidance on what to publish and what interpretations are desired by the regime (see Chapter 7).

In addition to open channels, the ruling groups in these countries have personal ties and informal connections with key newspapermen which they use to convey political guidance from time to time under this system of press organization because of the dependent status of the newspaper and the regime's influence over its personnel. Typically, when the regime wishes to convey specific guidance on a sensitive political subject, an information ministry official, party functionary or aide in the presidency, for example, will telephone a responsible editor in each newspaper to indicate the government's position. This position is not always accepted without discussion and some modification of detail, but the essentials of it will find their way into the press.[34]

These, then, are the guidance channels which the regime uses to convey policy on a daily basis to the mobilization press. It should be kept in mind that the guidance channels, control mechanisms, press structure, and political conditions described in this chapter are characteristic of the model from which individual press systems in these Arab countries may deviate in some details. In the following chapter we will analyze these countries more specifically, looking at the stages of development leading up to this system, but first we will look briefly at one country that has a mobilization system in order to see how individual countries can deviate from the basic characteristics outlined above.

THE EGYPTIAN PRESS

The above characteristics describe in a general way a type of press system which can be found in seven Arab countries. Of course there are differences among countries, some of which have been mentioned. Differences also develop over time, as the press adapts to changing conditions. In order to illustrate how far the press in practice can deviate from the common basic attributes they all share we shall look more closely at one country, Egypt, whose press has deviated farthest from the model and the others in this category.

The Egyptian press fits into the same basic pattern of relationships between journalism and politics, or between newspapers and government, that has been described above. It does not publish editorials attacking the basic tenets of the government's foreign policy or its basic principles—socialism, national unity and social peace—and all political discussion takes place within the framework of the policy of the state. Criticism of government bureaucrats for their failure to execute policy does appear in the press, but alternatives to the top leadership are not proposed.[35]

Nevertheless, the Egyptian newspaper is not a dull, completely predictable and slavish mouthpiece of the regime akin to Russia's *Pravda*, for example. The Egyptian paper has a style and vitality of its own, rather more so than the newspapers in Iraq, for example, which do have some *Pravda*-like qualities. The Egyptian newspaper is not just a government publicity sheet, and an Egyptian editor feels under no obligation to print the full text of yesterday's speech by the President of the

Republic, although he frequently does.[36] Government censors have been assigned to sit in newspaper offices at times of stress, such as during the years prior to the October 1973 war when tensions over the Arab-Israeli conflict were high. But even in those periods there was some give-and-take between censors and editors, the latter sometimes arguing against specific orders with which they did not agree.[37]

Egyptian newspaper editors have also been able to criticize the status quo in subtle and indirect ways. They have published short stories and even poetry by talented writers in order to convey criticism to readers through symbolic fiction. Some have also published economic analyses which describe existing economic difficulties in restrained and matter-of-fact ways that do not politicize the issues or blame the leadership but do make clear that there are problems. Even in political commentaries, some writers have been able to take gentle jabs at the system and the regime. In 1965 when Ali Amin was forced to leave the editorship of the paper he founded, he wrote: "I do not choose the songs I sing and I do not select the tunes [but] . . . I am infinitely optimistic. Many people are surprised at my optimism."[38] In short, the Egyptian press is not completely docile or subservient in the face of political realities. Indeed, there is evidence of vitality and professionalism in Egyptian journalism, though it is often restrained by the political system for the sake of current efforts by the leadership at unity in order to deal with overriding problems such as the Arab-Israeli conflict or economic development.

Egyptian daily newspapers are similar in content in that they deal with almost the same news stories and treat them with similar priorities. There are, however, clear differences in journalistic style and in the types of readership addressed. Al Ahram, which has a hundred-year history, tends to be more conservative in style, appeals more to government officials, businessmen, and university professors, while al Akhbar, which has a slightly higher circulation, is somewhat more sensational and popular, and appeals more to bureaucrats, students, and others who prefer its livelier approach. As the senior editor of al Akhbar put it, that paper tries to be "like the pretty girl who wears a new dress every day, and who turns heads when she enters a room. Al Ahram, on the other hand, is like an old man in a top hat and morning coat with a walking stick."[39]

Al Gumhuriyah, the third leading daily, until recently appealed especially to leftist intellectuals, workers, and others who like its tendency to stress Arab socialist ideological issues and leftist causes. The newspaper's editors were very proud that they still operated under a license issued in 1952 (the year of the Revolution) to Gamal Abdul Nasser. They tended to focus their attention on political commentaries more than news because, as one of them put it, since 1952 they have "always been influenced by the principles of the Revolution" (*mabadi' al thawrah*) more than the other papers, which focus on news.[40]

Beyond these stylistic differences, the Egyptian press has from time to time, and in certain limited ways, shown a bit of diversity and even some independence.

The diversity has been seen primarily in the non-daily periodicals. While Gamal Abdul Nasser was president (1953–70), leftist journalists were active in most of the media, but the monthly journal *al Tali'ah* became a special organ of the dedicated Marxists and the weekly *Rose al Yusif* was an outlet for irresponsible yellow journalism that carried the government's anti-imperialism and other policies to excess.

Following the death of Nasser in 1970, Anwar Sadat became president and the government subsequently showed a greater degree of tolerance for political discussion and criticism, certainly on the private level and to some extent in the press. At the same time, as Sadat developed his own policies in the post-Nasser era, the overall political complexion of the press shifted somewhat.

Muhammad Hassanain Haykal, who was President Nasser's confidant and by far the most influential journalist during the Nasser period, and who built al Ahram Publishing House into a multifaceted enterprise, stayed on as its head for three years after Nasser's death. More than a million people inside and outside of Egypt continued to read his weekly column "Speaking Frankly" (*Bisuraha*), in which he occasionally indicated his disagreement with government policy. After the October 1973 Arab-Israeli war, however, he expressed fundamental opposition to the way Sadat had conducted the war and to Sadat's direct appeal to the United States to solve the Arab-Israeli problem.[41] In February 1974 President Sadat, in his capacity as chairman of the Arab Socialist Union, finally removed Haykal from al Ahram, and Haykal after that concentrated on writing books and articles for publication outside Egypt.[42] Then in 1974 as Sadat implemented his policy of rapprochement with the West and criticism of the Soviet Union, the influence of Nasserites, Marxists, and other leftists in the press diminished, especially in the daily newspapers. Prominent journalists who had been exiled or jailed during the Nasser period were rehabilitated and given responsible press positions.[43]

In early 1974, the government announced the easing of press restrictions, and during 1974–75 columnists in various papers engaged in debates in print over the need for a revival of political parties, over Nasserism, over student discontents, and over freedom of the press itself. There was even some investigative reporting of official corruption.[44]

But the most outspoken criticism during the Sadat period continued to come from the non-dailies. The monthly *al Tali'ah* remained a Marxist organ, and the weekly *Rose al Yusif*, which became very popular with intellectuals, was also to the left of the mainstream. At the other side of the political spectrum, the two monthly magazines *al Da'wah* and *al I'tisam*, which had been suspended during the Nasser era, represented the views of the religious conservatives. When *al Tali'ah* and *Rose al Yusif* said the January 1977 rioting over consumer price increases was a spontaneous expression of mass disaffection, this clearly was out of line with the government's view that the rioting was inspired by radical elements. Shortly thereafter, the chairman of al Ahram Publishing House replaced *al Tali'ah* with a science magazine, and the editor of *Rose al Yusif* was replaced by a man more supportive of government policies, so both publications ceased carrying dissenting views.[45]

Shortly thereafter, however, the new political parties began to publish their own weekly newspapers, as they were permitted to do under the 1977 parties law. *Garidit Masr* of Sadat's center party which started on June 28, 1977, was totally supportive of the regime, but criticism of policies came regularly from *al Ahrar* of the rightist Liberal Party as soon as it began to appear on November 14, 1977, and even more so from the leftist Progressive Party's weekly *al Ahali*, which first appeared on February 1, 1978. During the spring of 1978, a rather lively discussion on several domestic and foreign policy issues took place in *al Ahali* and *al Ahrar*, in the People's Assembly, in the universities and elsewhere. But the party papers encountered serious financial difficulties in competing with the large publishing houses. In addition, *al Ahali* —which regularly criticized what it saw as growing income inequalities and other negative effects of the government's economic policy, the American connection, and corruption by prominent personalities—ran afoul of the Socialist Prosecutor who began on May 17 to seize issues for anti-democratic content, a charge that the court upheld. Meanwhile, in a referendum on May 21 President Sadat got approval for a new law banning political activity by Marxists, pre-revolutionary politicians, and others. He stressed in many public statements that he was committed to democracy, to freedom of the press and to party newspapers, as long as these were tempered by responsibility.[46]

Editors of the party weeklies continued their publication efforts through the summer of 1978, but by September all of them were gone, to a large extent reflecting the weaknesses of the new parties themselves. The religious magazines *al Da'wah* and *al I'tisam* did, however, continue their rather independent course, even criticizing the government's peace initiative as well as trends conservative Muslims found unhealthy in domestic life.[47]

What has caused the Egyptian press to show some diversity in style and to some extent in viewpoint and to carry occasional criticism of the government? Journalism is a fairly well respected profession in Egypt because of its long tradition and the fact that talented writers have devoted part or all of their careers to the press. Cairo newspapers and magazines have on their staffs some of the leading and best-known professional journalists, as well as some of the very best novelists, playwrights, and short story writers in the entire Arab world.[48] Working in the media is moderately prestigious, and the top positions in journalism pay almost as well as those in government. Some Egyptians have become prominent public figures through the press or through a combination of journalism, writing, and politics.

Secondly, among those who write or have written for the mass media, a wide range of personal political convictions and perceptions can be found. Each of the publications is likely to have on its staff a spectrum of individual views, from Marxist to conservative, and these views may emerge from time to time depending on the prevailing environment.

Thirdly, and most importantly, these journalists function in the Egyptian political environment which is not static but changing, so over time their fortunes change depending on how their views and their personalities fit with the times. The dynamics of government-media relations are based on the interplay between the regime, attempting to mobilize public opinion by using the journalists, and the latter, attempting to write and say what they want. The results of this interplay depend on personalities as well as policies.

The Egyptian press is not by any means an independent Fourth Estate. When Haykal spoke out too obviously in opposition to government policy he lost his platform. Other columnists denounced him for creating a "center of power" (*markaz quwwa*), a phrase used by Sadat to attack Ali Sabri and other opponents of the regime after 1970.[49] No one journalist emerged to the dominant position Haykal had held, but all of the chief editors fundamentally supported the government's policies.

Journalists who supported the government's policies were favored and appointed by Sadat to key press positions. Press critics were attacked by him publicly. But unlike Nasser, he did not treat opposition journalists harshly by imprisoning them or depriving them of their means of livelihood. Haykal is one example of that. And in 1973, when a large number of journalists were suspended from writing, they continued to receive their salaries. As Sadat said when he reinstated them, "I meant and still mean to give a warning. It has not been my aim nor is it my nature to harm any person in his work, profession or livelihood. . . . I want freedom of the press. At the same time I want it to be a dedicated press."[50]

Two years later, still involved in a discussion of press freedoms, Sadat recalled the event in a similar vein: "I did not dismiss anybody. It was disciplinary punishment. I said: shame, behave yourselves. Why? Because I am in a battle and a situation in which everyone is required to stand by their country—not by me personally—because it is their country. And on 28 September 1973 I came and said that all the journalists should go back to their newspapers."[51]

President Sadat endorsed press freedom, but he also called on the media to be responsible. As he put it in one speech, "If freedom of expression is sacred, Egypt is more sacred and I am not prepared to relinquish any of her rights."[52]

On another occasion in 1977, as the People's Assembly was discussing a new press law, he made clear that his concept of democracy required "public" control over the press:

> Today, thank God, 25 years after our revolution, our country has regained its constitutional legality. . . . We now have a state of institutions [dawlit al mu'assasaat] . . . the cabinet . . . the People's Assembly and . . . the judiciary. The fourth authority which we have created is the press. This is because the press has a great influence on public opinion. . . . We cannot allow our press, which shapes public opinion, to be controlled by an individual or by an opinionated and temperamental newspaper publisher, nor for that matter by a group of people who want to impose their will on the people. No, the press is the property of the people and will remain so.[53]

The system and structure of government-press relations thus remained fundamentally as described earlier in this chapter, although the style of managing it had changed somewhat and the government laid more stress on the goal of eventual press freedom. The Higher Press Council, created in 1975 to share ownership of the press with the ASU and encourage self-regulation, in fact did as much to reinforce the responsibility theme as it did to promote liberty,[54] and the party newspapers which were permitted to appear in 1977 were required to express their views within the carefully circumscribed framework of the national dialogue. These were changes in form but not in basic substance.

Thus while the Egyptian press structure fits into the category described in these two chapters, the dynamics of the relationship between the press and politics in Egypt are complex. Because of the existence of prominent personalities affiliated with the newspapers, the variety of views among them, and the changing political environment, the political tendency of the press is constantly undergoing subtle shifts while maintaining the same general direction.

Mobilization Press:
Development Stages

Seven Arab countries fit more or less into the model described in the previous chapter. Now we shall analyze in somewhat more detail how the press in these countries evolved into this type of system, since the evolution seems to have taken a remarkably similar course in all of the countries. A four-stage development process seems to have repeated itself, with some local variation, in each of the seven states. This chapter will describe those stages and the major reasons for their emergence.

In Egypt, Algeria, Iraq, and the Sudan the role of the press in the political process went through four similar stages of development. In the other three countries—Syria, Libya, and South Yemen—the press has gone through three of the same stages but has not yet fully entered the fourth, although for all practical purposes the basic system of the press is the same. For convenience we can label the four stages colonial, factional, non-partisan, and mobilization. In Table 3 we list the dates the press in each of the countries went through these stages. Understanding the complex set of factors behind each stage, however, requires more detailed explanation.

COLONIAL STAGE

Arab newspapers first appeared in all of these countries during a period of foreign colonial rule—usually Ottoman and then either British or French. The papers were established out of literary, commercial, political, or sometimes personal motives, and they tended to grow along with

TABLE 3
Phases of Press Development in Seven Arab Countries

	Colonial I	Factional II	Non-partisan III	Mobilization IV
Egypt	before 1920	1920–54	1954–60 (early Nasser pd)	since 1960
Iraq	before 1932	1932–63	1964–67 ('Arif Regime)	since 1967
Syria	before 1946	1946–58	1958–63	since 1963
The Sudan	1903–53	1953–58	1958–64 ('Abboud Regime)	
		1964–69	1969–70 (early Numeiry pd)	since 1970
Algeria	before 1962	July–Nov 1962	Nov 1962–Sept 1963	since Sept 1963
PDRY (South Yemen)	before 1960	1960–67	since 1967	
Libya	before 1951	1951–69	since 1969	

the nationalist sentiment and the pace of economic life. But the owners and editors had to be careful to keep the colonial administrator as well as the local government in mind. Thus the two major factors of the period were emerging nationalism which promoted the growth of Arab journalism, and colonial rule which tended to restrict it.

As early as the middle of the nineteenth century, an Arab press—that is, newspapers edited and published by and for Arabs—had already emerged in Egypt, Syria, and Iraq, all part of the Ottoman Empire. In Egypt, the first newspapers were organs of the regime, but non-governmental private papers appeared during the cultural and intellectual renaissance of the 1860s and 1870s, encouraged by the more liberal Khedive Ismail, who ruled Egypt from 1863 to 1879. Ismail suppressed any really critical voice, but discussion of social, political, and economic issues and debates between secular modernists and conservative reformists were aired in the newspapers. Ismail also backed at least one newspaper himself, in order to promote public interest in his administration's wider autonomy from the Ottoman Sultan.[1]

After Britain became a major factor in Egyptian politics by intervening in 1882, the press also debated the role of Britain, and during the next two generations newspapers became more political as nationalist feeling arose and parties were founded. A "virile party press appeared" after 1882, which was "lively, political and rebellious," although these early papers were not owned by the parties as such but merely patronized by them.[2] In several cases, a writer would establish a paper, and slowly, as other like-minded people were attracted to it, they formed a party which became active on the political scene. For example, Shaikh Ali Yusif's Hisb al Islah party grew up around *al Mu'ayyid* newspaper; the Hisb al Watani party developed after Mustafa Kamel established *al Liwa'*; and the Umma party emerged after *al Jaridah*.[3] Since the British were more tolerant of partisan papers than of organized parties, the former grew faster than the latter. Some papers, like the successful dailies *al Ahram* and *al Muqattam*, an evening paper, remained independent of parties and government. However, the discussion in these elite newspapers was still kept within strict limits by governmental restrictions, despite the proliferation of journals and the increasing political nature of them.[4]

Similarly, Syrian and Iraqi publishers were seriously encumbered until 1908 by strict Ottoman regulations enforced by local authorities, which hampered the free growth of journalism. Pressure from the Young Turks did force a relaxation of these strictures in 1908, so Arab newspapers proliferated in Syria and Iraq during the next decade. Young writers and politicians, with the ideas of nationalism, and many of them educated at colleges in Beirut, Cairo, Alexandria and Istanbul, started their own organs of Arab consciousness within the Ottoman framework. Nevertheless after World War I, Ottoman rule was replaced by French and British mandates in Syria and Iraq, respectively, and Arab newspapermen had to contend with their publishing restrictions. Journalism in Syria grew somewhat under the French mandate (1920–46), but the French used their mandatory powers to license for publication only those organs which generally supported their policies. Although writers and editors had somewhat more freedom in Iraq under the relatively lighter British mandatory administration (1920–32), they too faced some limits in political discussion beyond which they could not go.[5]

In Algeria, which the French administered with the intention of keeping it as a permanent Department of France, Arab journalism evolved under special colonial restrictions. During the second half of the nineteenth century, a large group of French settlers living in Algeria gained control of the economic, political, and cultural life so thoroughly that the Arab press was not able to grow. The political parties that became active after World War I did appeal to Arabs for support, but they were controlled by Europeans. All newspapers and most periodicals were owned by Europeans, printed in French, and ignored Arab news. These publications continued to prosper before and after World War II. By the time of independence in 1962 the seven dailies and most of the other publications in Algeria were published in French by Frenchmen; in addition, publications were imported from France in large numbers but the French administration restricted the importation of Arab publications from other Arab countries to keep out those which supported the nationalists.[6] These newspapers were not able to reflect Arab views, primarily because of restrictions imposed by the French administration, but also in some instances because of terrorist acts by the right-wing "Algérie Francaise" line. Only in 1960, after Paris had decided on self-determination for Algeria, did the French administration there allow publication of more moderate views.[7]

Arab nationalists were able to publish a few modest weeklies in Algeria in the years after World War II, but the French administration suppressed them in 1955 as the six-year war for independence was beginning.[8] Then the growing nationalist movement turned to underground newspapers as a means of mobilizing sentiment for independence. Algerian Arab journalists printed and circulated newssheets secretly, or smuggled them in from abroad. The leading nationalist organization, the National Liberation Front (NLF), began publishing its own party newspaper *el Moudjahid* in 1956, the year it gained the support of other Muslim parties. At first it appeared only in French, since even the nationalists communicated in that language, but starting in 1957 it also included some sections in Arabic. *El Moudjahid* was published in Tunis and smuggled into Algeria for secret distribution until June 1962, when the French High Commissioner allowed it to be sold openly in Algeria in preparation for independence a month later.[9]

The press in the other three countries—the Sudan, Libya, and South Yemen—began later primarily because of low literacy rates and an inadequate economic base, but also there it emerged and first developed under colonial rule. The first newspapers to appear in these countries were issued directly by the British colonial administration, usually in English and for resident British citizens.[10]

A bi-weekly Arab newspaper in Arabic called *al Sudan* was founded in the Sudan in 1903. Since it was owned by three Syrian journalists who also owned the then-famous Cairo daily *al Muqattam*, and since the Anglo-Egyptian condominium had been established over the

Sudan five years earlier, many Sudanese suspected that the paper was a mouthpiece of foreign interests. Two Greek merchants began publishing an English weekly a few years later, to which they added an Arabic supplement. Only in 1919, as literacy was spreading and the question of union with Egypt had become a live political issue, did the first indigenous Sudanese newspaper appear. *Hadarat al Sudan* (Sudanese Culture) pleased the British because it opposed union and supported the British administration. Even so, after the pro-unionist armed uprising of 1924 the colonial administration decided to restrict the scope of political and press activity somewhat.[11]

As a result, for more than a decade, Sudanese publishers turned their attention more to literary efforts.[12] British control over the press was relatively light, however. The Sudan government promulgated its first Press Ordinance in 1930, giving the British administrators licensing authority, but this was in practice very sparingly used. By 1935 the first Sudanese daily, *al Nil* (The Nile), had started, and the newspapers began to become more politically oriented. They reflected some of the popular discontent with the 1936 Anglo-Egyptian treaty for example. A second daily, *Sawt al Sudan*, started in 1940 as newspapers proliferated with the growing political consciousness. Political parties were formed after World War II and many of them were able to start their own newspapers.[13] This trend accelerated in 1953 as Sudanese political activity intensified for the February elections and Britain and Egypt declared their intention to end the condominium after a three-year transition period. As far as the press was concerned, the colonial stage ended then.

Press development in Libya and South Yemen was even slower, due primarily to the small size of the literate populations. Libya had no Arab-owned newspapers before independence in 1951, and the only Libyan journalists worked for British-owned papers. South Yemen (then known as South Arabia and Aden) produced only a few indigenous Arab newspapers, including one daily after World War I when the territory was still under British protection. As late as 1956, there was still only one daily in the country. But during the next few years more newspapers were founded and the Britsh colonial administration allowed them considerable freedom to say what they liked in their editorials. By the 1960s, the newspapers had proliferated—there were four dailies and fourteen others—and became more outspoken; in effect, the South Yemeni press had left the colonial stage even before achieving independence in 1967.[14]

FACTIONAL STAGE

When the press in these countries left the colonial stage, it moved into what we may call the factional stage. Newspapers became more active politically and—more important—the press became considerably diversified and competitive. Newspapers were backed by private individuals, families, political parties, or by government interests, and they could be distinguished from each other in tone, content, and editorial viewpoint. Concomitant with this factionalism was a degree of freedom from governmental restrictions for the press which was greater than in any other stage of its development in these countries. The government did impose restrictions including censorship from time to time, but the newspapers were relatively independent during this period.

This stage emerged because of changes in the political environment, and there are several factors which were conducive to the transition.

Lifting of Colonial Restrictions

Lifting of colonial-power restrictions on the press usually corresponded with the achievement of complete national independence from the colonial power, as in the case of the press in Iraq (1932), Syria (1946), Libya (1951), and Algeria (1962). But in the case of Egypt, British colonial control over the press was in fact lifted after World War I even though the British retained other rights in Egypt after that time. (Censorship imposed by the government during the second World War did protect the British again from Egyptian press criticism but this measure was temporary.) The same was true in the Sudan and South Yemen, where the factional press also began to emerge before the British were entirely gone because British colonial administrators stopped exercising rights in the press field.

Competition among Political Groups

The second condition for the emergence of the factional press was a political environment in which several parties and groups were openly competing for power. Individual newspapers were able to align themselves with specific parties or groups with which they sympathized, and in this way gain financial and other support for their publishing efforts. The government usually had affiliations with one or more newspapers, but they by no means controlled all of them since anti-regime elements had their spokesmen in the press as well. Some independent papers developed during this period, but many were linked with political factions and known to be editorial apologists for partisan points of view.

This condition was present in Egypt between World War I and 1954 because political parties and groups became more important and their feuding intensified and because a balance of three political forces emerged—the king and his parties; the Wafd Party as the only effective local opposition; and the British, who still retained some rights and privileges after the Treaty of 1936. In fact, the Wafd Party used its newspapers as a chief weapon of political agitation because there was no opportunity for the nationalists to challenge the British militarily, so they took advantage of the press freedom to make their views known. Egypt's largest circulation paper, *al Misri*, was close to the Wafd. None of the papers was revolutionary, nor did they threaten the basic political system—the 1923 constitution allowed the government to confiscate a newspaper to protect the "interests of the social system"—but there was considerable diversity and competition. Some owners and editors were privately wealthy, but many needed funds because of low advertising and circulation revenues, so they accepted subsidies from various interest groups which frequently showed in editorials and newsplay. Except for the interlude of wartime censorship, the press was able to criticize policies, expose corruption in government, and reflect diverse philosophies and interests. One observer in the late 1940s found that Egypt had a vigorous and diverse party press, as well as a few nonpartisan dailies such as *al Ahram*.[15]

During the factional-press phase in Syria (1946–58) the country experienced a high degree of partisan political activity, a rapid turnover in government, and a competition among contenders for power, all of which were reflected in the press. One observer noted that "the press is reorganized every time Syria gets a new regime" during this period.[16] There were many newspapers, virtually every one run by a politically oriented editor who had close ties with a party, interest group, influential family, minister, or even a foreign embassy. These patrons underwrote various interests across a wide spectrum, so there was "no such thing as independent newspaper in the real sense of the term."[17]

Similarly in Iraq during this phase (1932–63) there were periods of vigorous, open political discussion, and the press arranged itself along a broad political spectrum. Parties and individuals, competing for power in a relatively unstable political environment, sought support from newspapers in promoting their interests. There was rapid turnover in papers but diversity remained. In the first decade after World War II approximately half of the papers reflected opposition to the government, and between 1958 and 1963 there was considerable partisan debate in the press, although the framework of the debate shifted to the left in the latter period under Abdal Karim Qasim as Communist writers were given official encouragement. In 1962 there were twenty newspapers in Baghdad alone, one-third of them Communist backed and the rest of varying shades of political opinion.[18]

The Sudanese press passed through the factional phase twice, 1953–58 and 1964–69. The first phase began when Sudanese party political activity increased in preparation for the February 1953 parliamentary election, and by the time of full independence in 1956 the country had sixteen intensely partisan newspapers, including nine dailies. The National Unionist Party, which controlled the government after gaining a majority in the election, had the support of two leading dailies while the opposition Ummah Party was affiliated with a third. Party newspapers were effectively suppressed during the military regime of General Ibrahim 'Abboud (1958–64), but after his overthrow a measure of political competition was restored to the Sudan and with it came a revival of diversity in the Sudanese press. Before, during, and after the elections of June 1965, heavily contested by many parties including the Communists, the newspapers reflected many different viewpoints supporting and opposing the government. This competitive situation among parties and papers lasted until General Jafar Numeiry came to power in 1969.

In Algeria the factional phase in the press was very brief because the party system was so weak that parties did not last very long. The National Liberation Front (FLN) led the fight for independence from the French, and when that was achieved in July 1962, a variety of newspapers reflecting diverse interests appeared. The FLN brought its official weekly *el Moudjahid* to Algiers from Tunis now that it was legal to do so, the Communist-backed *Alger Republicain* which the French had banned in 1955 reappeared, and the newly formed Algerian Peoples Party began publishing its official organ. In addition, European-owned dailies in Algiers, Oran, and Constantine survived the transition to independence. This diverse press reflected public political discussion, including criticism of the government which was heard in parliament as the disparate elements that had led the revolution argued over policy. But no strong non-governmental parties or groups other than the Communist Party emerged. The regime banned the Communist Party and the newly formed Algerian Peoples Party (PPA) in November 1962, forcing their official newspapers to close. The new parliament of August 1963 included only delegates who were loyal to the government or eschewed public criticism.[19] Consequently when the new constitution issued that month proclaimed Algeria a one-party state, the press had lost most of its diversity.

In South Yemen and Libya, the press went through a factional stage resembling those described above, but in these two countries the basis was primarily competing individual personalities and informal groups rather than formal political parties. South Yemen had one Arab daily paper in 1956, but a decade later there were three more plus fourteen weeklies and fortnightlies. The British colonial administration allowed them considerable freedom, and their editorial policies covered a range from strong nationalist to pro-British. Most of them developed close ties to the increasingly articulate political factions or to private interests competing for attention as British authority waned. This relatively open diversity lasted until independence in 1967.

In Libya the factional phase in the press lasted for eighteen years (1951–69) on the basis of support by diverse private interest groups and a government which restricted but did not suppress them. The government published papers in Tripoli and Benghazi, and various competing private interests which had become politically active after independence found supporters in the press who developed dailies and weeklies in those cities too.[20] The press editorial spectrum ranged from conservative, religious, and anti-Communist to leftist Nasserite sympathies, and it included some criticism of the government.[21]

Governmental Restraint

The third factor behind the factional press was the existence of a national government which was unwilling and/or unable to impose severe restrictions on publications. Typically during the factional stage, direct governmental interference with the press fluctuated; there were short periods of government intervention, but the regime did not maintain or institutionalize it. It may have acted against one newspaper by revoking its license or prosecuting the editor responsible, but it did not permanently change the ground rules for all newspapers. The main reason for this was that there was an element of balance in the political system, so that the government faced political forces beyond its direct control which in effect guaranteed the continuation of critical nongovernmental voices in the press.

The governments did impose restrictions in emergencies such as

World War II and the first Arab-Israeli war, and from time to time they attempted to restrict the press for other reasons but without ending its basically factional nature.[22] The governments generally had legal authority, such as temporary suspension of a publication or arrest of an editor, to use against the newspapers, but because of the political situation these were used sparingly.[23] It was the post-colonial political balance of forces and the government's role in that, rather than legal or constitutional guarantees (such as the 1923 Egyptian constitution's guarantee of a free press) which was the key factor in maintaining the essential diversity and relative freedom of the press in this phase.

NONPARTISAN STAGE

The third stage of press development in these countries was characterized by a sharp reduction in diversity among newspapers, a muting of criticism, and a greater degree of support for the regime. Thus some of the key trends of the second stage were reversed, although much of the press remained in private hands. This stage was introduced by a zealous new revolutionary leadership group after it seized power. Three major steps brought about the transition.

End of Political Competition

First and most important was the sudden banning of competing political parties and private interest groups by the new leadership shortly after it seized power. Since the ruling group had power but its authority was not yet legitimized or fully established, it banned the parties in order to prevent any real challenge or organized opposition. The group's own political organization, whether pre-existing or created after the coup d'etat, was ordinarily proclaimed the only legal party. Naturally, as a consequence of this political move the party newspapers were banned at the same time, so that members of the outlawed parties would be deprived of their communication channel. This step effectively removed key underpinnings of the diverse and independent press.

Increased Governmental Intervention

Secondly, the new regime increased direct governmental intervention in the press, including its use of censorship of newspapers. The private papers continued to appear, but the government tended to take legal actions against them more frequently in order to make them adhere to the official political line.

Promotion of the Regime's Newspapers

And thirdly, the regime began to promote its own newspapers more as channels of communication and exhortation of the masses in the direction of its goals. Both of these measures were signs that the regime was sensitive to the political role of the press, concerned about evoking support from it, and strong enough to take such steps.

Egypt was the first of the seven countries to take its press into the nonpartisan stage, as it was first with all stages.

The military officers who seized power in Egypt on July 23, 1952, immediately abolished the monarchy, but almost as quickly they established their own "publishing house of the revolution," *Dar al Tahrir* (Liberation House), in order to make known the ideas and personalities of the new leadership. By September, Dar al Tahrir had begun publishing a bi-monthly magazine, *al Tahrir*. The magazine was anti-imperialist, leftist revolutionary in tone,, but supportive of the ruling Revolutionary Command Council. Several of the RCC members wrote for it, including Anwar Sadat and Gamal Abdul Nasser who were then still relatively unknown figures behind the presidency of General Muhammad Naguib. In December, the publishing house started its own daily newspaper, *al Gumhuriyah*, on a license issued in Nasser's name.[24] In January 1953 President Naguib announced the formation of a single new political organization, the National Liberation Rally, and banned all other parties and their journals as "prejudicial to the national interest."[25]

At the same time, the Revolutionary Command Council took direct action against the remaining influential privately owned newspapers. General Naguib increased press censorship when he became President of Egypt in September 1952. Colonel Nasser tried to lift censorship when he emerged as Prime Minister in February 1954, but the subsequent outburst of criticism from the unshackled newspapers caused him to reimpose it a month later, and censorship has been used periodically ever since. Small-circulation papers which had no impact on Egyptian political life, such as *Journal d'Egypte*, were allowed to stay in private hands.

The regime also used its licensing power and other legal weapons against uncooperative papers. The creation of a monopoly political party had lowered the amount of public debate over government policy, but still not enough to satisfy the RCC. Three private daily newspapers—*al Ahram*, *Akhbar al-Yawm*, and *al Misri*—were popular and way ahead of the RCC's *al Gumhuriyah* in circulation. The biggest, *al Misri*, had a circulation of more than 120,000.[26] It tended to reflect views of the recently abolished Wafd Party and was critical of the regime, calling for real parliamentary rule. In 1954 it openly criticized Nasser after other newspapers had muted their opposition. *Al-Misri* editors saw Nasser as a usurper of people's rights (as defined primarily by the Wafdists), and its editorials, under the heading "Back to your Barracks" directly attacked the RCC.[27] In April 1954 the RCC revoked the publishing license of *al-Misri*, and the Arab world's largest-circulation paper suddenly ceased to exist.[28]

At the same time, the regime took legal action against particular individuals who worked for newspapers. The RCC had the publisher of *al-Misri*, the Fatih brothers, tried before a revolutionary panel for "aiming to destroy the government," "spreading hostile propaganda," and otherwise acting against the national interest. The tribunal sentenced them to ten and fifteen years each, and the government seized their entire enterprise which had published other newspapers as well. The RCC had also jailed Ihsan Abdal Quddus, the editor of the well-known left-wing publication, *Rose al Yusif*, for a year. It dissolved the Press Syndicate and arrested several members, whom it accused of accepting large bribes from sinister elements.[29] Others were dealt with in similar fashion.

Thus the measures that the RCC took during its first two years in power—abolishing political parties and groups, censoring, closing newspapers and newspaper guilds, and jailing prominent newspaper men, and at the same time creating its own publishing house—had the combined effect of severely limiting any criticism of the regime and its policies. The RCC did not take over direct control of all private newspapers, but these other measures made it very clear to Egyptian journalists that they had to stay within certain lines in order to continue writing and publishing.

A similar pattern was repeated in other countries. When Syria merged with Egypt into the United Arab Republic in 1958, all political parties and their newspapers were banned in Syria as they had been in Egypt, and the regime-sponsored National Union was declared the only legal political organization.

The UAR government also imposed censorship in Syria and sponsored its own newspapers. As one observer described the result, in fact "the press spoke with one voice" during this period reflecting the lack of open political dissent in Syria.[30] Even after the military *coup d'etat* in Damascus in December 1961 led to Syria's withdrawal from the UAR, the various and competing political parties did not re-emerge to play their parts in the political system. The new ruling groups and others that came to power by *coup d'etat* prevented any public activities by political organizations which challenged their authority, so party newspapers also did not revive. The Syrian regimes continued censorship and the practice of sponsoring their own newspapers. After the September 1961 military coup led to withdrawal, some parties tried to resume political activity but boycotted the December elections. They were banned after the next coup in March. The Ba'th coup came a year later, in March 1963, and one wing or another of the Ba'th has ruled Syria ever since.

Similarly in Iraq, when Colonel Abdul Salam 'Arif seized power on November 18, 1963, he formed the Arab Socialist Union and declared it to be the only authorized political organization in the country, putting an end to the party press which had been active for three decades. Five months later, the 'Arif regime promulgated Press Law no. 53 which gave the government powers to censor publications critical of the administration, and to revoke licenses of newspapers publishing "whatever contributes a danger to the Republic and the internal and external security of the state."[31]

In Algeria and South Yemen, the first independent native government was formed by a revolutionary "National Liberation Front" which had led the fight to expel the colonial power. The Algerian FLN took over the country's leadership in the summer of 1962, and by November it was able to ban the Algerian Peoples Party and the Communist Party, forcing their official newspapers to close. The new constitution of August 1963 formally proclaimed Algeria a one-party state, and the new parliament elected in that month included only delegates who were loyal to the government or eschewed public criticism.[32] The press reflected this increased political uniformity, but the government also used censorship powers to deal with private papers which stepped out of line. At the same time, the National Liberation Front promoted its weekly, *el Moudjahid*, and during 1962 and 1963 established three daily newspapers and ten other publications, to spread the regime's point of view.[33] This system continued under the regime of President Houari Boumedienne (1965–78), and under that of his successor, President Chadli Benjedid (1979–).

In South Yemen, the NLF took over in November 1967 as the Brit-

ish withdrew; it established a Peoples Republic in which no political organizations other than the NLF were allowed, so party political papers
could not be published, according to the *New York Times*, December 1,
1967. The NLF began its own daily newspaper, *14 October*, as well as a
weekly, and the regime kept close watch on the private press, dealing
with criticism by legal means.

The press in the Sudan and Libya underwent a transformation of
a similar nature, but different in some details.

There were no political parties in Libya when Colonel Muammar
Qaddafi and his military group seized power from the monarchy there
on September 1, 1969, so he had none to ban and did not need to create
his own party. But Qaddafi established a regime similar to the others
mentioned above and he did not allow the development of any competing political organizations or party newspapers in the new republic. He
did start publishing the regime's own newspaper, *al Thawrah* (The
Revolution), to help explain his ideas; the paper disappeared in January
1972, but a new government daily, *al Fajr al Jadid* (The New Dawn),
began later the same year and carried on the campaign for the regime.
Qaddafi also used some of the powers of the government to undermine
the effectiveness of the private press. It sharply cut back on subsidies
that the monarchy had given the private press, and in January 1970 declared that only *al Thawrah* should receive the lucrative advertisements
placed by government ministries.[34] This put the other papers, including
the independent dailies—*al Raa'id*, *al Hurriyah*, and *al Haqiqah*—at a
disadvantage. Then in January 1972, Qaddafi's Revolutionary Command Council held "corruption of public opinion" trials which resulted
in the suspension of all newspapers and the revocation of publishing licenses for ten papers including *al Hurriyah, al Yawm, al Zaman, al Fajr*,
and *al Haqiqah*. The RCC has also used censorship and other legal
means to encourage conformity with its policies. The publications law
of June 17, 1972, for example, required that newspaper owners "believe
in the Arab revolution and abide by its objectives and the objectives and
principles of the ASU."[35]

In the Sudan, General Ibrahim 'Abboud led a successful military
coup d'etat on November 17, 1958; his regime banned all political parties and their official newspapers. 'Abboud started his own newspaper,
al Thawrah. The private papers that continued to appear were relatively nonpartisan in content and were kept in line by the strict government censorship which General 'Abboud imposed and under threat of
suspension which encouraged them to follow the official policy line.
For example *al Nil*, the Sudan's oldest newspaper, was suspended in

February 1960 for disagreeing with Abboud's policy.[36] The October 1964 revolution ousted 'Abboud and restored some party activity, taking the press temporarily back to the factional stage. But General Jafar Numeiry's *coup d'etat* of May 25, 1969, led, within a month, to the banning of all political organizations other than his Revolutionary Council, again ending the party-backed press. Numeiry used some of the powers of the government to influence the private press, which became less outspoken than before his coup, but he did not create his own newspaper to compete directly with them as other leaders had done in similar circumstances.

Thus in all of these countries a revolutionary leadership group was able to use governmental powers to restrict the press more directly than its predecessor regime, and by banning all competing political organizations it undermined one of the essential foundations for a diverse press independent of governmental control. In most places, the ruling group was also able to counter the press competition directly by putting out its own newspaper. By these means, it moved the press into the nonpartisan stage characterized by a greater degree of uniformity and of loyalty to the government.

MOBILIZATION STAGE

In the final stage of development, private newspaper ownership is ended, and all politically important papers are controlled directly by a political agent of the ruling group or its affiliate. They are all supposed to mobilize public support for the regime. This stage has been fully achieved in Egypt, Iraq, Algeria, and the Sudan. In Syria, Libya, and South Yemen a very similar situation has been brought about without the formal end of private newspaper ownership. What are the conditions that have led to the emergence of the mobilization press?

First, the ruling group, which came to power by means of revolution or *coup*, has established a reasonably firm hold on the means of coercion (such as military or police). It has also been in power long enough to eliminate all political organizations which openly competed for leadership. Nevertheless the leadership was aware that its authority had not fully been legitimated, and it was sensitive to even slight criticism and the possibility of dissatisfaction with its program.[37]

In this situation the leadership regarded the press as an important political tool and was concerned and impatient that the newspapers had not yet more uniformly and enthusiastically promoted the policies and ideas of the regime. It felt that the press should by then have begun to play its part more effectively to help implement important programs. As President Numeiry said when he announced the end of the private press in the Sudan, one year after seizing power:

> Most papers have gone to great lengths to appraise the course of the revolution, giving arbitrary interpretations. . . . They have thus ignored the principles and goals declared by the revolution. . . . Confusion and perplexity have been created according to the different explanations. . . . Certain newspapers have broken up speeches and statements by members of the RCC and ministers, . . . distorted those speeches and published fragments to convey the opposite sense from the original statements. . . . Certain newspapers have been concentrating on cleverly destroying the positive achievements of the revolution. They publish on the first page a report about an internal achievement . . . and at the same time publish on the same page another report to contradict the first, to slant it or to sow doubts about it.[38]

Although the opposition party press had disappeared with the abolition of political parties, still the national leadership was disappointed in the remaining private newspapers.[39] Added to this was disappointment that the newspaper published by the ruling group to propagate its ideas had failed to become more successful and popular than the existing private papers despite its advantages over them. *Al Gumhuriyah* in Egypt, *el Moudjahid* in Algeria, *al Thawrah* in Iraq, *al Ba'th* in Syria, *al Thawrah* in Libya, and *14 October* in South Yemen were all daily newspapers published by the revolutionary leadership after it took power, but none of them surpassed the private newspapers with which they had to compete. In Egypt, for example, *al Gumhuriyah* remained far below the established private dailies *al Akhbar* and *al Ahram* in circulation, and in Algeria the private *la Depeche* had more than four times as many readers as the FLN's *le Peuple.*[40]

The ruling group particularly felt the need for a uniformly supportive press in order to advance its revolutionary program against what it perceived as an unjust resistance. Observers of the Egyptian press, for example, stress the significance of the timing of the press reorganization there in 1960, just a year before the Egyptian government's nationalization of important sectors of the economy. The Nasser regime apparently became convinced it could not nationalize the economy if the press was "still in the hands of the capitalists."[41] President Nasser and his associates saw the owners of most of the newspapers as big capitalists who would resist and possibly openly oppose the coming socialist measures, and an explanation attached to the Egyptian press law said "public ownership of the means of social and political guidance is a way in the new society of prohibiting capitalist domination over the means of guidance, establishing democracy and the public ownership of the means of guidance, which is the press."[42]

The transition to the fourth stage of press development, in which the private press was abolished, was usually accomplished by leaders who espoused socialism and perceived themselves as engaged in a struggle for society against vested interests of capitalists. At the same time, these leaders adhered to a strongly nationalistic ideology which put great emphasis on a struggle against foreign influence, imperialism, and Zionism.

In Iraq, for example, the preamble to the 1967 law stated that it was necessary to abolish the private press because of "the current battle the Arab nation is waging against imperialism, Zionism, and reaction, which requires that the Iraqi press be guided on sound national lines to meet the responsibility of the battle, and in order to prevent infiltration of the press . . . [and to] disseminate sound ideas, provide true guidelines, and carry out constructive criticism in a manner that would preserve the state in the present exceptional circumstances."[43]

In the Sudan, President Numeiry declared that his takeover of the private press was necessary because some newspapers were "mere tools serving the objectives and goals of British imperialism," and "certain newspapers have become trumpets for saboteurs, publishing the fabricated reports of the imperialist newspapers which have launched a psychological war against the revolution."[44]

And when Algeria ended its private press, government-controlled Radio Algiers broadcast a commentary which said that the move would end "attacks on our country," praising it as "a great victory over hired pens, absurd tendentious propaganda," and "filthy psychological campaigns."[45]

The regimes in these countries, therefore, had firm control over the instruments of coercion but not of persuasion, which they saw—or said they saw—as remaining in the hands of reactionary forces. As long as these regimes had new revolutionary programs to implement, and since the private newspapers did not cooperate enough in that endeavor, they sought to take them over as a useful political tool which would help put their ideas across without interference.[46] Because their countries were not at war and such measures were difficult to justify these regimes did not wish simply to use broad censorship measures.[47]

Nor did they wish to make their move on the press appear to be the imposition of state control over the newspapers. (Egyptians, for example, take pains to argue that their reorganization of the press in 1960 was not "nationalization"; see Chapter 2.) They therefore transferred ownership of the private press into the hands of the ruling political organization, which they claimed represented "the people"—sometimes even avoiding the term "party" because that implies narrow representation.[48]

In Libya, South Yemen, and Syria, the ruling elite has not formally moved the press into the final stage by legally abolishing the private press. In these cases, however, the loyalty and active support of the press and the *de facto* disappearance of all significant private newspapers has been sufficient to satisfy the regime and it is not necessary to sanctify this situation in law. In Libya, the government forced the last of the private daily newspapers to close in 1972, and the only dailies which have appeared since that time are the regime's own, primarily *al Fajr al Jadid, al Jihad* and *al Ra'y*. Likewise in South Yemen the only dailies that in fact appear, *al Thawri* and *14 October*, are controlled by the National Front which rules the country. Neither country ever did have a well-developed party system or well-organized political groupings, so in contrast to the other countries discussed above, these two regimes probably find it unnecessary to take the legal step of officially abolishing the party and private press in order to make clear that only the regime has the right to publish.

The Syrian ruling groups have also not taken this final step to legitimize the government press monopoly which in fact exists. Syrian parties were banned in 1958, but when parties were included again in Syrian cabinets in the 1970s, their newspapers did not reappear. These parties, including the Communists and the Arab Socialists, were in fact not true opposition groups or organizations which in any way threatened and challenged the basic policies of the ruling Ba'th Party leadership. Instead, they were officially members of the so-called National Front, and in fact they followed Ba'th guidelines on all essential issues. Thus the *de facto* creation of a mobilized press, fully loyal and actively supportive of the regime, which had been established in 1963, continued. The Syrian journalist therefore finds himself in the same practical situation as does the Algerian journalist, for example, or the Sudanese. He knows he is required to give positive support to the essential policies of his government.

In Iraq, as in Syria, the regime has in recent years formed National Front governments including parties other than the Ba'th which are not true opposition parties and thus are not allowed to criticize basic policy. The Communists and the Kurdish Democratic Party have participated in the National Front in the 1970s, since they loyally support essential Ba'th Party tenets. In Iraq, these pseudo-parties have been allowed to resume publication of their own newspapers, *Tariq al Sha'b* (Communist Party organ) and *Taakhi* (KDP organ), but these papers are put out by the government's General Establishment of Press and Printing, just like the Ba'th Party's official organ *al Thawrah* and the government's *al Jumhuriyah*. The content of all four of these papers, and of the government's English-language daily, *Baghdad Observer*, reveals only minor differences in political opinion or in news presentation, and none on sensitive issues.[49] On these sensitive issues, the other two parties are in effect agents of the regime, which controls the press ultimately through them. The newspapers published by these parties are therefore very similar in content.

Thus we have seen that in all of these countries, the press has gone through a series of stages leading to the current situation in which it is more or less mobilized in active support of the ruling group. Two key related factors in this evolution were the relative strength of the regime and the existence of organized opposition groups which are able to function openly. Diversity in the press and competition among newspapers did exist during the factional stage following the lifting of colonial restrictions and before the regime acquired sufficient power to take control of the press. During this factional period, representational parties were active and their existence helped create necessary conditions for diversity in the press since some newspapers reflected opposition party views. Where the representational parties and groups independent of the regime were particularly weak, as in Algeria or South Yemen, for example, the factional phase did not last long and did not return once it ended. Elsewhere, in the Sudan, fissiparous tendencies in the political spectrum reasserted themselves in the mid-sixties into the re-emergence of political parties, and with them came a revival of a diverse and competing press—although both party and press competition ended again in 1969.

As these regimes grew stronger, they sought to create a press which was more uniformly and actively supportive, a goal they were able to achieve particularly after representational parties had disappeared. The regime's political organization, a solidarity party, became a favorite agent for newspaper control.

The parties which appeared in Syria and Iraq later as legitimate and legal participants in the political process did not lead to a diverse press in those countries because these were not truly representational parties advocating policies fundamentally at variance with those of the ruling group.[50] Similarly, the parties that were created in Egypt in November 1976 out of the three wings of the Arab Socialist Union, and which were permitted to publish their own papers, did not overnight create clear press diversity because policy differences among the parties remained small, and those journalists who were critical of the government had difficulty in publicizing their views (see Chapter 2).

As long as the regimes in these countries remain strong and dominate the political scene, not allowing opposition groups to form and to direct criticism against the government, and as long as the regimes continue to regard the press as important instruments for mobilization of the public the newspapers will probably remain as they are, basically similar in political content and differing only in style. If the political system in these countries evolved so that representational parties emerged and public debate on issues took place, a diverse press less subject to government influence would probably follow. A diverse and criticizing press (which would probably have greater reader credibility, although we have no survey data to prove that) can exist only if there is diversity in the political spectrum that can be expressed publicly. Such a diverse press would, in turn, give opposition groups the open forum they would need to challenge the ruling group in an open system.

4

The Loyalist Press

In six Arab countries—Jordan, Tunisia, Saudi Arabia, Bahrain, Qatar, and the United Arab Emirates—the press plays generally the same kind of role in the political process. We designate this type the loyalist press because its most prominent characteristic is that the newspapers are consistently loyal to and supportive of the regime in power despite the fact that they are privately owned. In this chapter we will discuss that and other characteristics of this type of press, and the major factors that have led to its emergence in these countries. As with the mobilization press we will focus on the daily newspapers and highlight the common features that apply to all six countries, but we will also mention deviations from the model.

Of the six countries, three have had daily newspapers only a short time: the UAE since 1970, Qatar since 1975 and Bahrain since 1976. Before these countries became independent in 1971, they had developed a non-daily press, but it was quite limited. In Bahrain, the paper *Jaridit al Bahrayn* began in the 1940s, *Sada al Usbu'* appeared in 1969, and another weekly *al Mujtama' al Jadid* followed a year later. Qatar's first weekly, *The Gulf News*, began in 1969, followed by *al 'Urubah* in 1970. In the Trucial States, which in 1971 became the UAE, the weeklies and monthlies *Akhbar Dubai*, *Ra's al Khaymah*, *al Shuruq*, *al Khalij*, *al Ittihad*, and the *Abu Dhabi News* all appeared in the few years before independence. The other three countries—Jordan, Tunisia, and Saudi Arabia—have had a much longer experience with a daily press. Most of the examples and specific discussion on this chapter, therefore, will be taken from the latter countries, although the newer daily the press in

71

the UAE, Qatar and Bahrain does seem to be following the same pattern (see Table 4).

PRIVATE OWNERSHIP

Generally speaking, the newspapers in these countries are in private ownership. They have not been taken over by political agents of the regime, as has the mobilization press, nor have they been nationalized directly by the state. Ownership by private individuals, families, and groups is one important structural characteristic of the press in these countries which helps to differentiate it from the press elsewhere in the Arab world.

There are exceptions to the basic rule of private ownership in these countries, but the exceptions are few—two dailies in Tunisia and one in the UAE—and they have special reasons. In Tunisia, two of the five daily newspapers, al 'Amal and l 'Action, are organs of the ruling Destourian Socialist Party (PSD), while the rest are in private hands. Both al 'Amal and the French language l 'Action are financed partly by the PSD, and PSD members occupy key positions on their editorial staffs as well as on their boards of directors.[1] On the basis of this one characteristic, Tunisia might seem to have a mobilization type of press. But the system in Tunisia results from a situation rather different from that in the mobilization press countries. President Habib Bourguiba, who has dominated the Tunisian political scene since Tunisia's independence in 1956, has had a personal interest in and association with party newspapers dating from the early years of his political career in the 1930s. In those days, he wrote for Destour Party papers which were predecessors of the current ones, and in 1932 he established his own politically oriented paper, l 'Action Tunisienne. It is understandable therefore that in the political system of independent Tunisia, which he has overwhelmingly influenced, he would have his political party continue to publish newspapers because he sees them as an important part of his political success.[2]

Tunisian party papers play a substantially different role in the political process from the role the mobilization papers play. The two party dailies in Tunisia were established long before independence, and continued in an unbroken line after Bourguiba achieved power. They were not created after independence merely as a means to help the new regime stay in office but were carried over from earlier days of political

TABLE 4
Major Daily Newspapers in Six Countries
(1976)

Name	Est. circ.	Location	First pub.
JORDAN			
Al Ra'y (The Opinion)	18,000	Amman	1971
Al Dustur (The Constitution)	20,000	"	1967
Al Urdun (Jordan)	1,000	"	1923
Jordan Times*	1,000	"	1975
TUNISIA			
Al Sabah (The Morning)	35,000	Tunis	1950
La Presse de Tunisie†	30,000	"	1939
L'Action†	27,000	"	1932
Al 'Amal (Action)	27,000	"	1957
Le Temps†	20,000	"	1976
SAUDI ARABIA			
Al Riyadh (Riyadh)	25,000	Riyadh	1965
'Ukaz	18,000	Jidda	1960
Al Madinah (Madina)	16,000	"	1937
Al Nadwah (The Forum)	15,000	"	1958
Al Bilad (The Country)‡	12,000	"	1946
Arab News*	10,000	"	1975
Al Yawm (Today)	5,000	Dammam	1959
Al Jazirah (The Peninsula)	4,500	Riyadh	1962
Saudi Gazette*	1,200	Jidda	1976
BAHRAIN			
Akhbar al Khalij (Gulf News)	10,000	Manama	1976
QATAR			
Al 'Arab (The Arab)	2,000	Dawha	1975
UNITED ARAB EMIRATES			
Al Wahdah (Unity)	3,000	Abu Dhabi	1973
Al Ittihad (Federation)	5,000	"	1970

*Published in English.
†Published in French.
‡al Bilad al Sa'udia, est. 1946, was renamed al Bilad in 1958.

competition by a man who made use of them as a political writer. More importantly, except for Bourguiba's two party newspapers, the rest of the press has remained in private hands.

The only other significant daily newspaper in these six countries that is not wholly in private hands is *al Ittihad* in the United Arab Emirates. This paper was established by Abu Dhabi in 1970 when it was still a Trucial State but approaching independence and seeking to advocate Abu Dhabi views. The paper remained in government hands after independence and the formation of the UAE federation in 1971, although in 1976 the government transferred it to a new semi-autonomous publishing house in order to make the government role and responsibility for content less direct. In the meantime, a number of other newspapers had appeared in post-independence UAE which were entirely in private hands: Rashid 'Awaida's daily *al Wahdah* (1973), Muhammad Suwaydi's weeklies *al Wathbah* and *Gulf Times* (1974), 'Abdul Fattah Sa'id's *Sawt al Ummah*, and Rashid Abdullah's *al Fajr* (1975). The press is overwhelmingly in private hands, although it receives government subsidies.[3]

In the other countries—Jordan, Saudi Arabia, Bahrain, and Qatar —the press is entirely owned by private persons. The Jordanian government established its own newspaper *al Ra'y* in 1971 alongside the private press for special reasons (see below), but that situation was only temporary and the paper was turned over to private owners in 1974.

NEWSPAPER CONTENT

The content of the press in these countries, particularly as it relates to political matters, has some of the attributes found in the mobilization press described in the previous two chapters. Like the latter, the loyalist press in each country tends not to attack the basic tenets of national policy as enunciated by the regime, it eschews criticism of the personalities at the top of the national government, and it exhibits little real diversity of treatment or view on important issues. There are, however, significant differences between the loyalist press and the mobilization press.

The loyalist press, like the mobilization press, does not question the major policies of the regime or attack the personalities at the top of the national leadership. Editors in these countries admit that their newspapers, in commentaries and in newsplay, support the official line and the head of government on all essential matters.[4] However, the loyalist papers are much more likely to criticize government services which the general public finds deficient, and print stories which put specific government officials in a negative light. This does not happen every day, and the criticism is gentle by Western standards, not in any case casting doubt on the top leadership. The Saudi press, for example, has criticized the Pilgrimage Ministry on some details of its handling of the annual pilgrimage, and Saudi papers have criticized the government schools for girls on their educational policies.[5] The Jordanian press has criticized officials for water shortages and failure to control inflation.[6] Most of the negative press treatment concerns local domestic issues, although occasionally it also deals with foreign policy issues of a secondary nature. The Tunisian press for example, does not discuss pros and cons on the sensitive issues of the Arab-Israeli conflict or Tunisian-U.S. relations, but it sometimes does on the less vital Asian or Latin American questions.[7]

In addition, the tone and style of the loyalist press differentiate it from other Arab newspapers. The loyalist press tends to be more passive. On the whole, it avoids some critical issues, it is slower to react editorially to events, and it tends to be more muted in its commentaries. It avoids the language and opinions of aggressive revolutionary journalism which are characteristic of the mobilization press, in which writers continuously do battle with enemies and evils, real or imagined, and loudly exhort the public on to victory for the goals of the regime. The loyalist press does take care to give adequate publicity to government activities and achievements, and from time to time inveighs against evils, but it does so generally not in such a strident, combative way, and its news treatment is more likely to be straightforward or even dull. Thorough and independent investigative reporting is rare.[8]

The loyalist press in each country lacks essential diversity among newspapers largely as a consequence of the support it gives to the regime on all fundamental issues. As one Saudi editor put it, "the newspapers are so similar they might as well be nationalized."[9] The content of the press on important political issues is in each country quite similar, despite the fact that nearly all of the newspapers in these countries are privately owned by individuals and groups.

In Jordan, for example, the daily paper with the closest ties to the regime tends to be more optimistic on internal and external problems, and responds more readily in defense of Jordan when foreign criticisms are voiced, while the other dailies tend to be somewhat more pessimistic, printing more news with negative overtones without becoming openly critical.[10] On sensitive subjects such as the question of the Palestinians, subtle differences in language give clues to underlying editorial views, but truly critical views are not expressed outright.[11]

Likewise, in Saudi Arabia the daily newspapers (seven Arabic, two in English as of 1976) differ in content from each other only in the amount of space they give to secondary stories and nonpolitical items.

For example, if the king makes a public statement or takes a public action, such as making a trip or receiving an important visitor, that news will be the top story on all front pages and the treatment will probably be verbatim from the government-controlled Saudi News Agency.[12] However, the Saudi dailies are slightly dissimilar in the amount of attention they give to particular subjects. Some papers typically carry more news about the Arab world and others carry more international news from outside the Middle East. Some focus on Islamic items, while others are strong on local stories or literary articles and features.[13] Even in Tunisia, there is little essential difference on major stories between the PSD-owned newspapers and the private ones. All of the Tunisian papers operate within the framework of national policy and on major stories take the bulk of their copy from the government-controlled Tunis Arab Press news agency. The non-PSD papers may add details and slightly different interpretations developed by their own reports. Also, the private press, especially the sister papers *al Sabah* and *le Temps*, have a slightly more aggressive style. However, on politically important subjects, the basic lines of the story tend to be the same in all papers.[14]

The same holds true for the nascent press in the small states on the Persian Gulf. In the UAE, the privately owned daily newspaper *al Wahdah* does not differ in politically important content from the government-owned daily *al Ittihad*. They have somewhat different styles, the former presenting more features and translations from foreign articles, while the latter is stronger on international news and has more original reports. The private weekly paper *al Wathbah* is a bit more aggressive and outspoken than the others, particularly on Arab affairs. But all of the new UAE newspapers support the basic policies of the UAE Government and give good, favorable coverage to UAE officials. In Bahrain and Qatar, comparisons cannot be made between daily newspapers because they each have only one, but the pattern is discernible among the non-daily papers. The Bahraini weekly *al Adwa*, founded in 1965, focuses on national events, and on foreign policy it takes a moderate Arab nationalist line; *Sada al Usbu'*, which appeared in 1969, is slightly to the left of *al Adwa*, while the weekly *al Mujtama al Jadid*, started in 1970, is slightly to the right. All of them, however, support fundamental government policies, as does the new daily, *Akhbar al Khalij*. Similarly in Qatar there are no serious political differences between the publications of the Dar al 'Urubah publishing house (the daily *al 'Arab* and the weeklies *al 'Urubah* and *Gulf News*) and those of the government departments.

FACTORS RESPONSIBLE FOR PRESS LOYALISM

If the press is basically in private hands in these countries, why are the newspapers so uniform in content and so supportive of the government? How does the government influence the press so much without controlling newspapers through partisan agents or direct ownership? Essentially the government has and uses influence derived from legal authority and its financial benefits, and this influence is effective because the press is susceptible to it and because of the political environment.

Government Influence Derived from Legal Authority

The governments in these countries have certain rights and powers which they can use to influence the press even though it is in private hands.

Saudi Arabia's current press law, promulgated in 1963, declares that the press is private and the state has no right to interfere with it except for the sake of the "general welfare." In these cases, which the law says will occur "rarely" (*nadiran*), the government has the right to stop a paper from publishing. The law also gives the government influence over personnel selection in the press. The Information Ministry can veto any candidate for the fifteen-member board of directors each paper must have, and it is the ministry which selects the board chairman and the paper's editor-in-chief from among a slate of candidates, nominated by the board.[15]

These legal powers to close the newspapers if necessary and to veto or select top personnel, are not used very often, but the fact that they are available helps give the government some day-to-day influence over the content of the newspaper. A phone call from the Ministry of Information is usually enough to persuade an editor to emphasize one story or downplay another. If the editor prints a news item which the ministry would rather have seen ignored, the ministry may levy a fine on the paper as a small punishment and a warning not to violate certain taboos. One Saudi newspaper has been fined, for example, for quoting a Syrian editorial calling for the elimination of "imperialist" interests in the Arab world—a reference that readers would take to mean U.S. business interests like the ones in Saudi Arabia. Another Saudi paper was chastised by the ministry for publishing news of anarchist demonstrations in the West—apparently regarded as too dangerous an example to talk about.[16]

Jordan's Press and Publication Law, first passed in 1953 and modified somewhat in 1955 and 1973, gives the government the authority to license all newspapers and magazines, and to withdraw the license if a publication "threatens the national existence" or security, infringes on the "constitutional principles of the kingdom," harms the "national feeling" (*al shu'ur al qawmi*), or offends "public decency" (*al adab al 'ammah*). The law specifically forbids publication of news about the royal family unless approved by it, of articles defaming religion or contrary to public morality or unauthorized military and secret information.[17]

The Jordanian government has used these powers occasionally. In March 1967, for example, after the press expressed dismay at the inability of the army to respond adequately to military raids across the border by Israel, Prime Minister Wasfi Tell declared that the newspapers had "failed to meet the level of responsibility expected of them" in the crisis, and he had all publishing licenses revoked. The government then issued new licenses on condition that the four Jerusalem dailies merge into two —ostensibly to improve the quality of the press, but the move was widely regarded as an attempt to evoke more support for the government through this warning.[18] Then in the summer of 1970, when the Palestinian commando (*fida'iyin*) movement seriously challenged the Jordanian government and actually took control over parts of the country, the government again used its legal powers against the press. It closed the two dailies *al Dustur* and *al Difa'a* on June 14 when they carried on their front pages a *fida'iyin* communiqué blaming the "reactionary regime" for the conflict. The government allowed them to reopen two weeks later because it was not strong enough to suppress the new fida'iyin daily *al Fatah*, which took their place and was a stronger critic. But after the final showdown of September, *al Fatah* disappeared along with the fida'iyin, and the government again withdrew the license of *al Difa'a* as a punishment.[19]

The Jordanian government rarely resorts to these methods. It is probably restrained in part by a concern that direct control would undermine the credibility of the government and of the press. Nevertheless, just the fact that the government can close a paper in a national emergency, or take it to court at any time, makes editors pay particular attention when the government complains to them about what they have published. As one Jordanian official describes the relationship, "in most cases the government simply has a talk with the paper's editor and asks it not to continue printing the offensive item, and this usually works."[20]

The Tunisian press operates under the same basic rules. The Tunisian Press Code affirms "freedom of the press" but limits that freedom where necessary "to protect society from anything injurious to tranquillity, security and public order," and "to protect the state and the constituted agencies of government against anything liable to cause foreign or domestic disorders."[21] The government has used these powers occasionally to suspend or close newspapers, but usually this is not necessary as the leadership can influence a newspaper's content simply by a phone call to an editor after he has printed something they do not like, asking him not to repeat the offense.[22] In the United Arab Emirates the press law focuses on the journalists, giving the government the authority to issue these journalists the required professional licenses, and to revoke these "without exploring the reasons."[23] Like the other governmental press powers mentioned above, this one is only rarely used, but the law's existence lends considerable weight to oral comments on newspaper content which the Information Ministry passes to editors from time to time. These comments are usually conveyed informally and privately because under the circumstances a quiet word is sufficient to bring results, and the government can refrain from open intervention which would undermine credibility.

Moreover, in times of national emergencies these governments can and do exercise even greater influence over press content, in the same manner, by asserting to editors that the national interest requires loyal support of the regime and its policies during the crisis. The continuation for over a quarter century of the Arab-Israeli conflict with its intermittent flareups of violence and periods of tension, makes this situation not uncommon.

Government Influence Derived from Financial Benefits

The government has another asset which also helps give it practical influence over press content. In all of these countries the government is a major source of revenue to the newspapers, in the form of official government advertisements, subscriptions for government employees, and in some cases direct subsidies. Because the government plays such an important role in the economy in all of these countries, the commercial tenders, personnel notices and other ads issued regularly by the ministries are voluminous, and typically they are the largest source of a daily newspaper's income.[24] Newspapers which encounter financial difficulties are frequently assisted at year's end with subvention payments. Neither the government ads nor the subsidies are explicitly tied to pro-government newspaper content, and there is usually no discernible discrimination in government distribution of funds. However, editors and publishers are just as aware of the government's carrot as they are of its stick, and the general effect of these financial arrangements is to increase their tendency to make their newspapers loyal to the regime.[25]

Susceptibility of the Press to Influence

Government influence over the private press in these countries would not be as great as it is, however, if the newspapers themselves did not have some particular characteristics that make them vulnerable. For a variety of reasons, these newspapers have not developed a strong tradition of independent journalism, or an independent financial base, to help them withstand government pressure to conform and be loyal to the regime. Publishers, editors and other newspaper staff members carry out their tasks not from a position of Fourth Estate strength based on an ethic of independence and a self-sufficient budget, but from a position of relative institutional weakness.

Saudi Arabia has had indigenous journalism almost since the beginning of the twentieth century, but its experience with modern-style newspapers and political reporting and commentary is not very extensive. In December 1925 the al Sa'ud family unified the country by adding the Western Province (Hijaz) to the Central and Eastern Provinces which it already controlled. Prior to that, the Hijaz had enjoyed a fairly active press for seventeen years, but virtually all of the newspapers were run by resident foreigners.[26] Then, during the first fifteen years of Saudi rule, the Hijaz press flourished under the leadership of Hijazi intellectuals, but the content of the press was almost entirely literary rather than news or politics. Even the official Saudi government journal *Umm al Qura* (which today is merely an official gazette of laws and decrees) in the beginning contained primarily literary articles, as did the private *Sawt al Hijaz* and *al Madinah al Manawarah* which were established in the 1930s. They all had financial difficulties, and all except *Umm al Qura* were suspended 1941–46 because of World War II.

It was not until the late 1940s that real newspapers began to emerge. Until that time, Saudi Arabia had lacked the economic base, literacy, secular education, commerce with other countries and interest in the outside world on a scale necessary to bring forth modern newspapers.[27]

Even then, these conditions appeared only in the Western Province, not in the rest of the kingdom. Both *Sawt al Hijaz*, which began publishing again under the name *al Bilad al Sa'udiyah* in 1946 and *al Madinah* which resumed in 1947, became news-oriented dailies and were published in Jidda, but there were no such papers elsewhere in the country for some time. It was the growth of the economy, improvement in printing and distribution facilities, and the growth of government ministries with their advertising needs during the 1950s and 1960s which led to the proliferation of daily newspapers at that time.

The individuals or families who founded these papers did so not to become rich, since the economic conditions were not right for that, but generally to participate in public life through this new medium. Editorials became bolder as owner-editors increasingly criticized the government for various shortcomings. Then in 1963 the Saudi government issued a new press law, which required that the newspapers be owned by groups of Saudis, not individuals or families. Individual and family pride in the development of an independent Fourth Estate was considerably diluted. The new groups that formed included mostly businessmen and others who knew little about journalism. Many regarded the paper as a business undertaking, but they soon realized that economic conditions were not right for making a profit. The owners did not invest very much in staff, or vigorously encourage quality reporting. Employees had to moonlight to make a living and many editors became discouraged about the profession. In this situation, it was often easier to do the minimum necessary to put out a paper which relied heavily on wire service copy and government releases, rather than to take chances in dealing with controversial subjects. Aggressive investigative reporting never developed, and editorial criticism became muted.[28]

Even Saudi Arabia's increased prosperity, which brought more money to the press in the late 1970s, has not changed this situation very much. For example, in 1978 when a new Arabic daily, *al Sharq al Awsat*, appeared, its Saudi publishers set up editorial offices in London staffed by Lebanese and Palestinian journalists in exile, printed the paper on the most modern equipment, and had it flown to Saudi Arabia every morning. But in content it was a Saudi paper in terms of its cautious treatment of issues sensitive in the kingdom.

In Bahrain, Qatar, and the United Arab Emirates, too, the press has so far failed to develop into an independent force for some of the same reasons. These are even younger states with even shorter press traditions than Saudi Arabia. They achieved full independence in 1971, and have had little time to develop indigenous journalistic talent. By 1975, five different newspapers (including two dailies) were being pub-

lished in the UAE by five different UAE citizens, but at four of the five
the top two editorial positions had to be filled by expatriates, mostly
from the Arab world.[29] Similarly, the Bahraini and Qatari press depend
heavily on expatriate journalists, especially Arabs. For example in Bahrain, 'Abdulla Mardi, publisher of the weekly paper *Sada al Usbu'*, attempted in 1971 to bring out a daily, but it failed after a few months
because it had a weak staff; then in 1976 when he made his second attempt with the daily *Akhbar al Khalij*, he took the precaution of bring-
ing in an almost complete staff of trained newspaper people from
Egypt, and the venture was an immediate success.

The press in Jordan, too, suffers from staffing problems, although
for somewhat different reasons. Professional journalism had developed
quite well in Palestine prior to World War II, but with the creation of
Israel in 1948 some of the leading publishers and editors fled to East Jerusalem where they began their careers again by establishing Jordan's
first daily papers.[30] The only newspapers being published in Jordan at
the time were two low-circulation Amman weeklies, *al Nasr* and *al Urdun*, and the latter had been controlled since its establishment in the
1920s by a Lebanese family. The Jordanian press slowly developed
competence and a measure of independence during the next decade and
a half, as new papers were founded and some freedom to criticize was
possible.[31] However, two events in 1967, a press merger and a war,
shook this still-fragile foundation. The first was the incident mentioned
above when the newspapers criticized the army's response to Israeli
raids and the government announced it would issue an executive order
reorganizing the press. The resulting merger came at a time when the
government was under increasing criticism not only at home but also
from some of the Arab countries—notably Syria and Egypt—for "weakness" on Israel.[32] The June 1967 war interrupted this reorganization but
later a merger of several newspapers into new ones did take place. The
war itself, which resulted in the Israeli occupation of East Jerusalem
and the West Bank area, caused most of the personnel of the Jerusalem
Arabic press to flee once again eastward. These dislocations resulted in
the emergence of two new dailies in Amman, *al Dustur* in 1967 and *al
Difa'a* in 1968.[33] Almost immediately the press was drawn into Jordan's
next political crisis, which was the regime's confrontation with a growing militant Palestinian commando movement. This crisis put considerable pressure on the Palestinian journalists, many of whom were among
the best trained and most qualified, but whose loyalties and professional standards were severely tested as the civil war intensified in 1970.
Many journalists became discouraged when the government closed *al*

Difa'a for siding too much with the commandos, and established a new paper, *al Ra'y*, to help promote the regime's viewpoint.[34]

One result of these upheavals in the Jordanian press has been to discourage talented Jordanians from entering the profession, and to help persuade a number of experienced journalists to leave the country, primarily to seek employment in the nascent media of the Arabian Peninsula. They were hired especially by government-owned radio and television there.[35]

This movement of skilled personnel from Jordan to the oil-rich Arab states points up a concomitant internal problem of the Jordanian press, which helps make it susceptible to governmental influence, namely the weakness of its financial base. Saudi Arabia and the UAE can pay good salaries to attract from Jordan the media talent that they lack, but this movement of personnel can adversely affect all the countries involved. The UAE and Saudi Arabia can afford to import foreign skilled labor, so the training of indigenous journalists tends to be retarded because the need is less urgent. On the other side Jordan, which had developed a small group of qualified journalists, lost some of them to these other states partly because it could not pay them enough, and the general skill level declined. The growing demand for competent journalists in the Arab electronic media has put additional pressure on the small pool of available talent, causing movements and dislocations in several countries.

The Tunisian press, too, has had financial and staffing problems which weakened its ability to withstand governmental pressures. An indigenous Arab press did develop in Tunisia during the years of the French Protectorate (1881–1956), primarily because a group of middle-class intellectuals and writers maintained contact with the Arab world and Arab culture. The Tunisian Arab press was, however, controlled, censored and restricted by the French, and although some Tunisians learned technical journalistic skills under the French, they did not develop experience in independent and self-sufficient media.

President Bourguiba began his own political career with the help of partisan newspapers which he edited, but the French closed his *l'Action Tunisienne* along with other nationalist papers in 1933. The French allowed these papers to reopen again in the late 1930s, but shortly thereafter put them under strict wartime censorship. They lifted this in 1947, and allowed a fair amount of press freedom during a period of good relations with France, but then after 1971 they reimposed censorship and heavy restrictions including the bans on Communist organs, in order to deal with the growing nationalist movement. Thus

French colonialism did not leave a vigorous climate of independent Tunisian journalism behind when it ended in 1956.

Nor did the institution of the press ever develop a strong financial basis in Tunisia. In 1961, for example, the leading French-language paper, *la Depeche Tunisienne*, was forced to close for financial reasons, and other smaller papers have had difficulties also.[36] These have contributed to the vulnerability of the press to governmental influence.

Political Environment

The most important factor of all behind the status of the press in these countries, however, is that the political environment in which the press must function has been conducive to non-diverse, relatively passive, and politically conformist newspapers.

The nature of the press reflects the facts of political life in these countries. The press has developed along similar lines in these countries because key factors in the political environment are similar enough to have helped create the necessary conditions for it. Differences of course exist among these political systems, but the following characteristics are found in common.[37]

Jordan, Tunisia, Saudi Arabia, Bahrain, Qatar, and the UAE have no independent parliament, and no instututionalized political opposition. No fundamental public dissent is expressed in any way. Only Jordan has a parliament, and it ordinarily does not express fundamental disagreement with government policy. Therefore, as an editor in one of these countries put it, "there is no opposition *[mu'arada]* in the nation so there is no opposition press."[38] The people believe they are not free to say what they think in public, so the newspaper editors are generally not anxious to use their papers to violate or even test that prevailing norm.[39]

The governments in these countries are essentially authoritarian, backed by elites who support some reforms but generally favor perpetuation of the political, economic, and social status quo. They are not revolutionary regimes which seek sweeping changes, and they require from the public passive acceptance of their rule more than anything else. They do promote such changes as the expansion of education, improvement of health and welfare services and public works, as well as continued economic prosperity. They expect any public comment on these efforts—including all treatment in the press—to be favorable, and government ministers tend to be very sensitive to criticism of their respective spheres of endeavor. They take it personally.[40] But the primary requirement from the public and the press is absence of criticism and at least passive acceptance of whatever the regime does. The ruling elites are not controlled by public opinion, though they consult it privately.[41] Neither the establishment nor the general public insists on the right to free public debate of politically important issues, so there is no such debate in the press. In Jordan, for example, government officials point to efforts among non-governmental political leaders to restrict the press even further as an indication of the lack of interest in a freer press.[42]

This environment of public consensus puts considerable pressure on newspaper editors and writers to conform, that is, to support the political status quo and the regime. The government does not need to use censorship with any frequency because the press is sensitive to the political environment and regulates itself to conform with the general consensus and climate of opinion.[43] As one Tunisian editor put it, "a national Tunisian policy has been chosen [by the ruling elite] and all newspapers are supposed to support it. They are only free within that framework. This is a system typical of a developing country."[44]

In fact, some observers believe that the habits of journalistic conformity to the public consensus are so strong that self-regulation is even stricter than it needs to be, that newspaper editors in these countries conform more than they need to. It is difficult to know, however, whether or not editors in these countries could be bolder and more critical of the status quo than they are. In any case it is clear that the public consensus acts as a strong restraint on the freedom of the press in these countries. And lest any journalist forget that, the government does usually make certain to remind the press periodically of its responsibilities in furthering the "national interest" at a time when economic development and other major problems must be faced. As the Saudi Minister of Information put it during a visit to the offices of one of his country's leading private daily newspapers, the "common goal" of the government and the press is development of the kingdom, and Saudi journalists are "called upon" to put forward opinions beneficial to this goal.[45] The importance of the public consensus factor becomes particularly clear when one examines earlier periods in these countries when the public consensus and government control were relatively weaker, and the press was more diverse and independent.

In Saudi Arabia, for example, the press was more outspoken and contentious in earlier periods when the political situation was less stable and the government weaker. Between 1909 and 1925, the press was de-

veloping in the Western Province (Hijaz) at a time when that area was
under the rather loose control of the Hashemite government of Husayn
in Mecca acting for a remote Ottoman sultan, and 'Abd al Aziz al Sa'ud
was expanding his control over territory to the east. One leading newspaper in Mecca openly criticized Husayn's rule, while another in Jidda
defended it.[46] During the next fifteen years, most Hijazi newspapers
had partisan political tendencies including Arab nationalist, Hijazi nationalist and—after the 1924 capture of Mecca by 'Abd al Aziz al Sa'ud
—pro-Saudi. But this political ferment in the press ended after the al
Sa'ud family captured the Western Province in 1925. The Hijaz became
politically stable as it was joined to the al Sa'ud domain covering most
of the Arabian Peninsula. The newspapers which prospered turned
away from politics and became preoccupied with literary concerns.[47]

The Saudi press underwent another period of limited political diversity during the late 1950s as the country experienced its first major
surge of modernization resulting from oil revenues. The economy and
the government administration grew rapidly, and the burgeoning press
—especially in the kingdom's commercial center of Jidda—attracted a
number of highly respected writers, some of whom began to criticize
various aspects of public life. In 1957 the government began to act
against newspapers which printed editorials it found objectionable; it
closed the newspaper al Adwa' for openly attacking Aramco and the
royal family, and al Riyadh for advocating more rapid development of
democratic instututions, for example. In 1958, as rumors of rivalry between King Sa'ud and Crown Prince Faisal began to circulate privately,
some of this was reflected in newspaper columns which made subtle
comparisons between the two princes. The government decreed a
merger of four papers into two, and in 1960 banned four prominent
writers from writing in the press—moves which clearly signaled official
determination not to let criticism go too far, and which helped mute the
outspokenness. Then Faisal's accession to the throne in 1964 brought a
considerable measure of stability and consensus to Saudi politics which
were reflected in a more quiescent press.

Similarly, in Jordan and Bahrain, the press became bolder, more
outspoken, and independent of the government in periods of domestic
ferment and relative weakening of governmental authority. In Jordan,
these periods coincided with and were fueled partly by greater criticism
in parliament. The Jordanian press during the civil war of 1970 reflected the growing deterioration in governmental control over the Palestinian radicals as an anti-regime Palestinian daily newspaper al Fatah
appeared and strongly attacked the regime, while existing newspapers

gave increasing space to news and commentary unhelpful to the authorities. They were giving honest expression to previously repressed sympathies but also they were intimidated by the growing power of the Palestinian militants.[48] Then when the government forcefully restored order in the fall of the year, and suppressed the Palestinian rebellion, the radical Palestinian newspapers disappeared and the others became more supportive of the regime. In Bahrain, the short-lived experiment with an elected parliament, 1973–75, also saw a brief upsurge in press outspokenness, reflecting the political debate and ferment that parliamentary activity unleashed. The December 1973 election results revealed more radical and leftist strength than most conservatives had anticipated, and the liveliness of the debates in the assembly surprised and irritated the government. When the government suspended the assembly indefinitely in August 1975, and parliamentary discussion of controversial issues such as security legislation ceased, the press also became more bland in content.

GUIDANCE MECHANISMS

In the loyalist press system, the regime does not have at its disposal the mechanisms for guiding and influencing that exist in the mobilization system and derive from ownership of the press by a political agent of the regime. Since the loyalist press is in private hands, the regime must use indirect methods to influence newspaper personnel. These methods have already been alluded to in this chapter, but we shall summarize them here.

The most common mechanism ensuring newspaper loyalty to the basic policies of the regime and to its top leadership is anticipatory self-guidance based on sensitivity to the political environment. The editors and other journalists usually know, without any specific guidance, what the regime expects them to say in their newspapers and they usually comply for the reasons outlined in this chapter. Secondly, the regime makes known, through public acts such as statements of policy or appointments of personnel, what is important to it and what the official line is. These acts, publicized first through official press releases and by the government-owned radio and television, are recognized as important by journalists in the private press who treat them accordingly. Occasionally the government will specifically praise a newspaper for "balance" and "objectivity," a pat on the back designed to signal approval of the editorial line.[49] Thirdly, in all of these countries the government operates a national news agency which indirectly gives the private press guidance signals each day by the way it treats and comments on the news.[50]

Fourth, government officials in these countries from time to time contact newspaper personnel informally and privately to make clear on specific issues what government policy is, what the regime would like to have emphasized, and what is sensitive. And finally, the government has some powers under the law which it uses on those relatively rare occasions when it believes direct action must be taken against a disloyal newspaper.

In summary, the press in Jordan, Saudi Arabia, Tunisia, Bahrain, Qatar, and the UAE is basically loyal to the regime and non-diverse, despite the fact that it is privately owned. Although the regime does not control the newspapers directly through a political agent as in the mobilization system, it does evoke loyalty to its policies and top personnel because of the legal, financial, and especially the political conditions under which the press functions. The newspapers do not aggressively promote revolutionary change as they do in the mobilization system; instead they loyally support the non-revolutionary regimes which hold power in these countries. The means of government influence over the press and the reasons for their effectiveness, as well as the style of the press itself, is unique to the loyalist system.

5

The Diverse Press

A THIRD MAJOR TYPE of press system has appeared in the Arab world in modern times. It can be called the diverse press because its most significant distinguishing characteristic is that the newspapers are clearly different from each other in content and apparent political tendency as well as in style. They are all privately owned and reflect a variety of viewpoints. In mobilization or loyalist press systems similarities outweigh any differences among papers within one country, but the opposite is true with the diverse press. The degree and quality of differences among newspapers is difficult to quantify or describe precisely, but regular newspaper readers perceive them quite easily.

Substantial diversity in the press implies that at least some of the newspapers, if not all, print news and opinion that is not supportive of the regime in power. Newspaper readers in this system have access to a greater variety of information than do readers of the loyalist or mobilization press, where all newspapers uniformly support the regime's basic policies and leaders. The diverse press is therefore relatively free, even if individual newspapers may be strong promoters of the regime, because some newspapers are somewhat independent of the regime and because the reader has more information and opinion to choose from.

The clearest and most consistent example of this type of press system has been seen in contemporary Lebanon. Kuwait and Morocco have also developed press systems which in many respects follow patterns similar enough to put them in this general category, too, although with some qualifications because the Kuwaiti and Moroccan newspapers also have some of the loyalist press characteristics. In addition, as we have seen above (in Chapter 3), the press in seven other countries passed through a factional stage characterized by diversity and relatively greater freedom, before it developed further to become mobilized. The diverse press seems to be a type which can and does emerge in the Arab world in various places, at various times.

What are the conditions under which this system emerges? In the case of the factional stage of the mobilization press, we have seen that three major factors helped diversity develop: the end of colonial restrictions, the appearance of openly competing political factions, and a national government which exercised restraint in dealing with the press. When the competition among political groups ended in those countries and the government intervened more directly and forcefully in the publishing business, the factional phase and substantial diversity ended. Similarly in Lebanon, and to a degree in Kuwait and Morocco also, the key factors seem to be these: political pluralism, patronization of the newspapers, and a relatively restrained approach to the press by the regime.

By political pluralism we mean the existence of readily identifiable groups or factions with distinguishable philosophies or approaches to public policy. This pluralism may manifest itself in organized political parties or in other forms, but the public can discern some clear choices among alternatives within the basic national consensus. Some of these groups establish direct or indirect ties with specific newspapers, creating a symbiotic patronization or sponsorship arrangement which —as we saw in Chapter 1—is not uncommon in the Arab press. Since the basic political system has manifest elements of pluralism in it, this is reflected in the press, as competing groups sponsor different newspapers. The regime in power may participate in the patronization process, sponsoring its own newspapers, but for the system to work it must show restraint in the exercise of governmental authority and political power over the press. The government may from time to time take legal or other action to restrict the press, but it does not go so far as to silence criticism totally or create complete uniformity.

Looking more closely at the system of a diverse press, we see that conditions which gave rise to it do vary from country to country; there can be many reasons for pluralism and for governmental restraint. Likewise the degree to which the system is in effect varies also. So to understand its dynamics we must examine individual cases. First we will take Lebanon, since the press has come the closest to the model and has sustained these characteristics over the longest period of time. The Lebanese civil war, which began in the Spring of 1975, quieted down somewhat in late 1976, but continued sporadically into 1979, threatening to destroy totally the political basis on which the press had functioned for more than thirty years. If that happened the press system would have changed too, but after many months of fratricidal strife the basic structure of the press remained as it had been. After discussing that structure, we shall turn briefly to the Kuwaiti and Moroccan types.

THE LEBANESE PRESS

Lebanon has more newspapers than any other Arab country. Although it has a population of only three million, there are over four hundred valid licenses to publish periodicals, including approximately fifty for daily newspapers and forty-five for political weeklies. Not all of these publications appear all the time—in the 1970s about thirty dailies appeared regularly, and this number fell below twenty during the civil war. The quality of the papers varies considerably; a few may be the best in the Arab world, while some are among the shoddiest, most irresponsible, scurrilous papers anywhere. Some have very small circulations, numbering in the hundreds, but others are read widely at home and abroad. Lebanon has the highest literacy rate of any Arab country, and it has been estimated that daily newspapers are read by three-quarters of the adult population on a regular basis. In addition, Lebanon exports a large percentage of its newspapers to other Arab countries. In normal times, more than twenty Lebanese dailies are read somewhere outside the country, and seven or eight have for years distributed more outside than inside Lebanon.[1]

Lebanese newspapers are not only numerous but taken as a whole they present readers with the widest variety of opinion and the most complete collection of information on a given topic of any Arab press. All significant currents of Arab thought can be found represented in the Lebanese press. Readers of the Lebanese press believe that most publications with political content have one political bias or another which they can detect in the news selection as well as in the editorials.

They usually attribute this bias to a secret understanding of some kind between a newspaper's editors and a specific Lebanese political faction and/or foreign groups. They infer this secret understanding from the content of the paper since editors as a rule do not admit that they have any such connections. Indeed, even the editors themselves typically accuse each other of receiving hidden financial subsidies or other benefits from political patrons in return for support in the paper. As one editor put it, "with so many newspapers in Beirut, they must receive subsidies to stay alive"; he repeated the common characterization that the papers may not be bought but they are "rented" *(ma'jurah)*.[2]

But the typical editor denies that *he* biases *his* paper in return for a subsidy. And when the Education Minister declared that "all our newspapers and all our journalists can be bought, sold, and hired," for example, the President of the Lebanese Press Syndicate felt compelled to respond with a strong attack on the minister and defense of the press— without denying the charge.[3]

There is no doubt that patronization of the press for political purposes does take place in Lebanon although it is impossible to determine the extent or precise nature of these connections. In some cases, the editorial tendency of a paper may be determined in large part by the personal attitude and philosophy of the publisher and only secondarily or marginally by any outside connections or subsidies. A few newspapers, such as *al Nahar* and its French language sister paper *l'Orient-le Jour*, have achieved sufficient variety and balance within their own pages so that observers have difficulty identifying a clear bias and some even call them objective. Other papers change their political orientation frequently so that it is difficult to categorize them except as opportunistic.

For purposes of illustration, Table 5 gives some indication in simplified form of the variety of political tendencies that were observed by readers in the leading Lebanese dailies in 1975. Observers generally believe they can detect political tendencies in the dailies on three levels: national politics and religious affiliation, regional politics including the Arab-Israeli question, and international relations. The table lists the twenty-one highest circulation papers from among the Lebanese dailies which appeared regularly just before the civil war together with circulation estimates and a simplified annotation indicating the orientation their readers generally perceive.[4]

During 1975 and 1976, the Lebanese civil war modified the list of leading newspapers and their political orientations somewhat, but the basic phenomenon of a broad spectrum of views, and patronization—or presumed patronization—by many different groups persisted as a prime characteristic of the Lebanese press.

For example, it was assumed by readers of the Lebanese press that *al Nida, al Sharq, al Safir,* and *al Kifah* had connections with—and probably received subsidies from—Russia, Syria, Libya, and Iraq, respectively. Similarly, *al Hayat* was thought to have Saudi and conservative Lebanese backing. Readers believed that *al Amal* and *al Jaridah*

TABLE 5
Leading Lebanese Daily Newspapers
(1975)

Name	Est. circ.	First pub.	Predominant orientation & readership	
			Religious	Political
Al Nahar (The Day)	55,000	1933	Greek Orth.	independent, often pro-West
Al Anwar (The Lights)	40,000	1959	Greek Orth.	moderate Arab national-ist, pro-Cairo
Al Muharrir (The Liberator)	35,000		Sunni	rejectionist, radical Arab nationalist, anti-West, anti-U.S., anti-Cairo
Al Hayat (Life)	18,000	1946	Shi'ite	independent, conserva-tive, moderate Pales-tinian, pro-Saudi
L'Orient–le Jour*	18,000	1924 (1934)		independent, gen. pro-West
Lisan al Hal (The Spokesman)	8,000	1877	Greek Orth. mod. Christian	pro-West
Al Amal (Hope)	7,000	1938	Maronite	Phalange Party organ, Lebanese nationalist, pro-West, anti-Communist
The Daily Star†	6,000		Shi'ite	gen. pro-West, but also pro-Palestinian
Al Bayraq (The Flag)	4,500	1959	Maronite	independent opportunist, rightist Christian
Al Jaridah (The Newspaper)	4,000	1953	Roman Cath.	moderate, conservative, Lebanese nationalist
Nida al Watan (Call of the Nation)	3,000		Maronite	conservative Maronite, pro-Saudi, pro-West
Al Nida (The Call)	3,000	1949	Shi'ite	Communist Party organ, pro-Moscow
As-Safa (Purity)*	3,000		Catholic	independent
Al Liwa' (The Banner)	3,000	1939	Sunni	radical Arab nationalist, rejectionist
Al Sharq (The East)	3,000	1938	Sunni	anti-West, anti-U.S., pro-Syrian
Al Yawm (The Day)	2,500	1938	Sunni	moderate Arab national-ist, pro-Cairo, anti-West
Al Safir (The Mediator)	2,500	1974		radical Arab nationalist, anti-West, rejectionist, pro-Libyan
Al Kifah (The Struggle)	2,000	1950		pro-Iraqi
Al Sha'b (The People)	1,500		Sunni	leftist, pro-Moscow
Le Soir†	1,500	1947	Armenian Orth.	independent, gen. pro-West
Sawt al 'Urubah (Voice of Arabism)	1,000		Sunni	Najjadah Party organ, moderate Arab national-ist, gen. anti-West

*Published in French.
†Published in English.

must have Lebanese nationalist financing of some kind, while Palestinians and Pan-Arab nationalists supported either *al Muharrir* and *al Liwa'* or the more moderate *al Anwar* and *Sawt al 'Urubah*. Some papers, however, were more difficult to categorize so neatly because they showed mixed tendencies. For example the now-defunct *Daily Star* and even *al Jaridah* were frequently pro-West on international questions, but individual columnists often expressed strong criticism of the United States, especially in the Arab-Israeli question.

The many weekly and other publications which appeared before the civil war, and the ones which survived or emerged after it, cover the same broad spectrum of political orientations as these dailies. Competition and rhetorical conflict among them has been vigorous and lively, as has the criticism and defense of the government's policies and leaders. This type of press has developed in Lebanon because of the particular political circumstances in that country and the way that journalism emerged over the years. What are those circumstances?

Development of Press Patronization and Diversity

Lebanese newspaper journalism began in the middle of the nineteenth century, when the territory was under Ottoman rule. Although newspapers had appeared earlier in Egypt, Beirut has the longest continuous press history, and because of its early emphasis on education it had a higher concentration of newspapers from the beginning. The first Arab daily was started in Beirut in 1873, and about forty other newspapers and periodicals appeared there between 1870 and 1900. The first newspapers were elitist, written by and for intellectuals, whose liberal ideas frequently got them into trouble with Ottoman authorities. They were influenced by Western, particularly French, ideas and journalism, and their publications—in French or Arabic—often resembled contemporary French journals.[5]

Periodic strict censorship, especially during the reign of Sultan Abdal Hamid (1876–1909), caused some journalists to flee to Egypt where they could establish newspapers with fewer restrictions. But after the more liberal press law of 1909, Lebanese newspapers were able to play a definite role in the Arab nationalist movement. Their activities were still watched by the government, however; in May 1916, for example, sixteen of the thirty-one Arab leaders hanged in Beirut and Damascus for demanding independence and stirring up public opinion were journalists.[6]

Under the French Mandate (1920–41), more newspapers appeared, and many became politically involved, although the French maintained and even tightened controls on the press. By 1929 there were many papers in Lebanon, and some editors risked suspension, fines, or jail because they called for independence in their editorials. For example, the government suspended one leading daily fifteen times between 1933 and 1939 because of its criticisms of the Mandatory Power and its campaigns for constitutional government.[7]

In 1943, Lebanon became essentially independent, but France in fact retained some powers, and authority to regulate the press was not turned over to the Lebanese until 1946, when French troops finally withdrew. The newly independent Lebanese political system was based on a careful balance of a variety of interest groups, which has been maintained to this day, and which underlies the system of the press. Lebanon has always been a refuge for minorities, particularly religious sects, who maintained their autonomy and frequently competed vigorously against each other. An unwritten agreement of 1943, now referred to as the National Covenant (al mithaq al watani), was made between the two outstanding Christian and Muslim leaders. All groups and factions accepted a de facto coexistence which entailed, among other things, the proportional allotment of high political offices on the basis of factional membership. The competitive balance underlying the Lebanese polity is not only among confessional groups, but among secular ideological, social, economic, geographic, personal, and family ones as well. Thus Lebanese democracy was "not the rule of the demos, but simply the distribution of guarantees to the recognized factions coexisting in the country of the means to defend their minimum interests."[8]

The Lebanese press reflects these multiple divisions. In addition, disagreements among political officials, which result from splits and the necessity of coalition government made the state relatively weak against organized interest groups. The Lebanese "system provides a relatively open opportunity for participation by all who desire it."[9] In such an environment, newspapers proliferated, many become highly political, and most reflected interests of special groups or parties. As one chief editor put it, "there are so many contending influences on the press that it stays free." Another leading editor proudly declared in the years before the civil war, "the message of Lebanon to the world was always one of dialogue," and this was carried on intensively in the press.[10] The newspapers frequently came into conflict with the government, but in contrast to most other Arab states, the government was not able to reduce the level of dissent or diversity significantly.

The Lebanese press was relatively strong from the beginning of the modern era. It exposed the corruption of the first regime after independence, and accused the government of rigging the elections of 1947. The government reacted by imposing more restrictive press regulations in 1948. The press objected to this, and the government suspended seven complaining newspapers in one day; the newspaper syndicate reacted by calling a general strike and boycott of government news.[11]

In 1952, a continuous press campaign by a number of newspapers against the government played a major role in focusing public discontent to such an extent that President Bisharah al Khuri resigned in September. The pro-Socialist newspaper *al Anba'* declared in an editorial in June, headlined "The Foreigners Brought Them; Let the People Expel Them," that al Khuri had been put in power by foreign elements. The government reacted by having the paper suspended for eight months and its editor jailed for fourteen months. Eight other papers joined the attack, simultaneously republishing the offending editorial as a "news story," and the government took action against them also. By late July, thirteen papers had been suspended. The newspapers by this time had joined together to form a syndicate for self-protection and self-regulation; at one point, it declared a sympathy strike in protest against the government action, blacking out the entire press for several days.[12]

The new government which came into office in September 1952 was grateful to the press and passed a more liberal publishing law which lifted most of the restrictions in October. But the editors did not stop their criticism. In fact, the power of the press increased during the 1950s, especially as politicians and groups recognized its value as an ally in their battles. As their importance grew, the number of newspapers increased rapidly, so that before long Beirut alone had more than fifty dailies, many of them "thriving on sensational news and patroned by different leaders or groups." The Press Syndicate itself requested a limitation on this expansion, and a legislative decree in April 1953 set minimum standards and a ceiling on the number of newspapers.[13]

From time to time, in spite of some self-regulation, the government has stepped in to exercise direct control over the press. During the 1958 civil war, the government suspended several opposition papers— two defied the ban by publishing in the rebel-held Basta District of Beirut—and also used its power to censor specific items in the press. But even when censorship is imposed, the Lebanese papers usually show their independence by publishing with blank spaces as a signal to readers that they have been restricted—a practice generally not allowed elsewhere in the Arab world.

The severity of the 1958 crisis also led the government to ban the importation of some foreign publications, particularly Egyptian and Syrian, and on a few other occasions the authorities have stopped single issues, although as a rule there are no such restrictions and virtually any foreign publication can be found in Beirut.[14]

The Lebanese press law of 1962 continues to be valid with some amendments. It does prohibit the publication of "news which endangers the national security, or unity or frontiers of the state, or which degrades a foreign head of state." The Lebanese press has over the years tended to interpret these rules somewhat liberally and to see to its own observance of them. The 1962 law supported the Press (owners') Syndicate and Writers' Syndicate, and provided for a self-regulating body. The government has ordinarily not found it necessary to intervene directly, since the press syndicates functioned well in practice.[15] This law has helped reinforce in the press a "high degree of freedom," and Lebanese editors are proud of their practice of self-regulation, which has usually avoided government censorship.[16] When the press fails to regulate itself, the government sometimes steps in, following judicial procedures laid down in the law. The 1974 amendment to the press law did away with preventive detention of newsmen and made the civil courts responsible for press violations. Before that, a special press tribunal had had jurisdiction. From time to time these courts have handed out prison sentences and fines, usually for slandering the army or a foreign head of state, or occasionally for revealing military secrets.[17] On these occasions, the government may ask a paper to refrain from publishing a specific item because it would endanger national security. In such a case, the paper would leave a blank space on its page and editors would discuss among themselves whether the request had been proper; and they would publicly protest if they believed it was not.[18] The Lebanese government has also used the technique of making general appeals to the press, "to be more careful than usual because of present circumstances," as the prime minister said in June 1972 during a delicate stage in intra-Arab discussions about Israel and the Palestinians.[19]

The Lebanese civil war, which began in early 1975, created special pressures on the press as it did on all Lebanese institutions. Lebanon's "social mosaic" which had provided the pluralist base of an open democracy for thirty years, began to come apart over economic and social issues, over the allocation of shares of political power, over the proper role of the Palestinians in Lebanon, and other questions. Contending factions became frustrated with the dialogue in the press and parliament and sought to achieve their ends by violent means. Divisions cut across different lines—religious, rich/poor, Arab nationalist/ Lebanese nationalist, pro- and anti-Palestinian—and national leaders lost enough of their control so that private militias took over the streets and revealed the inability of the state to keep order.

Most of the major daily newspapers continued to appear, but with fewer pages and virtually all of their space devoted to strictly Lebanese events. Distribution of each paper became restricted to the area or areas controlled by the paper's supporters, as Lebanon and particularly Beirut became divided along geographic lines into enclaves. The level of responsibility and veracity in the press diminished as the crisis worsened; those papers lacking ties to patrons with armed militias became circumspect or went out of business while the rest became more vociferous. Journalists, like national political leaders, at first remained immune to deliberate physical attack but in January 1976 the top editors of two important dailies died as the result of raids on their newspaper offices that may have been politically inspired. The Minister of Information, himself a prominent editor, issued only a mild reproach after the raid but did nothing, showing the government's powerlessness to protect journalists or anyone else.[20]

In the fall of 1976, agreement was reached among major Arab countries to establish an Arab Deterrent Force to help the Lebanese government restore order. Syria, which had sent its own military units into Lebanon during the peak of the civil war, was dominant in the ADF as Lebanon began to return to normalcy. While some of the Lebanese press supported Syria and the ADF, a number of newspapers were critical of developments. In December 1976, Syrian troops of the ADF occupied the offices of several newspapers, including the independent daily *al Nahar* and the pro-Libyan daily *al Safir*, which suspended publication. A few weeks later, the ADF allowed the restricted papers to resume publication. But in the meantime, the Lebanese government had issued a decree imposing pre-censorship on the press, giving the Directorate General of Public Security the power to preview everything before publication. The Interior Minister declared that no one should publish "material stirring up sectarian strife, . . . instigating actions endangering public safety and security, [or] . . . causing arguments leading to a renewal of fighting." First violations were punishable by fines and imprisonment, second violations by rescinding the license to issue the publication.[21]

The Lebanese government thus had decided that self-regulation was not sufficient and direct censorship had become necessary, because the internal situation was still not fully settled. But the guidelines as laid down by the Interior Minister were only somewhat more specific than those already existing in the 1962 press law, and it is significant that the censorship decrees specified an explicit judicial procedure through the courts for dealing with violations. It is true that the Lebanese press in 1979 was more circumscribed than it had been in 1973 before the civil war, but it still was able to express criticism of the government, and its disputes with the authorities were adjudicated in court.

Moreover, even the civil war did not destroy the characteristic multiplicity and diversity of the Lebanese press. Of the twenty-one most widely read dailies which existed in 1975, nine were no longer being published at all in 1979, and eight others were still below their 1975 circulation levels. Nevertheless, several new dailies had emerged, of which three were going strong as of 1979, and one of these had even climbed to second place in circulation. Equally important was the fact that clear differences in orientation of the various newspapers, across a considerable spectrum, had also returned by 1977 and were still present in 1979. (see Table 6)

TABLE 6
Leading Lebanese Daily Newspapers
(1979)

Name	Est. circ.	Religious	Political
		Predominant orientation & readership	
Al Nahar	40,000	Greek Orth.	independent, usually pro-West
Le Reveil* †	20,000	Maronite	Phalangist, pro-West
L'Orient-le Jour†	15,000	Greek Orth.	independent
Al Amal	15,000	Maronite	Phalangist, pro-West
Al Anwar	10,000	Greek Orth.	rightist, pro-Syria
Al Safir	9,000	Shi'ite	leftist, pro-Libya
Ike*‡	6,000	Sunni	independent
Al Ahrar*	4,000	Maronite	radical right, NLP, pro-West
Al Bayraq	4,000	Maronite	rightist
The Daily Star‡	3,500	Shi'ite	pro-West and pro-PLO
Al Sharq	3,000	Sunni	pro-Syria
Al Liwa'	1,000	Sunni	pro-Libya, -Iraq, -PLO, anti-West
Sawt al 'Urubah	800	Sunni	Najjadah Party, anti-West
Al Nida	600	Shi'ite	Communist Party organ
Al Sha'b	500	Sunni	pro-Moscow

*New daily, appeared after 1975.
†Printed in French.
‡Printed in English.

The basic political and religious orientations of the twelve daily papers which survived or revived were not changed very much. Although all papers tended to be more supportive of Syria which dominated the Arab Defense Force occupying Lebanon, the fortunes and misfortunes of the papers did not follow a major unifying pattern. The two older papers which were able to surpass their 1975 circulation figures were of totally different political orientations: the Phalangist, pro-West *al Amal*, and the radical leftist *al Safir*. The pro-West Greek Orthodox *Lisan al Hal* was gone, but the new and successful *Reveil* had the same tendencies. And the pro-Iraqi *al Kifah* was gone, but *al Liwa* was still defending Iraq, among other causes.

Lebanese weekly magazines, like the daily newspapers, have exhibited a variety of political and religious orientation which has not been erased by the civil war. The number of weeklies was reduced by the unsettled conditions in the country, but as of 1979 there were still more than a dozen weeklies with circulations of over one thousand copies each, and they represented a fairly broad range of editorial opinion. In addition, several publishers had moved their headquarters from Beirut to Europe during the civil war, so that Lebanese-owned weeklies were being published in Paris and London and not only read by expatriate Arabs but also sent into the Arab countries, including Lebanon, from there. In 1979, the Arabic-language weeklies *al Mustaqbal, al Watanal 'Arabi*, and *al Nahar* were appearing in Paris, and *al Hawadith* and the English-language weekly *Events* were appearing in London. Presumably these will all move back to Beirut after the situation in Lebanon stabilizes. The Lebanese civil war was a traumatic event for the press, as it was for other institutions, but fundamental press characteristics did survive.

Two factors have made the Lebanese press probably the most free in the Arab world. First, the state failed to silence press criticism to the extent that other Arab states have, and the press has developed a measure of self-regulation to protect itself as an institution. And second, the continuation of the pluralist society and confessional democracy was and is reflected in the genuine diversity of the Lebanese press. The Lebanese newspaper reader may not always find objectivity in one newspaper, but taken as a whole, the Lebanese press provided him with a broad spectrum of views and news unparalleled in the Arab world, and from which he could make his own choices.[22] This press system was built on a political base of institutionalized pluralism which other Arab countries lacked. But as that base crumbled, the press became more limited to functioning as a narrow channel of communication among members of one group, and it became more irresponsible and tied to agents of violence. Newspaper diversity remained because Lebanese pluralism turned to fragmentation, but the loss of national unity undermined the national role of the press.

THE KUWAITI AND MOROCCAN PRESS

The press systems in Kuwait and Morocco have some structural similarities with the press in Lebanon, and also a few differences.

Kuwait produces a large number of newspapers for its size, and the quality of its press reached a remarkable level during the 1970s. By 1979, seven daily newspapers (five in Arabic, two in English) with an estimated domestic circulation of over 100,000 were being published in Kuwait, although the population was still under one million and adult literacy was only 60 percent. In addition, sixteen weeklies and an equal number of other publications were appearing in that country. All of the dailies were known outside of Kuwait, where they sold another 26,000 copies. They were popular in the Gulf states but some had gained readers elsewhere in the Arab world also.

Morocco, too, has a relatively large number of newspapers. In 1979 it had ten important dailies (five in Arabic, five in French) with a total circulation of more than 240,000 copies, and it had dozens of other publications. It is true that the quality of the Moroccan press does not match that in Lebanon or Kuwait. Its journalism is relatively weak —it has neither a long tradition of journalism like Lebanon nor the money to hire outside talent as Kuwait does.[23] Nevertheless, the three countries do share other press characteristics.

Diversity among Newspapers

The press in Kuwait and Morocco, as in Lebanon, is basically in private hands, and it shows a significant degree of diversity.

In Kuwait (see Table 7), it has developed a degree of diversity, competition and outspokenness which put it in a special category distinguishable from the press systems discussed in previous chapters. These characteristics make the Kuwaiti press somewhat similar to the Lebanese, although in Lebanon they are more pronounced and newspaper traditions are more firmly established because the press began seventy-

TABLE 7
Kuwaiti Daily Newspapers
(1979)

Name	Est. circ.	First pub.	Predominant orientation
Al Qabas (The Beacon)	30,000 (23,000)	1972	free enterprise capitalist, politically objective, Kuwaiti nationalist
Al Siyasah (Politics)	20,000 (16,000)	1965	moderate, pro-government, less emotional than others, pro-Egyptian
Al Ra'y al 'Amm (Public Opinion)	20,000 (16,000)	1961	conservative, monarchist, Kuwaiti nationalist, anti-Communist and pro-West but critical of U.S. Mideast policy
Al Watan (The Homeland)	17,000 (15,000)	1974	liberal, critical of government, democratic including free speech, pro-Syrian
Al Anba' (The News)	20,000 (14,500)	1976	capitalist, establishmentarian, critical of government and of U.S. Mideast policy, rival of *Siyasah*
*The Kuwait Times**	10,000 (7,500)	1961	middle of road, focus on non-Arab affairs
*The Arab Times**	7,000 (3,000)	1977	liberal, popular, focus on regional news

*Published in English.
Sources: Circulation figures, from informed observers, are the best obtainable, but they should be considered estimates. Other data is from interviews and from Mruwa, *Al Sahafah*, pp. 403–405, and USIA "Media Directories" for Kuwait. Kuwait domestic circulation in parentheses.

five years earlier. It seems that the relatively young Kuwaiti press—the first publication of any kind appeared there in 1928—is tending in the direction of the Lebanese press, although its political environment is somewhat different.

Kuwait's oldest successful dailies are *al Ra'y al 'Amm* and *al Siyassah*, both having been established in the 1960s. *Al Ra'y al 'Amm* maintains a uniform and consistent editorial policy, strongly supporting the royal family while criticizing individual government officials and public figures opposing communism and Arab socialism (especially that of the Iraqi Ba'th Party) and advocating ties with the West, while defending Kuwaiti independence and frequently expressing unhappiness with American Middle East policy. *Al Siyassah*, on the other hand, tends to be somewhat more outspoken, liberal and diverse in its interpretation of events. It tackles a variety of problems with vigor, and a considerable variety of viewpoint is expressed in its editorials, subjecting public figures of any persuasion to its close scrutiny. Its well-known chief editor, Ahmed Jarallah, specializes in interviews with Arab leaders. Some of its writers have shown sympathy for Marxist interpretations and for the radical Arab regimes in Iraq and South Yemen. However al Siyassah does tend to support the ruling family, and it tends to advocate moderate courses of action, treating issues in a less emotional fashion than other papers do.[24]

However al Qabas, a paper with a different editorial approach, is even more successful than these two. Established in 1972, in four years it had achieved the highest circulation of any daily. Al Qabas does not advocate any one political line but seeks to satisfy all Kuwaiti factions. It is rather liberal and fairly objective in its presentation of news and commentary. Financed by a group of local businessmen, it gives especially good coverage to economic matters, giving emphasis to Kuwaiti business interests. It tends to use think pieces and translations from the foreign press (including the Israeli) more than its competitors, and it gives more space to Palestinian writers.

A fourth daily, al Watan, shows somewhat more concern for foreign affairs, especially the Gulf area, than the others. It is an advocate of democratic concepts including free speech and the free exchange of ideas, giving writers with diverse views access to its pages. It has often been outspokenly critical of the Kuwaiti government. Finally, the fifth and newest Arabic daily, al Anba', which has strong ties with the Kuwaiti business community, is a staunch advocate of capitalism and Arab family traditions, and it has been an outspoken critic of governmental policy. Its chief editor, who is related to several prominent politicians, sometimes engages in polemics with other dailies, especially al Siyassah, which heightens the contrast in content and view between al Anba' and the other papers.

Kuwait's English-language daily, The Kuwait Times, has existed since independence, and it presents a moderate, liberal point of view. Its long-time competition, the more conservative Daily News, ceased publication in 1976, when Abdul Aziz Masa'id sold it to the al Ghanim family, which was unable to keep the publication going. But in 1977 al Siyassah Publishing House sold The Kuwait Times and began a new liberal English daily, the Arab Times, which has a lively style. And just like the dailies, Kuwait's weekly publications also present a spectrum of viewpoints and orientations, including liberal, and extreme and moderate conservative, trade unionist and promanagement, Kuwaiti nationalist and Arab nationalist, Ba'thist and even Marxist.[25]

The Moroccan press, too, is spread quite widely across a political spectrum in that country. Three dailies high in circulation in 1979, for example (see Table 8) represent views other than the government's. Two of them, *al 'Alam* and *l'Opinion*, are Arabic and French sister papers published by the Istiqlal party, which for many years was in the opposition but as of 1979 was in the government. They are the two oldest dailies in existence—*al 'Alam* was started in 1944—and like the Istiqlal party itself, they have been part of the political scene in independent Morocco for so long that they are virtually part of the establishment. They are regularly critical of the status quo, however. They call for redistribution of wealth, social justice and educational reform. They are strongly nationalistic at home, calling for rapid Arabization, and on international questions they strongly support pan-Arabism and Third World positions, sometimes more outspokenly than the government does. *Al 'Alam* appeals most to the moderately educated middle and lower-middle classes while *l'Opinion* tends to be read by a better educated and slightly wealthier group.[26]

Even more successful as a critical voice is the daily *al Muharrir*,

TABLE 8
Moroccan Daily Newspapers
(1979)

Name	Est. circ.	First pub.	Predominant orientation
Al Muharrir (The Liberator)	40,000	1971	Socialist Union of Popular Forces, anti-government
Al 'Alam (The Flag)	45,000	1944	Istiqlal party, critical of government, nationalistic
L'Opinion*	45,000	1965	
Le Matin*	50,000	1971	pro-government, monarchist, establishmentarian (Ahmed 'Alawi)
Maroc Soir*	35,000	1971	
Al Anba' (The News)	7,000	1963	Information Min.
Al Mithaq al Watani (The National Pact)	5,000	1976	pro-government (Ahmed Osman)
Al Maghrib (Morocco)	8,000	1978	
Al Bayan (The Dispatch)	2,000	1972†	Party of Progress and Socialism, pro-Communist
Al Bayane*	5,000	1972†	

*Published in French.
†Weekly paper, 1972–76.
Sources: Mruwa, *Al Sahafah,* pp. 224, 397–402. Stuart H. Schaar, "The Mass Media in Morocco," *American Universities Field Staff Reports* (New York, 1968), p. 8.

published by the Socialist Union of Popular Forces (USFP). The USFP party, which was formed by a group of politicians who broke with the Istiqlal party, and its organ *al Muharrir*, are critical of the government's economic and educational policies and its European and American ties. The paper tends to use standard socialist rhetoric in many of its articles and headlines, and it appeals especially to university students, younger professionals and government employees.

The government's policies are defended by two successful dailies, the Casablanca morning and afternoon sister papers *Le Matin* and *Moroc Soir*. Both are published by Moulay Ahmed Alaoui, a former minister who is a relative of King Hassan II, and who regularly writes editorials himself. In news selection and commentary, their tendency is to support the monarchy, the Establishment, business and private enterprise, and they are relatively more friendly to Western countries. Two other dailies, *al Maghrib* in French and the Arabic and *al Mithaq al Watani*, also support government policies. However, their tendency in 1979 was to favor Prime Minister Ahmed Osman, a political rival of Ahmed Alaoui's, so their content was somewhat different from that of *Le Matin* and *Maroc Soir*. The daily *al Anba'*, published by the Ministry of Information, is consistently pro-government. The latter three have the advantage of being able to scoop the competition with government news, and they present a supremely optimistic tone which contrasts with that of the other papers.

Finally, a pair of daily papers published by the Party of Progress and Socialism (PPS) has not achieved the high circulation figures of the other dailies mentioned above, but they nevertheless add significantly to the spectrum of press views found in Morocco. *Al Bayan* (The Dispatch) in Arabic and its sister paper *al Bayane* in French both speak for the Marxist PPS and reach a significant sector of the Moroccan reading public.

Criticism and Government Restrictions

In Kuwait, the press tends not to go as far as the press in Lebanon in its attacks on the government. The Kuwaiti press is forbidden by law from criticizing the ruler (*amir*) or quoting him without authorization, and it may not publish information which would "affect the value of the national currency or create misgivings about the Kuwaiti economy," or advocate the overthrow of the government by force.[27] However the press still has considerable freedom to criticize. Between the press law amendments of 1972 and 1976, the government could not take direct action to suspend a newspaper which broke the rules but could only

take it to court; in practice this is a long drawn-out process, which reduced the number of governmental actions and gave the press additional
freedom.[28]

The August 1976 press law amendment gave the government the
power to suspend or cancel a newspaper (a) which served "the interest
of a foreign state or organization," (b) which "obtained any sort of assistance from a foreign state," or (c) if "its policy contradicts the national
interest."[29] The Ruler of Kuwait decreed this press amendment at the
same time that he suspended the parliament and strengthened security
laws. His Prime Minister explained that Kuwait had reached a "serious
turning point" in its democratic experience and "negative aspects" had
to be corrected. He said: "with unlimited freedom the press became
irresponsible. . . . Giving it freedom without controls have made some
papers obedient instruments in the service of objectives alien to our
country, which work to corrupt society, propagate self-interested rumors and sow trivialities and sedition among our ranks."[30]

The Kuwaiti government does use this new authority to take action against newspapers for certain controversial editorials and some
news items which have political significance. But as a rule the actions
are relatively mild, involving brief suspensions by the Information Minister for less than three months rather than longer suspensions or cancel-
lations which the Council of Ministers was empowered to order.[31] Pre-
censorship is not used except in a national emergency such as the 1967
war, and censorship of imported print materials is as rare as it is in Lebanon. The Kuwaiti press continues to challenge the regime and the government's primary means of influence is persuasion.

In Morocco, too, the press enjoys some freedom to criticize the
government and the politically powerful. Since 1956, when Morocco
gained its independence and colonial controls on the press by France
and Spain were lifted, the Moroccan newspapers have as a whole shown
a consistent willingness to criticize and debate the issues. The government has not always tolerated this criticism and from time to time has
used various legal and political means against individual newspapers.
Each time, these measures evoke protests from the editors and publishers in question, so there has been a kind of ongoing tug-of-war over how
far the press can and should go.

Moroccan press laws provide for fines and prison terms for offenses against the royal family, the public peace, the morale and unity
of the armed forces and police, and external security.[32] The King has expressed his pride in freedom of the press in Morocco, but he has ex-
horted journalists to act with responsibility: "The educative role of the

press, in the period that we are now passing through, imposes on it the maximum of honesty, of loyalty, of probity in publishing information. . . . To utilize press liberty to accumulate verbal violence and ties is not only a dishonorable act for their authors, but it is an act of treason toward the Moroccan people."[33]

The government uses this reasoning—that the state must "ensure and safeguard" the climate of liberty—to justify its interventions against some newspapers. This has not gone unopposed; in 1959, when the government decreed new regulations allowing for penalties for some press offenses, the Istiqlal Party suspended publication of its five newspapers in protest against this "infringement of free press." But the government continues to play a role in regulating the press. For example, in December 1959, the leftist paper *al Tahrir* published an article accusing royal palace personnel of refusing to allow a group of National Resistance leaders to meet with the King; its banner headline was: "Those who drove out colonialism yesterday are themselves driven away today." That and subsequent critical editorials demanding a purge of the administration led to the arrest of the paper's chief editor and managing director, for committing an "offense against the political and religious institutions of the kingdom." However, in December 1960, when the government announced a new press code giving it more authority to suspend papers, a press strike led to the rescinding of the code.[34]

The competition between the Moroccan government and opposition newspapers increased during the political crises of the 1960s. Some papers were vehemently critical of government policies and officials, but the government made regular use of its authority to seize and censor individual papers. The suspension of the Istiqlal daily *la Nation Africaine* in February 1965 for publishing an anti-monarchical quotation from a nineteenth-century Egyptian philosopher led to a parliamentary crisis and an amendment to the press code cancelling the government's power to suspend or ban a newspaper, but this in turn sparked the king's decision to take personal control of the government in June. The "state of exception" was lifted in July 1970, but the government continued to act against the opposition press with suspensions and arrests of editors.[35] Most Moroccan journalists however welcomed the government's suppression in 1971 of the French-owned Mas Group newspapers. The Mas dailies *La Virgie Marocaine* and *Le Petit Marocain* had survived the transition to independence, and their circulations were three to four times that of next leading daily, *al 'Alam*, because of the quality of journalism and objectivity of news coverage. The Mas Group papers had consistently opposed independence before 1955, and had even called for the deposition of Sultan Muhammad V, applauding his exile in 1953. But just before his return in 1955 they suddenly switched sides and supported him. After independence, they avoided all political involvement and fulfilled a strict information function; because of this and the relatively smooth transition to independence, they were able to continue publishing.[36]

Their continuation was, however, an irritant to many Moroccans, especially to the opposition Istiqlal and other political groups which resented this "foreign press" succeeding in their country. The press code of 1958 required—at the request of the Istiqlal—that all papers had to be controlled by Moroccan nationals, but the government did not enforce this rule against the Mas papers. In 1963, the National Press Union filed suit against the Mas papers, and the court agreed that they were being published illegally, but levied only a small fine against them. An Istiqlal attempt to pass a law against them in June 1965 was diverted by the government's "state of exception."[37] Finally, on October 7, 1971, the government revoked the licenses of the two Mas Group dailies, and by November 1, *le Matin* and *Maroc Soir* appeared to take their places. The new papers were published by the staffs of their predecessors, but new Moroccan chief editors were installed to take full responsibility for editorial decisions.[38]

Government actions suspending newspapers briefly for specific violations of the press law continued, and in the mid-1970s at times became almost a monthly occurrence for such opposition dailies as *l'Opinion* and *al Muharrir*. But the papers do not tire of continually testing how far they can go, and in the process considerable open debate on issues takes place.

WHAT CAUSES DIVERSITY AND RELATIVE FREEDOM?

What are the reasons behind the diversity and relative degree of freedom in the Kuwaiti and Moroccan press?

The newspapers tend to be owned by active, ambitious men, who see the press as a means to make their voices heard and to increase their political and economic power. In Kuwait, *al Ra'y al'Amm* is a family-run paper, published and edited by a prominent Kuwaiti who headed the foreign affairs committee of parliament until its abolition in 1976. *Al Anba'* and *al Qabas* were founded by leading groups of Kuwaiti businessmen who had ties with different families and sectors of society. *Al*

Watan is owned by a group of wealthy landlords and contractors, while *al Siyassah* is run by a young journalist with excellent connections in Kuwaiti and some foreign government circles. All of these people have a personal stake in their newspapers so the orientation and style of a paper is influenced by their personalities.[39]

In Morocco, too, individuals with political interests feel they gain by the promotion of their ideas through their newspapers. The clearest examples of this are *al 'Alam* and *l'Opinion*, the two Istiqlal Party newspapers. The Chief Editor of *al 'Alam* is a central committee member of the Istiqlal, Abdel Karim Ghallab, who has quite distinct political views and ambitions. He is one of Morocco's best journalists and at the same time a leading opposition politician. The chief editor of *l'Opinion*, Abdel Hafid Kadiri, is also an Istiqlal politician. Both of them use the papers to reach Istiqlal Party members with political opinions and analyses, and they regard the press as extremely important because as opposition politicians they feel their access to the government-run radio and television is denied. They even regard the government-operated distribution company as biased against them and inadequate, so they use their own party channels to distribute their papers to members.[40] Similarly, the other pair of wide-circulation dailies, *le Matin* and *Maroc Soir*, are run by Moulay (prince) Ahmed Alawi, a cousin of the King, and they clearly reflect his monarchist, loyalist views. They represent an obvious political counterbalance to the political attitudes conveyed in the Istiqlal papers, a result which 'Alawi has intended. And a newer daily, *al Mithaq al Watani*, tended in 1979 to represent the views of Prime Minister Ahmed Osman, a rival of Alawi's. Finally, the newspapers *al Muharrir* and *al Bayan*, too, are in effect used by their chief editors as political outlets for their own partisan views. The two parties which back them, the USFP and the now-illegal Communist Party, respectively, have been restricted in their activities by the government, so the chief editors are even more anxious to exploit their newspapers as channels for political expression.[41]

Secondly, the political system in the country is such that this open competition and rivalry is possible. In Kuwait, the National Assembly was not a fully representative democratic institution, but in the mid-1970s it held more vigorous debates on sensitive issues and publicly expressed considerable criticism of government policy. Not only were the major merchant families well represented but the leftists, trade unionists and the Arab nationalists had articulate spokesmen there whose views are amplified in the press. The Kuwaiti government still retains considerable authority, but it diminished over the years as the parliament became stronger and more outspoken, enhancing press freedom. This trend was stopped in 1976 with the abolition of parliament and promulgation of a stricter press law.[42] The Ruler announced that the measures had to be taken to preserve national unity, and his prime minister said that government work had become impossible because ministers and officials were preoccupied with "attacks and unjustified charges" in the National Assembly. Despite the 1976 measures, however, Kuwaiti politicians remained active and the courts upheld the right of the press to criticize officials, so something of the political debate remained.[43]

In Morocco, too, the political system helps make press diversity and competition possible. This system allows a degree of political competition to prevail in the open; as one observer notes: "Morocco is one of the rare countries in Africa where political opinions and associations are almost completely free and open. . . . [Laws] permitting the exercise of executive judgment, such as those forbidding any attack on the 'principles of the monarchy,' have been called into operation on a very few occasions to limit freedom of the press."[44]

It is not a completely open system like the Lebanese, but there has been a clearly defined political spectrum in Morocco since independence in 1956. At that time, Sultan Muhamed V recovered full sovereign powers in treaties with the French and Spanish, but he set up a government containing representatives of a number of different parties including the Istiqlal and the Democratic Independent Party. Since the parties were legitimate and open, it was natural that newspapers emerged reflecting their diverse views. Journalism in Morocco had begun in the nineteenth century but it had taken on a strong nationalistic political tone in the 1930s when nationalist leaders tried to use the press against the colonial French.[45] After independence the papers were regarded as political tools. One observer puts it this way: "As newspapers were considered the very heart of politics, representatives of every political tendency attempted to publish at least one, and sometimes two or three papers in Arabic to advance the views of their leaders."[46]

The Istiqlal maintained its position as the loyal opposition, but it was unable to dominate the nationalist movement. The Communist Party and some other small ones such as the Popular Movement were also active, as were several trade union organizations and most of these groups sponsored newspapers. The Communist Party was outlawed in 1959, but much of its leadership and membership was later allowed to join together in the so-called Party of Progress and Socialism which came out with a new Marxist-oriented newspaper. The government and its supporters also promote newspapers.[47]

Thus several political groups compete for power under the watchful eye of the King, who has periodically allowed general elections and the formation of parliaments. Although the political process in Morocco sometimes is paralyzed by this "rich variety of interest groups and parties . . . translating demands into sloganistic appeals that decisionmakers cannot reconcile,"[48] the vitality of the press is maintained by this active pluralism. Thus it is possible for the Moroccan newspapers to be called "certainly the most diverse and interesting press in North Africa."[49] Observers agree that the diversity is based on the underlying political competition that takes place in the system.

The third factor behind the Kuwaiti and Moroccan systems is governmental sensitivity to its international position, which seems to make it more tolerant of a lively and diverse press.

In Kuwait the government is quite conscious of the fact that the country is a very small state surrounded by larger and more powerful neighbors, and even the resident population of the country is more than half non-Kuwaiti. As a consequence, the government has adopted a circumspect policy of cooperation with everyone and toleration of virtually all important political movements in the area. The fact that every newspaper has non-Kuwaitis in influential positions—usually Kuwaiti journalists are in the minority—reinforces the toleration of diverse viewpoints. Also, both the government and members of parliament like to point with pride at the country's free and vigorous press.[50]

The Moroccan government, too, is sensitive to foreign opinion. Many Moroccan leaders including the king support the continuation of press freedom partly because the press is free in Europe, and the European countries, particularly France, are still looked upon as models to be emulated in many ways. Despite the nationalist anticolonial hostility directed against France in the 1950s, the influence of French culture is still strong in Morocco and this is one manifestation of that phenomenon. It must be added, however, that the Moroccan press has not lived up to the expectations of the Francophile elite that support press freedom, so many educated Moroccans still prefer to read le Monde or other French newspapers.

Thus the press systems in Lebanon, Kuwait, and Morocco have a degree of diversity and freedom which set them apart from the other press systems in the Arab world. There are significant differences among these three systems; the Lebanese press (in normal times) exercises considerable self-regulation and is relatively free from government control, while the Kuwaiti and Moroccan newspapers operate within stricter boundaries. Nevertheless they all reflect a political diversity and a degree of open debate in the political system itself which make press diversity and freedom possible.

6

Arab Radio and Television

Radio and television in the Arab world are typically monopolies under direct government supervision. There are a few exceptions, and in the past there have been more, but the rule in the 1970s is direct government operation and ownership of radio and TV. Thus organizational patterns for these media are much less complex than for the press, and they are more uniform throughout the Arab world.

There are several reasons for this. First, the minimum cost of establishing a radio or television system is much higher than the minimum cost of establishing a newspaper, and thus it is far beyond the capability of nearly all private persons in these developing countries. Secondly, this high cost encourages the pooling of resources, or a monopoly, and because these media reach beyond borders and literacy barriers, the government has a much greater interest in controlling them or at least keeping them out of hostile hands. Anyone with a printing press has the technical capability of reaching the literate elite, and while this is seen by the government as a potential threat, it is not nearly as great a political threat as a monopoly radio station broadcasting to millions. Radio and television, which have the potential of reaching every single person in the country, and many outside it, instantaneously, are regarded by Arab governments as too important to be left to private interests. There has been very little argument in the Arab countries against this basic claim of government.

Thirdly, radio and television are newer media, and the trend toward greater authoritarian control over all media that we have seen in our discussion of the press, has affected these newer media more because they have no tradition of independence to uphold. Television, which was not established under Arab control anywhere until after 1956, arrived in an era of declining press diversity, when even newspapers were being standardized and mobilized. Radio, which began in the West around World War I and in a few Arab countries shortly after that, did not really develop in many Arab countries until after World War II. In some places, radio began during a period of press factionalism, diversity and relative independence, and at that time radio too had a large degree of independent, private influence. But it developed and expanded in a period when governments were encroaching on press freedom, and this made governmental control of radio that much easier.

Individual countries had different experiences with radio and television because of unique local factors that influenced these media. But many of the Arab countries first acquired these media when the country was still under European colonial influence. The British and French colonial administrators tended to put them under governmental control from the start, both because they sought to use them as instruments of colonial rule, and because their experience at home in France and Britain had been with government-sponsored electronic media. When these colonial powers departed, they usually turned over broadcasting facilities to the newly independent governments, which were content to maintain them as governmental institutions.

There are also other, minor reasons for governmental control of the electronic media, such as the scarcity of broadcast frequencies and the difficulty of finding and training qualified personnel. But the main factors are the intense government interest in the media as political instruments, the high cost, the lack of tradition as independent entities, and in some cases the precedents set by colonial administrators.

The authoritarian approach to broadcasting in the Arab countries is further seen in the general lack of concern for the size, nature and interests of the audience. Arab radio and television stations rarely carry out any research into listening or viewing audiences. Programs are not shaped to fit precise needs and desires of the audiences but rather they are designed by broadcasting personnel and government officials who decide what the public should have. Listener and viewer mail gives them some flavor of the public reaction but even that is not a determining factor in program decisions.[1]

Advertising is carried on radio and television broadcasts throughout the area, but it is quite restricted and commercial broadcasting exactly as conducted in the United States does not exist. The most common arrangement is for the radio or TV program to carry a cluster of advertisements at specific times, carefully placed between programs to avoid interruptions, and without any sponsorship connection. These advertisements do bring revenues which help cover broadcasting budgets, but usually the government has to provide the bulk of the station's income from receiver license fees or other sources.[2]

A handful of stations in the Arab world depend almost entirely on advertising revenues. Dubai has both commercial radio and commercial television stations, which derive their incomes from advertisements and which exist alongside the government-operated non-commercial ones. Bahrain's television was established as a commercial venture under contract with an American firm, although now the Bahrain Government operates it directly. And three of Egypt's eleven radio services carry advertisements, including the Middle East Radio whose light programming and abundance of ads make it resemble American programming in some ways.[3] Finally, both of Lebanon's television stations are operated on a commercial basis—these will be discussed separately below.

Despite the fact that most Arab radio and television systems are under direct control of the government and therefore exhibit similar organizational characteristics, there are some differences among them in the political roles they play. Systems that exist in the eighteen Arab countries can be divided into three groups, roughly parallel to the groupings of press systems discussed above. The seven countries which have developed the mobilization press system outlined in Chapters 2 and 3—namely Algeria, Egypt, Iraq, Syria, Libya, South Yemen, and the Sudan—have also treated radio and television in a manner similar enough to put them into one group. These seven governments have exercised the strictest control over the electronic media and have pushed their development as instruments of political communication most strongly. The style and tone of programming in these countries, while not the subject of detailed objective surveys, seems, to observers, to differ from those of the second major group, comprising all of the other Arab states except Lebanon. These ten states also have governmental control over broadcasting but it is somewhat more relaxed and development of these media has not been pushed as rapidly given resources available, nor for the same purposes.

These two main groupings can be labelled the mobilization type and the governmental type of broadcasting system, and they include all Arab countries except Lebanon, which presents a special case and will be considered separately.

THE MOBILIZATION SYSTEM

The seven Arab states discussed in Chapter 2 have tended to give higher priority to the development of the electronic media than have other Arab states with comparable resources. They have shown greater appreciation for radio and television as instruments to reach and mobilize the mass of the population which is still illiterate. They have devoted a greater share of their resources to radio, and have been earlier to establish television systems.

Radio

When the revolutionary regimes came to power in these seven countries, they devoted a great deal of attention to radio, promoting its expansion so that it could be used as a political tool to mobilize the masses and propagate the official line.

Egypt has the most extensive and powerful radio broadcasting system in the Near East and Africa. In the 1970s more than 2000 program personnel and 2500 engineering staff, working in 43 studios in the broadcast building in Cairo put out more than 1200 radio hours each week in fourteen services, eight of them for domestic audiences. Powerful transmitters made these programs audible all over Egypt and in most of the Arab countries as well, even on medium wave. This system was built essentially after the revolutionary regime came to power in 1952 and decided to stress radio broadcasting as an instrument of policy. A private firm had started radio in Egypt as a purely commercial venture in the 1920s and the monarchy had not devoted much attention to it for political purposes. Even when the government ended the private contract with Marconi in 1947 and increased government intervention somewhat, this was done primarily because of nationalist pressures; the control of radio was given to a semi-autonomous board of governors whose supervision was relatively loose.[4]

The new Egyptian leadership which seized power in 1952 found only a modest 72kw medium wave radio facility, no shortwave and a small broadcasting staff. It began immediately to build up this capability and ensure control over it, putting radio under the new Ministry of National Guidance which invested large sums to boost signal audibility and expand programming. The new regime also abolished the monarchy's receiver license fee to expand the audience by removing this cost barrier.[5] In less than a decade, the government increased transmitter power 28-fold, providing good reception throughout the country and abroad. During the 1950s, programming expanded to include not only the General Service but also the "second" program of cultural fare for intellectuals, and "With the People" aimed specifically at workers and peasants to provide political indoctrination as well as practical information. The European Program was developed in six foreign languages along with the Sudan Corner and Voice of the Arabs; later the Koranic, music, youth, Hebrew, Palestine, and Middle East Broadcasting programs were added to reach other special groups in Egypt or abroad. Programs designed for domestic audiences alone increased from 18 hours per day in 1952 to 72 by 1960 and more than 120 in the late 1970s, when 85 percent of urban adults reportedly listened to the General Service alone.[6]

The Egyptian government also developed radio as a powerful instrument for reaching foreign audiences (see Chapter 7), but radio expansion was primarily caused by a desire to communicate government policy more effectively to all Egyptians. The regime promulgated a broadcasting law which required the Egyptian Broadcasting Corporation to "strengthen the national consciousness . . . participate in the educational campaign among the people . . . deal with social problems and exhort adherence to moral and ethical values."[7] The effort had a political and social purpose.

Similarly, the other six countries discussed in this section also expanded their facilities relatively rapidly after revolutionary regimes came to power there and took over more direct control of radio.

In Syria, the government through its Broadcasting and Television Corporation established radio transmitters all over the country in the 1950s, boosting power from 13.6 to 150kw, and in subsequent years increased that even further. Its Home Service grew to 18½ hours daily, and other services were promoted also.[8] In Iraq, real expansion of radio broadcasting took place immediately after the July 1958 revolution, when the new regime was engaged in propaganda battles with Egypt and Syria, and was trying hard to make Iraqis and other Arabs understand its point of view.

The pattern repeated itself elsewhere. When the Sudan became independent in 1956, the new regime transferred control of broadcasting from a semi-autonomous committee of leading Sudanese personalities over to a governmental department. This department devoted considerable effort to turning a low-power station reaching only 11,000 of the country's 11 million people 8 hours daily into a nationwide network on the air 17 hours each day. Then during the 1960s, the revolutionary groups which forcibly replaced the European colonial regimes in Algeria and South Yemen, and which took over from the monarchy in Libya, all gave high priority to making the radio facilities more effective and more controlled. In Algeria and South Yemen, these groups fought battles over the radio stations themselves during the liberation struggles, and then immediately after independence the facilities were rebuilt and expanded under tight supervision of the ruling National Liberation Fronts. In Libya, the group of army officers which seized power in 1969 immediately made the Libyan Broadcasting Service responsive to direct orders from the new Revolutionary Command Council and began planning for increased listener coverage.[9]

Television

Television, too, has on the whole been promoted more energetically by the revolutionary regimes in these seven countries than elsewhere in the Arab world, when differing resource levels are taken into consideration. These countries have tended to establish television systems earlier than other Arab countries because their governments were especially anxious to exploit the new medium for political purposes.

Table 9 shows that except for Lebanon (a special case), most of the states with mobilization press systems inaugurated national, Arab-controlled television systems before the rest of the Arab world. Only South Yemen and Libya lagged behind the group, and this was because their revolutionary regimes did not come to power until 1967 and 1969, respectively.[10]

The first Arab-controlled television system was opened by Iraq in May 1956. This was a modest facility of 500 Watts with a program devoted largely to entertainment for the Baghdad audience. When the revolutionary government replaced the monarchy two years later, it boosted the station's power and increased the political content of the programs, drawing partly on the support of the Communist countries for this. New transmitters were built throughout the country, allowing the audience to grow considerably: by 1961 there were 50,000 receivers and by the mid-1970s there were 350,000.

Egypt and Syria began their television systems in 1960 as separate entities after attempting without success to launch a joint enterprise under the aegis of their short-lived political union. The Egyptian government expanded coverage during the 1960s to major populated areas by building twenty-nine transmitters and subsidizing the purchase of com-

TABLE 9
Inaugural Dates of National Television Systems

Mobilization systems	Others
Iraq 1956	
	Lebanon 1959
Egypt 1960	
Syria 1960	
Algeria 1962 (French 1956–62)	Kuwait 1962
The Sudan 1962	Morocco 1962
	Saudi Arabia 1965
	Tunisia 1966
Libya 1968	Dubai 1968
	Jordan 1968
South Yemen 1969 (Brit. 1964–67)	Abu Dhabi 1969
	Qatar 1970
	Bahrain 1972
	Oman 1974
	Yemen AR 1975

munally owned receivers in many poorer locations. As with radio, the Egyptian government built television facilities on a grand scale, fitting out eleven TV studios in Cairo with the latest equipment and hiring 2500 program and more than a thousand technical staff.[11] Meanwhile the Syrian government was busy erecting transmitters outside Damascus in Homs, Aleppo, and then in other provinces in order to reach the bulk of the population. The number of TV receivers in Syria grew as a result to 42,000 in 1961 and 425,000 by the mid-seventies.

The nationalist revolutionary groups which ended colonial rule and came to power in Algeria and South Yemen also promoted television and turned it to their own political uses. The nascent Algerian political system which the French had operated since 1956 in Algiers was heavily damaged by both sides during the course of the liberation struggle, but the new regime in 1962 immediately began to rebuild it and to redirect its content politically. French extremists destroyed the Oran transmitter to prevent the Algerians from hearing de Gaulle, but in 1963 RTA asked the French ORTF to help them rebuild. In South Yemen, the regime that came to power with the hasty departure of the British in 1967 found the modest British-run station so badly damaged, and its own financial situation so weak, that it took nearly two years to begin telecasts again. But a deliberate expansion has taken place in this country under tight political control of the new government, so that three transmitters served more than 21,000 receivers in the mid-seventies. The South Arabian Broadcasting Service, established in 1954, began TV in August 1964, and by 1966 there were 16,000 TV receivers in the country.

The Sudanese government, also facing financial problems and a vast geographic territory to cover, nevertheless pushed ahead with television in 1962 under the Abboud military regime, which had a political purpose in doing so. Abboud was out in 1964, but television received another impetus after President Numeiry came to power in 1969. The government improved service to the Khartoum-Omdurman area so that by the mid-1970s more than 70,000 receivers were in use there including many in clubs and other organizations; and a special effort in the Blue Nile area with transmissions and government-supplied receivers boosted viewing there too.[12] Finally in Libya, the monarchy had for years not felt any need to build a national television system even though thousands of Libyans could watch foreign TV programs from the American base at Wheelus or from Italy or Tunisia. The monarchy only started television modestly in 1968 and in less than a year the revolutionary group which seized power made television one of its priorities as an instrument of control and mobilization. Colonel Qaddafi and his Revolutionary Command Council expanded transmitter capacity and politicized programming, while in 1970 he presided over the closure of the American Wheelus air base and its TV system, which had been broadcasting programs for resident U.S. military personnel that were seen by some Libyans.

Mobilization Programming

The regimes in these seven countries have generally made more effort than governments elsewhere in the Arab world to make radio and television programming convey political messages to the masses of the population. As one observer says of the Sudan, for example, the government "uses television very frequently to get messages across to the Sudanese citizens and to mobilize and control public opinion when major issues arise. The style which is used on such occasions is direct and obvious exploitation of the medium."[13] The politicized programming generally has revolutionary overtones, advocating substantial and rapid change at home or abroad, and is open and explicit such as the Libyan

Information Ministry's published statement on broadcast objectives: "To embody the Arab revolutionary objectives of freedom, socialism and unity and to permeate such objectives in the minds of the people; . . . to bind the Arab struggle for liberation of the occupied territories with the cause of liberation and freedom in the Third World."[14]

For example, Sudanese television and radio tend to devote large portions of their newscasts to the latest achievements of the Numeiry government and to his activities, followed by interviews or other features documenting the benefits that such changes have brought. Then on special occasions, such as Sudanese National Day (May 25), these media begin weeks ahead of time drumming up enthusiasm for the event by rebroadcasting highlights from previous such events interspersed with slogans taken from standard socialist rhetoric. Plays with political lessons—such as the perfidy and evil of the capitalist, the threat of the imperialist and the urgent need to oppose Israel—are broadcast using the best acting talent available.[15] Such programming is carried out with varying degrees of intensity and skill in all seven of the countries being discussed here.

Probably the most effective, subtle and well-executed political programming of this sort is done in Egypt, where radio and TV personnel seem to have a much lighter touch than in Iraq, for example. The Egyptian regime first concentrated on radio in the 1950s, building powerful internal and external services, then it turned in the 1960s to TV as a supplementary means to reach Egyptians. President Nasser used both to evoke enthusiasm for the social, political, and economic changes he was promoting and contempt for the domestic and foreign enemies he was fighting. Regular listeners understood quite clearly from news and commentaries and from features, drama and music programs what direction his policy was taking and who his friends and enemies were. To cite but one domestic example, radio and television between October and December 1965 broadcast the lengthy trial and confessions of the eighteen Muslim Brotherhood members who had plotted against the regime, and the presentation clearly drew the moral for the audience that the regime wanted to be drawn.[16] As for foreign affairs, the electronic media launched numerous campaigns against "imperialism" in the form of the Baghdad Pact, Glubb Pasha, the Suez Canal Company, Israel, and for Arab unity and socialism.[17]

Egyptian broadcasters in both media, but particularly in radio, at times displayed excessive zeal in promoting the official line, and credibility suffered—especially at the time of the June 1967 war—so that these media subsequently became more restrained. But the Egyptian leadership has made it clear that radio and television, like the press, are to continue "to participate along with all the organs of the state in educating men capable of shouldering the burdens of the new stage" of the revolution. The small amount of program material that does carry criticism of governmental policies is usually couched in humor or innuendo for which the Egyptians are famous.[18]

Each of the seven countries discussed in this section aggressively uses the electronic media to convey political messages, usually in support of leftist, anti-imperialist Third World themes. It follows that these are the countries which have provided the bases for Palestinian nationalists to broadcast their political appeals for support among Arabs for the liberation of their homeland. Despite the similarity in name of the Palestinian program—in recent years uniformly "Voice of Palestine"[19]—and the appearance of an independent station in each of these countries, however, these programs are broadcast over national transmitters and are carefully monitored by the host government. Consequently their content conforms to the policy requirements of the host, and when they step out of line they go off the air.[20] Indeed, the seven broadcasting systems are not immune from conducting air wars with each other because of tactical policy differences even though there are similarities in their philosophies and in their uses of the media.[21] In any case, the political content of the programming remains unmistakeably inspired and guided by the regime.

Politically motivated programming tends to be most obvious and pervasive on Iraqi and South Yemeni radio and television.[22] Algerian, Syrian, and other broadcasters sing similar tunes but generally not in quite so strident a manner. Some of the material is acquired from Communist sources, but much is locally generated and all is shaped to fit local conditions, and government policies.[23] In all these countries, however, at least half of the material carried on the electronic media in normal times has no immediate political implications. Indeed all of these countries acquire non-political entertainment films and tapes from many sources, especially American, and they broadcast these alongside political material which is often hostile to the United States. Thus it is a common experience for audiences in these countries to watch an evening TV newscast laden with reports deliberately putting America in a bad light, and then view a Hollywood film or TV series such as "I Love Lucy," "Mod Squad," or "The Bold Ones."[24]

Nevertheless, the governments in these seven countries tend to be more concerned about alien political ideas reaching their populations via the airwaves. The Ministries of Information make certain that all of the imported foreign films used on the mass media are nonpolitical or politically acceptable, and they have even tried to block listening to some foreign radio broadcasts. Some have tried to jam the incoming signal of the British Broadcasting Company's international program, for example, or they have warned the public not to have their minds "poisoned" by the "lies" of Western broadcasters. An editorial in a Libyan newspaper, for example, declared that the Arabic Service of the BBC, Voice of America, and Deutsche Welle have "confused Arabs' thinking by psychological warfare. They induced the Arab individual to entertain suspicion regarding his course . . . to obliterate the Arab individual's morale . . . [they] disseminate rumors, lies, and misleading political news."[25]

GOVERNMENTAL BROADCASTING

Except for Lebanon, radio and television in the other Arab states have tended to be slower to develop, and the programming style is less intensely and aggressively political. The major reason for the difference is that the governments of Morocco, Tunisia, Jordan, Kuwait, Saudi Arabia, Bahrain, Qatar, the United Arab Emirates, Oman, and North Yemen seem to be less interested in active social engineering of the masses and therefore they are less intrigued with the media as tools for social change, than are the regimes in the seven countries just discussed. These ten governments—all of them monarchies except Tunisia and Yemen—have shown some awareness of the political importance of the electronic media for reaching the masses, so they have seen to it that radio and television are in government hands. But they have generally not pushed as hard as the "revolutionary" regimes to expand the reach of radio and TV as a priority matter, nor have they explored all the possibilities of program politicization. They have devoted relatively more attention to other development projects.

Radio

The first Arab radio broadcasting in any of these countries began in the 1940s, and in most of them it started much later. The Jordanian government in 1948 took over the Ramallah transmitters built by the British in Palestine but it did not expand these facilities substantially until the mid-fifties when it found itself under attack by broadcasts from Cairo because of the Baghdad Pact and Glubb Pasha. This radio war helped encourage Jordan to build new transmitters in Amman in 1956. The loss of the West Bank including Ramallah to Israel in the 1967 war undercut Jordan's radio capabilities, however, and the government has not given broadcasting a very high priority in the distribution of its scarce resources. Skilled Jordanian broadcasters have also left the country, further weakening the system as they sought better-paying jobs in the Arab states of the Persian Gulf.

North Yemen also began radio broadcasting shortly after World War II; it too lacked the money to invest in the medium and it was also totally lacking in trained personnel. The government showed little positive interest so that still in the mid-seventies this country had only a rudimentary broadcasting system and only 90,000 receivers distributed among more than five million people. The other states of the Arabian Peninsula have had the financial means to devote to broadcasting but they have been relatively slow to do so. When Saudi Arabia opened its first radio station in 1948, it was only audible in the Jidda-Mecca area. The Saudi government, conscious of its international role as protector of the Islamic holy places, developed its shortwave radio capability aimed at Muslims in Indonesia, Pakistan, and elsewhere, but it did not push domestic radio particularly strongly. It did not open a radio station in Riyadh, the capital, until 1963, or in Dammam for Eastern Province audiences until 1967.[26]

In neighboring Kuwait, radio broadcasting began in 1952 but it was only heard 2½ hours per day and this increased very little until the country was fully independent nine years later. After 1961 the program and audience did grow substantially, a fairly easy task in such a city-state with abundant oil revenues. Further south, in the small Arab emirates of the Persian Gulf and in Oman, there was no Arab-controlled broadcasting before the late 1960s except in Bahrain which opened a modest facility in 1955. The British, responsible for foreign affairs and defense in the area until 1971, operated a radio station from Sharjah starting in 1966 but the Arab rulers saw no pressing need to have radio stations for their own people. Then in 1968–69, anticipating full independence and competition for international attention, the oil-rich states of Qatar and Abu Dhabi opened their own radio stations. The new federation of the United Arab Emirates took over British radio facilities in 1971 and Ras al Khaimah, one of the constituent states, expressed its independence from the federation by opening its own station in 1974. Oman had no radio station at all until after 1970 when the new sultan deposed his reactionary father and opened the country up to the outside world.

Thus it was primarily external pressures of competition among neighboring states, manifesting themselves after the British departure, which induced these small states to invest some of their oil wealth into radio facilities. These rulers purchased large transmitters and fancy studio equipment, and they imported radio talent, not so much to communicate government policies on specific issues to their own populations as to convey to the world the image of independence, sovereignty and national identity which they felt their small countries needed. The rulers saw them as external symbols of power more than as internal instruments of communication and certainly not agents of social change.[27]

In North Africa, the leadership in Tunisia and Morocco also did not push government-controlled radio as much as Arab revolutionary regimes did. Morocco was fully independent in 1956, but it was not until 1959 that the government closed the private commercial radio stations and took over control of all broadcasting to create a national network.[28] The Tunisian government which took over at independence in 1956 put radio under a government department but gave it some autonomy. Not until 1964, when President Bourguiba had a member of the Tunisian ruling party's Political Bureau appointed director of Radio Télévision Tunisienne did the government clearly show its concern for tight policy control. The government did expand radio facilities somewhat, but a survey in 1973 showed that as many as 25 percent of urban Tunisian adults still did not listen to radio even once a week.[29]

Television

Arab-controlled television did not come to any of these ten countries until after 1961, and it generally lagged behind TV development in the other states. The Kuwaiti government, which had oil revenues to spend on the medium, was the first of the ten to go into it. But the newly independent Kuwaiti government at first allowed a wealthy private entrepreneur to establish a small television station and only after this had begun operating did it take over and start to develop a government-run system. With abundant resources and ideal geographical conditions the government was able to provide a good signal for all 900,000 inhabitants of this country without any difficulty.

The government of Saudi Arabia began television broadcasts only in 1965 after some delays, and the five major urban areas were not covered by the network until November 1969. The Saudis had sufficient funds to do it sooner, but conservative elements strongly resisted introduction of the new medium altogether, and the government hesitated to push because of unknown social consequences. Finally, however, the government saw that television might be a substitute for public cinemas (which were and still are banned), and it accepted as inevitable a medium that other countries had enjoyed for years.[30] The decision to inaugurate Saudi television was also spurred by international broadcasting considerations. Cairo radio broadcasts were at the time critical of the Saudi government and widely listened to by Saudis, so television was seen partly as a self-defense measure. And when the Saudi government in 1969 opened the largest antenna in the Middle East in Dammam with a pair of 12.5kw transmitters, its motive was not so much to give Eastern Province Saudis a better TV picture as to reach Kuwait, which had had television for nearly a decade.[31]

Similarly, the other Arab states on the Persian Gulf felt this same urge to compete with electronic media. In 1968, before any of the small lower gulf emirates had television themselves, many people were buying TV receivers to watch Kuwaiti and Aramco (Dhahran) television. Bahrain and Qatar at that time had respectively an estimated 7500 and 2500 receivers for that purpose. This cross-border competition helped encourage Dubai, Abu Dhabi, and Qatar to use their surplus oil revenues to open showcase television stations in 1968, 1969 and 1970, respectively. The governments of neighboring Bahrain and Oman, not so wealthy, had other priorities and did not open their TV stations until 1972 and 1974; also, the former was a private commercial venture for the first three years.[32] Finally, North Yemen, the poorest state on the Arabian Peninsula, opened its television system in late 1975 but then only because the Abu Dhabi government offered to finance the entire enterprise. The Yemeni government had shown no urgent desire to invest in television itself.[33]

In Morocco and Tunisia, too, the governments were encouraged to install local television systems because of TV growth in neighboring countries, rather than because of any urgently felt need to create a domestic information channel. Both countries became independent in 1956 but did not establish television until 1962 and 1966, respectively. For years Tunisians and Moroccans living in Mediterranean coastal areas had been able to tune in to European broadcasts, and after 1962 some could see Algerian TV as well. The Tunisian and Moroccan governments could not lag far behind in promoting this most modern symbol of statehood.[34] Finally, the Jordanian government in 1968 opened its own television system after the Jordanian population had acquired more than 10,000 TV receivers in order to see programs from several neighboring countries. As with most of these conservative governments, the impetus to begin TV came from external pressure rather than from any internal concerns or an ideological propensity to create an instrument to reach and mobilize the population for social change. The latter does not seem to exist in these states.

Programming

The content and style of radio and television broadcasting in these ten states tend to be characterized by less politically motivated programming, with more entertainment and popular culture. The newscasts and public affairs features do consistently present evidence of the latest achievements of the government, and extol the virtues of the top personalities. And the Ministries of Information do provide the editors with guidance on political programming which is followed. But the guidance is often of a negative variety, instructing editors to ignore sensitive issues rather than to exploit certain themes for their propaganda value. Editors who carefully avoid taboo subjects are given more freedom to do programs the way they wish.[35] With the exception of President Bourguiba during the first dozen years of Tunisian independence, the national leaders in these countries tend not to exploit the electronic media for direct personal communication with the masses the way the leaders in the revolutionary states do. Nor is it common for these radio and TV stations to launch aggressive campaigns promoting political themes in commentaries, features, drama, and song. Programming is much more bland and the vast majority of it is nonpolitical.[36]

As an inside observer in one of these countries put it, "the government does not even think about using the electronic media for political mobilization. It doesn't push specific issues on radio or television. It simply turns the media over to technocrats it trusts, and monitors the result."[37] Because of the prevailing political atmosphere in these countries (discussed in Chapter 4), the broadcast personnel are cautious about anything political, preferring to avoid all problems with the government. Since there is no open political opposition in nearly all of these countries, anti-regime views are not generally reflected in broadcast programming at all. Even in Kuwait and Morocco, where some political opposition functions in public, it has only limited access to radio and television—far less than to the press. Also, these government-operated facilities tend to be more careful about criticizing foreign governments than do the media in the other Arab states.[38]

For example, the Saudi Arabian government established its television system with modest educational and entertainment motives in mind, rather than political programming. When it proved difficult to fill the many hours of TV time with appropriate educational programming, editors turned to imported entertainment footage. In Qatar, an official of Qatar Radio explained that its purpose is to "push forward the march of civilization and spread cultural and social consciousness among the citizens. . . . The radio station is a window through which the listener sees the world."[39]

Even Jordanian electronic media are relatively low in political content and tend to stress entertainment, despite the fact that Jordanians and Israelis—at war since 1948—can see and hear each other's radio and television. It is simply not characteristic of the Jordanian government to politicize its media radically in order to mobilize the population for change.

The constraints on broadcast programming in these ten states are in many cases cultural rather than political. In Saudi Arabia, for example, Saudi women in the late seventies still do not appear on television because social custom requires that they wear veils in public. They are allowed to speak on radio, but both media observe other social and cultural taboos, too. Similarly, broadcast editors in the other countries are careful not to violate local social customs and mores. They generally rely heavily on imported films and tapes, especially entertainment material from the West, but these are all carefully checked before use for social and cultural as well as political suitability.[40]

LEBANESE BROADCASTING

Lebanon is a special case among Arab broadcasting systems, as it is among Arab press systems (see Chapter 5).

Lebanese Radio is the only one of the mass media that is owned and operated by the government. Since radio was established in 1938 by the French Mandatory authorities, who insisted on controlling it completely, the newly independent Lebanese government had no difficulty in taking it over completely as a monopoly when the French withdrew from the country in 1946. The French established the precedent of governmental radio, so the Lebanese officials were able to retain it.[41]

Control of radio was exercised at first by the Ministry of Interior, then by the Information Ministry, but the Lebanese government was relatively slow to push expansion of the medium. During the first years of operation by the Lebanese government, the number of radio receivers remained below 50,000, or fewer than 5 per 100 inhabitants. The government did not devote the necessary funds to transmitter expansion until the early 1960s, when finally the signal reached the entire country and listenership was able to grow substantially; still, a 1974 survey showed that more than a quarter of the adult population did not listen to Lebanese Radio even once a week.[42]

The Minister of Information and his Director General of Information control editorial policy of Lebanese Radio directly. They assure that politically important programming conforms to governmental guidance. However, newscasts generally do not follow any discernibly consistent policy line and usually they present issues in a straightforward and balanced manner. Also, most of the program time is devoted to entertainment and features which reflect no particular political coloration.[43]

Television in Lebanon, like the press, is in private hands. Lebanon is the only Arab country whose TV networks are wholly owned and operated by private commercial interests. Television was begun in June 1959 by the Compagnie Libanaise de Télévision (CLT), a commercial enterprise established by Lebanese businessmen with some French shares. By the 1970s, coverage included Beirut, some of its suburbs and Tripoli, and had expanded from its original two channels to four. A second company, La Télévision du Liban et du Proche-Orient ("Tele-Orient"), founded by another group of Lebanese businessmen with some British support, started telecasts in 1962. This company also extended its geographic coverage rapidly, and expanded programming from one to two channels. Both networks broadcast throughout the evening and offer a choice of programs in Arabic, French and English. The number of television receivers grew accordingly from 60,000 in 1961 to more than 400,000 in the mid-seventies.

Both CLT and Tele-Orient depend on advertising income, and commercials take up proportions of air time comparable to American TV although the scheduling is different. Advertising in Lebanon, as in Europe, tends to be grouped together before and after programs rather than interrupting them; also, firms tend not to be allowed to sponsor specific programs as they do in the U.S. The Lebanese government does have the authority to issue broadcast licenses for television, and under the terms of the licenses it can set editorial policy guidelines for news and special events coverage. The government has, however, tended to exercise this right only as a veto power over sensitive issues in times of political crisis. The news is written and edited by TV editors, using local reporters and international news services rather freely. They are careful to avoid favoring one group over another, or criticizing a foreign power, so their political material tends to be much more bland than the press.[44]

The two Lebanese television stations merged their news departments in 1962, but they have otherwise resisted attempts at coordination. They remain commercial rivals. The bulk of their programming is non-political, and nearly three-quarters of it is usually imported film or videotape. Foreign interests have not diminished over the years, either. The French supply considerable material to CLT and their role in that station has become so important that recent license agreements have been negotiated directly between the French and Lebanese governments. Tele-Orient, for its part, is more dependent on American and British support and a major shareholding interest of Lord Thompson of Fleet Street, London. CLT uses the French SECAM color technique, while Tele-Orient uses the German PAL color system.[45]

The Lebanese civil war, which began in 1975, fragmented broadcasting even further. The various Lebanese factions became increasingly interested in the electronic media for explaining their views as lines hardened geographically and the partisan newspapers were unable to circulate freely. At first the factions did not attempt to take over the broadcast stations by force, just as they had at first left the newspaper offices alone. One new radio station began broadcasting from a clandestine location, calling itself Voice of Lebanon and clearly supporting one of the major protagonists in the struggle, the right-wing Christian Phalange Party. Another new clandestine station went on the air calling itself Voice of Arab Lebanon, which attacked the "facist Phalange" while supporting leftists and Palestinians.[46]

Then on March 11, 1976, when Brigadier General Abdal Aziz al Ahdab announced that he had seized power in Lebanon from President Sulaiman Franjieh, the regular Lebanese radio and television systems were split into two competing sections. General Ahdab took over the medium wave and FM radio transmitters, and from the studios in central Beirut he began broadcasting on 989 and 836 kcs as well as three FM frequencies. He also saw to it that the CLT television company, located in the Tallat al Khayyat area of Ras Beirut which he controlled, broadcast pro-Ahdab Arabic newscasts each night. Meanwhile, supporters of President Franjieh—who refused to resign his presidency—

continued to control the main medium- and short-wave radio transmitters in the predominantly Christian area north of Beirut. They beamed radio broadcasts from there on 836 kcs (like Ahdab) and on three short-wave frequencies. The Franjieh group was also able to control the Tele-Orient TV facilities because they were located in the Beirut suburb of Hazmiyyah which was under Christian control since the beginning of the crisis. The Tele-Orient version of the evening news was clearly biased in favor of Franjieh and thus contrasted sharply with CLT's news.[47]

By the end of May 1976, General Ahdab had resigned, and "his" radio and TV stations had taken on the political biases of the Lebanese Arab Army (LAA) which controlled the area. For the next six months, Lebanon had radio and television stations separately supporting the LAA and Franjieh factions.

Many Lebanese could hear and see both the pro-coup and pro-Franjieh programs, although the former were more audible and visible in central Beirut and the latter more so outside the city.

In addition, some of them could hear other radio stations which came intermittently on the air as mouthpieces of various Palestinian, leftist and Christian groupings. According to listeners on the spot, broadcasts of these smaller stations tended to be much more strident and inflammatory in tone and content, while the broadcasts of the two main factions, produced by experienced broadcasting professionals, were deliberately more restrained and responsible. They were all, however, clearly partisan in commentary and news selection because of the serious political struggle in which their patrons were engaged.

By the end of 1976, however, a new Lebanese president was installed in office, the security situation was improved, and the opposition elements had lost control over the main radio and television transmitters. The Phalangist broadcasters went underground and set up a clandestine radio transmitter which they used for several hours each day on three frequencies. This "Voice of Lebanon" continued into 1979, broadcasting in English and French as well as Arabic, and it made an effort to keep up the attack on the government and the Palestinians, but the technical quality of its transmission was poor so its audience was quite small.[48]

Thus with the lessening of violence in the Lebanese Civil War after 1976, the extreme factionalism that resulted from it subsided, and broadcasting reverted to a more normal situation. The government again controlled the main radio station, and private interests not opposed to the government resumed control of television.

Sources of Foreign News Available
to Arab Audiences

WHICH ARE the most important channels of foreign news for Arab media? Who controls these channels and how do the channels themselves affect the news content by filtering of various editors and other gatekeepers along the way? What are the various different channels available, and how have they developed their networks into the Arab world?

In examining the news channels, we shall analyze not only economic, political, and technological factors that have shaped them, but also historical factors which have had a bearing on their functioning in the Arab countries during the period following World War II. The discussion will focus on the character and diversity of news available to an Arab editor about countries other than his own, such as, for example, news concerning the United States. It will note the various filters the news must go through to reach Arab editors—or Arab audiences directly, as in the case of international radio broadcasts.

Arab media editors use a variety of news sources every day. For domestic news stories concerning only events in their own country, these sources are generally the most important: the national news agency; governmental ministries; staff reporters and freelancers; radio (for the press) and newspapers (for radio and TV); and magazines and other sources.

For foreign news stories, however the most important sources used by Arab editors are: world news agencies; Arab and other news agencies; foreign radio broadcasts; foreign video services (film and videotape for TV); newspapers and magazines; foreign embassy releases and materials; correspondents stationed abroad; and television and other sources.

The use of one or another type of source varies, of course, depending on the nature of the story itself and other factors. But generally speaking, the five world news agencies are the mainstays of foreign news operation, followed by Arab and other news agencies, foreign radio listening and (for TV news editors) video services. Arab correspondents stationed outside their own countries and reporting back to their newspaper, or radio or TV station, (as contrasted with news agency correspondents) are very few in number, and do not therefore provide a major share of the foreign news in the Arab media. Finally, note that some of these news sources, such as foreign radio broadcasts, are available directly to Arab audiences, while others, such as news agency tickers, are filtered by editors and in some cases by government officials.

We will look in some detail at each of these news sources starting with the five world news agencies and then examining smaller non-Arab and Arab news services, and other sources.

THE WORLD NEWS AGENCIES

More than forty news agencies supply news to the Arab media. Five of these—the British Reuters, the French AFP, the Russian TASS and the American AP and UPI—are considered world agencies because they maintain networks of offices all over the world for the collection and dissemination of news on a daily basis. The rest are more limited in geographic scope to certain regions or to one country.[1]

It should be noted that Arab editors depend very heavily on the four Western news agencies for foreign, particularly non-Arab news. These four were established well before any Arab news agency existed, so they created news flow patterns early, and then they were able to maintain much of their position because they provided services that could not be duplicated.

The Early Anglo-French Monopoly

Until after World War I, the British and French controlled all important sources of news entering the Arab World from the outside, including news from America. They established themselves in the nineteenth century as the sole foreign news suppliers to this area because of their colonial activities there.

British colonial interest in Cairo, Khartoum, Aden, and Muscat led to the construction of a cable network from England to those Arab cities as early as 1860. The private news service operated from London by Julius Reuter established a monopoly on news collection and dissemination in the British territories of the Eastern Arab world, first along this cable route and then elsewhere including Iraq and Palestine.[2]

Simultaneously the private news service operated out of Paris by Charles Havas was opening offices in Rabat, Tunis, and Algiers as the French government assumed colonial responsibilities in those cities. At the end of the World War I Havas developed a monopoly over foreign news coming into Syria and Lebanon when France was named mandatory power over those countries. In 1945 Agence France Presse took over from Havas, and because it is an autonomous French government corporation it was able, according to observers, to establish a "virtual monopoly over the flow of news in the territories of France Ontre-Mer."[3]

The American News Agencies

The American news agencies Associated Press and United Press (later United Press International) helped break the Anglo-French monopoly in the years after World War II. By 1952, they were the leading news agencies in Kuwait and Saudi Arabia, and they served eleven papers in Egypt, two in Jordan, six in Lebanon and several in Syria and Iraq.[4] This happened because the Arab media editors were seeking to diversify their sources and break out of the restricted colonial connections, and because the American agencies offered a competitive fast and accurate service of international news. They also operated their teletypes 24 hours a day, offering subscribers a larger volume than AFP and Reuters which only ran 15–20 hours a day. The Arab media were growing rapidly during this period, and their audiences were becoming increasingly interested in international news, so editors sought to meet this demand by subscribing to these useful additional world services. And the 1956 Suez crisis, which discredited the British and French in Arab eyes, helped turn more editors away from Reuters and AFP to the American wire services.

Arab editors saw some similarity between AP and UPI and frequently chose one or the other. The Associated Press, as the world's largest news agency, was able to offer excellent news coverage, photos and features which persuaded Arab customers in a number of countries (Kuwait, Saudi Arabia, Jordan, the Sudan, Iraq, and, after the British gave up their special rights in the Persian gulf states, there, too) to choose AP over UPI. United Press, on the other hand, made a special effort to break into Francophone Africa with a French language service which the Algerian, Moroccan, and Tunisian media subscribed to.[5]

The Soviet News Agency

The Soviet news agency TASS (Telegrafnoie Agentstvo Sovetskovo Soiuza), which is an organ of the Soviet government, expanded its services into the Arab world particularly after 1956. Before that, only few leftist or Communist editors in Lebanon were using TASS regularly, because its news copy was not considered objective and because TASS had not made much effort to enter the Arab world.[6] In the 1950s, TASS representatives sought to extend their news service in the Arab countries. They were helped not only by the desire of Arab editors to diversify their sources, but also by political events such as the 1956 Suez crisis and a growth of "anti-imperialist" sentiment which the USSR was able to capitalize on. Thus TASS initiated daily teletype news service in Cairo, Damascus, and Amman in the fall of 1956.[7] The expansion of TASS was also helped by economic factors: they usually offered TASS free of charge, at least at first, a tempting arrangement for Arab editors facing rising costs with limited budgets. Marxist editors in some places encouraged their papers to install TASS tickers, and in other countries—such as North Yemen in the 1960s—the government made a deliberate decision to bring in TASS as part of an effort at good relations with Communist states, although local Communists were quite restricted.

In an effort to spread the Soviet version of the news abroad more effectively, the USSR in February 1961 created a second news agency which it soon offered as a bonus to Arab clients. Agenstvo Pechati Novosti (APN, or Novosti) was a government bureau which provided information about the USSR which Soviet embassies and TASS offices in the Arab world promoted as a supplement to TASS. Although it was not regarded as any more objective than TASS, it was free, and it gave Arab editors one more supplementary source of information to consider—so many took it.

In the early 1960s, TASS and Novosti established themselves in Morocco, Tunisia, Libya, the Sudan, and Kuwait. After successfully entering the Arab countries a gratis basis, they attempted to charge a nominal fee for regular news bulletins, features, and photos. Some Arab subscribers bought this package but others did not, or were slow in paying, and usually the services continued anyhow. By the mid seventies they had outlets in every Arab country except Saudi Arabia and the UAE. TASS reports relating to the United States took up 17 percent of its copy volume, and much of this was negatively biased. But the volume of news distributed by TASS in this area was far below that of the other world agencies; for example in the same year it was only 10 percent of AP's output and one-quarter of the others'. For that reason, and because many Arab editors regarded the material as "pure propaganda," it was not used regularly except in countries which had close political relations with the USSR, such as Iraq and Syria.[9]

Reuters and AFP Remained Competitive

Despite the loss of their monopoly positions, and the various problems and competitors they faced after World War II, both Reuters and AFP worked hard to retain leading roles in the distribution of news to Arab media. They succeeded primarily because they were able to give Arab editors what they needed; this sometimes meant tailoring the service to local Arab needs, which the American services tended not to do.

First of all, both Reuters and AFP split their service to the Middle East from their service to Africa, offering each area separate selections of news items chosen with local interests in mind. Many Arab editors regard them as more relevant to their interests than are the American services. Secondly, AFP had a strong position in North Africa and in Lebanon because its bulletin is in French; Reuters sought to imitate that by developing a special African service translated into French. AFP, by the same token, had its Middle East bulletin translated into English in order to make it more accessible to editors there. More importantly, both developed Arabic language services during the 1960s. In 1964, the Arabic Regional News Service was established in Beirut to translate and distribute Reuters news in Arabic throughout the area.[10] Then in 1969, AFP made an agreement with Egypt's Middle East News Agency (MENA) to translate AFP into Arabic and distribute it throughout the entire Arab world. Reuters also contracted with MENA to translate its bulletin for Egyptian subscribers.[11] These Arabic bulletins were of great importance in making the services useful to Arab editors.

Television News Services

The bulk of the foreign news material going into the Arab world is words and still photos which travel by wire or wireless to customers' receivers. Television, however, requires a special kind of news service— motion pictures or videotapes—which a number of West European companies in particular have been able to supply reasonably well. The British company Visnews has been the most successful in providing filmclips and videotapes quickly by air to many Arab television stations. After the West European countries started their Eurovision pool in 1954, and the East Europeans followed suit with their Intervision pool in 1960, television materials became more readily available for Arab customers. For the television stations in North Africa, which were linked with Europe by microwave, access was relatively simple and the material moved at a regular pace rather early. For television stations in the Eastern Arab world, Visnews and other suppliers had to ship the filmclips and videotapes by commercial air. Although this method was slower, television stations in the Sudan, Saudi Arabia, Kuwait, on the Persian Gulf and even South Yemen subscribed to the service and used the materials regularly despite the fact that they were sometimes two to three days old by the time they were telecast.[12]

Other Non-Arab News Sources

Aside from the five big agencies, a number of other international wire services attempted to develop outlets in the Arab world after the mid-fifties. Some of the government controlled news agencies in the communist states did manage to persuade Arab editors, particularly in the so-called socialist states, to take their material on a regular basis, either through exchange agreements with the local Arab news agency or through gratis handouts. The Yugoslavian agency Tanjug was able to do this in a number of states primarily because of Arab interest in Tito as a Third World Leader. Peking's New China News Agency (NCNA), the Czechoslovakian Press Bureau (CTK), and East Germany's Allgemeine Deutsche Nachrichtenagentur (ADN) found customers in several Arab countries, and representatives of news agencies from Hungary, Poland, Bulgaria, Romania, Cuba, North Korea, and Vietnam are also active in the area. But the usage of their materials seems to be relatively marginal.

Likewise some smaller non-Communist agencies have sought to

enter the Arab world but with limited success. West Germany's Deutsche Presse Agentur (DPA) has better success than most because through Cairo's MENA it offers (like AFP) an Arabic service to the whole Arab world.[13] The Italian and Spanish agencies have some outlets in the Arab world but they are little used.

By the 1970s, therefore, Arab editors had access to a wide variety of non-Arab sources of foreign news. A typical Arab country in 1950 had only one or two sources, and they were mostly AFP or Reuters, but twenty-five years later it had tickers of all five world agencies plus regular services of several smaller ones.

The editor's usage of these sources, however, seems to favor heavily the American, French, and British agencies. The American ones did well because of the volume and quality of their material, and because of Arab interest in U.S.–related events.[14] The French AFP and British Reuters did well because they managed, despite the problems noted above, to continue to provide services useful to Arab editors. Unlike the American agencies, which had one overseas service in English for the entire region, AFP and Reuters split the Near East and Africa services tailoring each to the needs of local editors, and they offered the material in Arabic as well as English and French. These efforts paid off, keeping the British and French services fully competitive with the American ones. Moscow's TASS, on the other hand, only did well in those places and at those times when close relations with the USSR made it necessary for editors to use it consistently. But in general, the clear favorites among non-Arab news agencies were the American, British and French ones. In fact, as Table 10 shows, the British and French were able to at least retain leading positions in most of their former colonial areas.

Therefore by the 1970s, Reuters, AFP, and one or the other of the American news agencies had subscribers in nearly every Arab country. All of them provided to Arab editors a considerable amount of news related to Western countries including the United States. In July 1975, for example, U.S. news averaged 29 percent of AFP's output to Near Eastern customers and 22 percent of its output to its North African customers. The Reuters figures were 32 percent and 16 percent. The American agencies, of course, did even better, because they are U.S.–based and because their copy is more voluminous. The AP for example, in 1975 provided 50 percent more news related to American subjects than Reuters or AFP Near East services did and 2½ times as much as their North African services did.[15] Arab editors thus have a wealth of U.S.–related material available to them.

TABLE 10
Rank Order of Significant Sources of Foreign News for Arab Media
(1975)

	British	French	American	Other Western	Russian	Other Communist
FORMER BRITISH SPHERE OF INFLUENCE						
Egypt	1	4	2	5	3	6
The Sudan	1	X	2	X	X	X
Jordan	1	3	2	X	X	
Iraq	3	2	X	X	1	X
South Yemen	1		X			
Kuwait	2	3	1	4	5	
Libya	1	3	4	X	2	
Bahrain	X		X			
Qatar	1		2			
UAE (Truc. St.)	1		2			
Oman	1					
FORMER FRENCH SPHERE OF INFLUENCE						
Tunisia	2	1	3	5	4	6
Morocco	3	1	2	5	4	6
Algeria	X	1	X	X	X	X
Lebanon	2	3	1	4	5	6
Syria	2	X	X	X	1	X

Source: Data from USIA "Country Data Sheets" for 1975 and 1976 and from interviews with news agency personnel in New York, London, Paris, and Washington. Numbers indicate rank order for the country's media as a whole; Xs indicate that the service is used but the ranking is unclear.

ARAB NEWS AGENCIES AND FOREIGN NEWS

By the mid-1970s, news agencies had been established by each of eighteen of the Arab states. But they were quite different from the Western news agencies just discussed, both in purpose and in actual function.

The real primary purposes of these eighteen organizations when they were established were: (1) to improve the dissemination of information about the national government and the country, and (2) to improve the government's control over the acquisition of incoming foreign news. All of the eighteen are organized as departments of their national governments and directly responsive to official policy guidance. Thus they were intended primarily to disseminate and control domestic information, and were not created to collect foreign news. A few of them developed networks and exchanges which got them secondarily into foreign news gathering, and we will examine that development. But we shall first examine the essential characteristics of these institutions.

Table 11 lists the eighteen Arab news agencies in the order in which they were established.

TABLE 11
National News Agencies in the Arab Countries

The Sudan	1946	Sudan News Agency (SUNA)*
Egypt	1956	Middle East News Agency (MENA)
Morocco	1959	Maghreb Arab Presse (MAP)
Iraq	1959	Iraqi News Agency (INA)
Tunisia	1961	Tunis Afrique Presse (TAP)
Algeria	1961	Algerie Presse Service (APS)
Jordan	1965	Jordanian News Agency (JNA)
Syria	1965	Syrian Arab News Agency (SANA)
Libya	1966	Jamahiriah News Agency (JANA)†
Lebanon	1966	Lebanese News Agency (LNA)
South Yemen	1968	Aden News Agency (ANA)
Saudi Arabia	1971	Saudi News Agency (SNA)
Yemen Republic	1971	SABA News Agency (SABA)
Qatar	1975	Qatar News Agency (QNA)
Oman	1975	Omani News Agency (ONA)
UAE	1976	Emirates News Agency (ENA)
Bahrain	1976	Al-Khalij News Agency (KNA)
Kuwait	1976	Kuwaiti News Agency (KUNA)

*The Sudan Press Agency was established in 1946 and replaced in 1960 by SUNA.
†The Libyan News Agency was created in 1966, and the name was changed to Arab Revolutionary News Agency in 1975, then to JANA.

Disseminating National News

The first underlying motivation for establishment of these eighteen government-run news agencies was a desire to improve the dissemination of news about the nation and the government. There was a feeling in all of these countries that misunderstandings and distortions existed, and that these needed to be set straight.

For example, the Tunisian news agency TAP was established because, as one of its directors put it, "We had been depending on foreign news agencies to distribute Tunisian news abroad, and while that was not false it was not presented from the Tunisian viewpoint."[16] The management of the Moroccan agency had a similar explanation for the creation of MAP: "While the world's press is served by big news agencies like

AP, AFP, Reuter, TASS, and UPI, there is a need for each country to set up and develop its own agency, to present its own viewpoint, supply the national press and organizations with news, and to send abroad news of the country from the national point of view. North Africa was completely dependent for news on foreign countries. . . . The influence of foreign organizations on Maghreb news distributed by them never satisfied our national need. Sometimes it was deformed or not even mentioned."[17]

The advent of television only intensified the dissatisfaction. The Arab States Broadcasting Union, created to help deal with the problem, publicly complained about Arab television station dependence on the British company Visnews for TV films.[18]

This feeling was not confined to government officials alone, but was also shared in many respects by professional Arab journalists. For example the Middle East News Agency was established in 1956, the year of the Suez crisis, when Egyptian journalists saw Western news agencies as particularly biased. The largest publishing houses in Cairo joined together to create MENA in order to take the "Arab viewpoint" into account in news selection. MENA began as a private venture, but in 1962 was taken over by the government.[19] Journalists in several countries who advocated the establishment of an Arab news agency usually thought it was needed even if it had to be a government institution, saying, "national poison is better than foreign poison."[20]

In some of the Arab countries, this widespread interest in presenting the national viewpoint was translated by the regime in power into a more intense and aggressive effort to develop a news agency as a propaganda instrument for the government's policies. The Algerian APS, for example, was established in 1961 by Algerian journalists in exile in Tunisia during the Algerian war, as a section of the information department of the National Liberation Front (FLN), in order to help spread the Algerian view of the war. After independence in 1962, APS moved to Algiers but it remained under the FLN and the Algerian president explained that it had a propaganda purpose: "It is clear that this agency cannot be simply an organism for the diffusion of facts, but it must be above all political and ideological, in the service of the nation and of all the vital forces of the country. To accomplish this mission, the APS must collaborate closely with the party, the government and all national organizations."[21]

The Iraqi, Syrian, South Yemeni, and (post-1969) Libyan regimes have taken a similar view of their national news agencies as primarily tools for political mobilization. The Libyan regime in 1975 even changed the name of its news service from the neutral "Libyan News Agency" to the "Arab Revolutionary News Agency" in order to symbolize its activist political purpose. But the majority of the Arab regimes regard their news agencies as necessary simply to fill gaps and correct misunderstandings they believe exist in knowledge of their country and government.

Finally, an Arab news agency representing Palestinian interests and not connected to any individual state, must be mentioned because it emerged after 1967 and became an important source of news and opinion for Arab media. It too was established for the same kinds of reasons just discussed. The Palestine Revolutionary News Agency (*wakalit anba filistin althawrah*, WAFA) was created by the Palestine Liberation Organization in the aftermath of the 1967 Arab-Israeli war as Palestinian nationalism and dissatisfaction with the status quo burgeoned. Centered in Beirut, WAFA opened branch offices in a number of Arab capitals which passed on to local media the daily bulletins of news, commentary and official statements emanating from the PLO. As a WAFA spokesman described it, "The Agency was established in order to express the line and principles of our revolution and the triumphs of our fighters, and to expose the plots and trafficking of renegades, agents and enemies."[22]

Enemy number one, of course, is Israel, and number two, judging from the content of WAFA output, is the United States. "Agent" includes those Arab governments who do not support the PLO avidly enough and "renegades" are generally the Palestinians who fail to adhere to the dominant PLO line.

Controlling Incoming Foreign News

The second purpose of these agencies is to help improve the government's control and influence over incoming foreign news. In practice, the eighteen Arab countries divide into three somewhat different approaches to carrying out this function.

In eight Arab countries—Algeria, Iraq, Libya, Oman, the Sudan, Tunisia, and the two Yemens—the national news agency is the only organization in the country which is permitted to subscribe to foreign wire services. All incoming foreign news must go through the national news agency, which selects and sometimes edits the items which are passed on to the press, radio and television. This arrangement gives the national agency editors, and the government for whom they work, considerable potential for controlling foreign news. They are, in effect, powerful gatekeepers who can screen out some stories and enhance the importance of others to suit their political purposes. The media editors, who are themselves gatekeepers, have less freedom of choice under this system than they would if they had direct access to foreign wire service copy. A Tunisian TAP official explained his editorial mission this way: "We guard against lies about Tunisia and take care to avoid disturbing public opinion" (tashwish fi ra'i al 'amm). His counterpart in the Sudan gave an example: "SUNA is a government agency so incoming stories that contain negative adjectives about Sudanese leaders are deleted."[23]

In a second group of nine Arab countries—Bahrain, Egypt, Jordan, Morocco, Kuwait, Qatar, Saudi Arabia, Syria, and the UAE—the national news agency does not have a monopoly on the acquisition of foreign news, because the media are permitted to subscribe directly to AP, or TASS or any of the others. But in these countries the national news agency is the only domestic news agency permitted, and since it is an organ of the government it has considerable influence over useage of foreign news in practice. This is a more subtle kind of gatekeeper function which is performed by example and by indirect guidance rather than by direct filtering of foreign information. The newspaper editor may have his own AP teletype machine for example, and be able to read a particular story as written abroad, but if the story has any political implications he will probably look at the national news agency ticker for clues as to what the government thinks of the story.

Thus the news selection, editing, and backgrounders by the national news agency in practice serve as a guidance channel for the media on a daily and even hourly basis. Media editors examine the official statements it carries, and look at its government sponsored versions of current news stories in order to obtain guidance as to how the regime would like them to be treated.

Finally, there is a third system at work in Lebanon, a country whose media in many ways follow unique rules. The Lebanese News Agency (LNA) is a government organization like its counterparts in the rest of the Arab world, but it does not have a monopoly and its influence on incoming foreign news is quite weak. Well before the LNA was established in 1966, several small and competing commercial news agencies emerged in Lebanon, and they—typically—reflected a spectrum of different political orientations. These orientations are not entirely stable, and the agencies also come and go, but the competition remains.[24] The Lebanese media editor, therefore, can often learn from LNA how the Lebanese government views a particular story or event, but he has access to many other interpretations not only from foreign but also from domestic sources, so he is more free to choose a version that suits him.

Collecting Foreign News

The Arab news agencies have been far less effective—and less interested—in making a major effort to collect foreign news for domestic media. With one exception, the eighteen Arab states have not, either individually or collectively, developed a truly international wire service with complete facilities for collection and dissemination of news quickly and on a multilateral, international scale.

The one exception is Egypt's Middle East News Agency (MENA). During the 1960s and 1970s, MENA developed an international capability and a staff of nearly 300 journalists, becoming the dominant agency of its kind. MENA is the only Arab news agency which has news ticker subscribers in every Arab country, and it maintains offices in nearly all of them. The MENA Arabic newscast runs 18 hours a day for Arab customers, and the English and French cast also runs 18 hours for European and African customers. MENA has its own correspondents throughout the Arab world, and also in Paris, London, Belgrade and Washington. It has contacts with seven foreign news agencies—those of Qatar, Oman, East Germany, Saudi Arabia, Iran, the Philippines, England, and France—to transmit their copy over its vast network of teleprinters. It also has agreements to exchange television materials with ten Arab and three Western organizations, and to exchange photos with twenty-one agencies.[25]

MENA is the only Arab organization which has this kind of an international network. A few of the other Arab news agencies have correspondents outside their home countries but they are rarely quoted as a source except on events in their home countries. There have been efforts at least since 1951 to establish multinational news agencies in the Arab world in order to deal with the bias which Arab journalists perceive in international news agency content.[26] But these efforts have not affected the flow of media materials in any major way, despite the hopes of their sponsors.

Pan-Arab discussions over the years did result in the establishment, in 1969, of the Arab States Broadcasting Union. The primary motivation for the creation of the ASBU was not news acquisition, however, but information dissemination. As the agreement put it, the main objective was "to acquaint all the peoples of the world with the reality of the Arab nation, its potentialities, hopes, aims and concerns."[27] The ASBU negotiated especially with Eurovision and Intervision, the television associations of West and East Europe, respectively in order to increase the exchange of TV materials. But these efforts have not had the intended impact on news flow. A formal survey conducted by ASBU in 1971 found that there was still very little cooperation among Arab states in acquisition of television news.[28] The exchange with Eurovision has grown somewhat since then although it is still modest and heavily in a West-to-East direction. For example, a March 1976 study of TV news flow between Eurovision and the Egyptian television system, probably the most active of the Arab stations, showed that Eurovision had sent 161 items to Cairo that month, of which fifteen had been used, while Egypt had sent only one item to Europe and it had been used. The Eurovision contribution to Cairo TV's news program amounted at that time to 5 percent, while the regular news agencies contributed 15 percent.[29]

Aside from the ASBU, North African Arab journalists have tried particularly hard to create cooperative arrangements but also limited success. When a group of Moroccan journalists established their national news agency MAP in 1959, they intended it to be a North African regional service jointly controlled by the four countries, and they reserved stock in it for Algeria, Tunisia, and Libya pending their adherence to the agreement. But the other three countries never joined because of political differences. On 1970, Morocco, Tunisia and Algeria did establish a television exchange system called "Maghrebvision" with the intention of joint production and coordinated telecasting. But in practice, cooperation has been limited to strictly non-political materials, and even those have been criticized by audiences. Exchanges of materials for television also take place on a bilateral basis between other Arab countries but the volume is not great. Lebanon and Egypt have been leading suppliers. Egypt, for example, in the mid-seventies was sending about twenty items monthly to Syria, Jordan, and the Sudan, but receiving half of that from them.[30]

It should also be noted that the Arab states have given some attention to satellite communication for news exchange. By 1977 fourteen of the eighteen Arab states had satellite ground stations, and in February 1974 the Arab Information Ministers meeting in Cairo passed a resolution approving an Arab satellite project. Their plan is to launch an Arab communications satellite which can handle two television channels in the first five-year phase, 1978–83, and eight in the second phase 1983–88. Start-up costs are estimated at over $150 million. The headquarters of the project will be in Saudi Arabia.[31]

Many Arab states have also supported, at least in principle, the creation of a Non-Aligned News Agencies Pool. The Fifth Non-Aligned Summit Conference held in Colombo in August 1976 decided that such a pool would be established. Arab governments endorsed the idea for some of the same reasons that had led them to create their own national news agencies. As the Egyptian Minister of Information said to the Co-ordination Committee of the Pool during its inaugural session in Cairo in January, 1977: "For a long time international news agencies [have been] serving the political and economic aims of the great powers and ignoring news related to developing countries, a matter that constitutes a great danger for freedom of expression and freedom of the press."[32]

The non-aligned pool operates by members submitting news items to Yugoslavia's agency Tanjug which in turn retransmits them to customers around the world. A 1977 study of pool materials showed that of the twenty-six actual participants, ten were Arab national news agencies and an eleventh was the Palestinian WAFA; Egypt's MENA was second only to Tanjug in the volume of its contributions. In fact, because of this high Arab participation in the pool, the Arab-Israeli conflict and other matters of vital interest to the Arabs take up a disproportionately large share of the actual pool output.[33]

These various Arab attempts to increase the flow of news have however had very little impact on the acquisition of news related to the United States, for example. Indeed it is remarkable how little effort has been made by the Arab media, individually or jointly, to establish their own news collection systems in America. Scores of news agencies, newspapers, and radio and television stations all over the world have their own correspondents in Washington, New York and elsewhere in the United States, reporting on American developments of interest back home. Prior to 1975, the only full-time Arab-sponsored news collection activity in the entire United States was one small office in the United Nations which sent reports to one Arab newspaper and four TV stations, and this bureau did not attempt to cover all the major American events of interest to Arabs, but focussed on UN activities with special emphasis on the statements of Arab diplomats before various UN bodies.[34] Finally in 1975 the Middle East News Agency sent a correspondent to Washington, and he was the first Arab journalist to cover U.S. national news full time for Arab media. Some Arab editors and media officials believe much more should be done, and although the situation has improved, the contrast between the number of Arab and other correspondents covering Washington is striking.[35] But the Arab media do not seem inclined to do much more to collect American news, or to build a news agency of the types found elsewhere.

There are several reasons for this. First of all, conditions in the West that led to the creation of international news agencies, have not existed in the Arab world. In the West, the international agencies were established "in countries where the press was particularly developed . . . because the readers of the numerous newspapers there wanted news from all parts of the world."[36] They emerged at the time when the newspaper in Europe and America was beginning to change from an elite-oriented party organ to a mass-circulation commercial enterprise, which needed increasingly better news sources to attract readers. The high cost of foreign news collection forced these Western newspapers to join together to form news agencies, and these agencies in turn to create a world-wide cartel, in order to make international news networks possible. These conditions have not existed in the Arab world, where the press, for the most part, has not developed into the mass-circulation, commercially oriented type.

Secondly, the Arabs have not imitated the Russian example of a government-controlled world news agency, either. TASS was created after the Russian revolution by a regime which laid great stress on propaganda and the control of news and information, both news going abroad about Russia, and news coming in the Russian people. The Arab media have not developed under such a centralized, totalitarian system, although the primary motivation behind Arab news agencies has been information dissemination. No one of the Arab regimes sees itself as leader of world revolution as does the Soviet government, and none gives such high priority to control and exploitation of information media that it has created a worldwide correspondent network.

Thirdly the lack of financial resources available for the creation of an international Arab news agency has also been a factor. The cost of overcoming the technical and other barriers to the fast provision of news useful to the world's media is enormous. A few wealthy Arab states such as Kuwait or Abu Dhabi could probably afford to establish such a news agency, but their conservative regimes have not shown much interest in such projects. They are content with dependence on the international news agencies' material as filtered through their own editors.

Why have the Arab states not joined together to form an Arab news agency with a truly international network? The answer to this lies in conditions that have hampered the other efforts at political union among Arab states. Despite cultural and linguistic commonality, policy differences including those dividing socialist from other Arab states, have prevented them from coming together to establish a news agency which, to Arabs, would have so much political importance. Under present economic and political conditions, a pan-Arab news agency would probably have to be government controlled, and it would have to abide by strict policy guidelines. But it is difficult to agree on those guidelines and the administration of a news agency satisfactory to all Arab regimes. In times of tension between two Arab countries, for example, information cooperation stops entirely and even news agency offices are closed for political reasons.[37] Governments have thus been too sensitive about the political importance of daily news coverage to turn control of it over to a supra-national body.

Finally, the prior existence of several functioning world news agencies with excellent links to the Arab world has undoubtedly helped prevent the creation of one more world agency by the Arabs themselves.

OTHER SOURCES OF NEWS AND INFORMATION

There are three other important sources of news and information in addition to the various news agency channels discussed above. These other sources are used regularly by Arab media editors. But unlike the news agencies, they are also accessible to the general public in the Arab world—at least they are to some extent, depending on local restrictions and other factors. The three sources are: foreign radio and television broadcasts; foreign publications; and information distributed by foreign embassies.

Foreign Radio and Television Broadcasts

A number of radio stations, both Arab and non-Arab, have been important sources of news to Arab audiences. Arab media editors regularly use foreign radio broadcasts as sources of news, and the general public can listen to such broadcasts from other countries. Of the non-Arab broadcasters which have programs in Arabic and can thus be understood by significant numbers of Arabs, the British Broadcasting Corporation and the Voice of America are the most widely listened-to (see Table 12). Both stations have diverse programming in Arabic including news, features, commentary and entertainment, and they have reasonably strong signal strength so they can be heard throughout the Arab world.[38] In recent years, Radio Monte Carlo, a commercial station that broadcasts mostly contemporary popular music interspersed with short news bulletins, has developed a broad listenership in the Arab world. The other non-Arab stations which broadcast in Arabic—including

France's ORTF, Radio Moscow, Radio Peking, Bulgaria, Albania, Czechoslovakia, and East Germany—have never achieved popularity, apparently because they were not competitive on medium wave with an interesting program.[39]

Some Arab radio stations have developed regular audiences throughout the region or in part of it. Cairo's General Service and international Voice of the Arabs clearly have taken the lead in this competition. Egypt broadcasts more hours abroad than any country except Russia and China. Its transmitters have strong signals which reach many countries in the daylight hours and virtually all Arabs after sundown (when signal propagation conditions improve), and its sophisticated programming and the importance of Egypt make it popular. Listeners throughout the area have since the 1950s tuned in to Cairo to hear the best Arab music, the latest political move by the Egyptian government, and commentaries by well-known journalists. Cairo broadcasts, on several different types of program, also deal with news and commentaries affecting the United States, using international news agency material tailored to fit Egyptian government interests, and official statements from Cairo as well as government-approved commentaries. Egyptian broadcasters (see Table 12) concentrate on Arabic broadcasts to the Arab countries, leaving their other languages for non-Arab audiences. Eleven programs emanate daily from Egypt which can be heard in Arabic by Egyptian and other Arab audiences.

This is far more air time than that of the Arabic services of the ma-

TABLE 12
Egyptian Radio Broadcasts

Program	Hours per week
General Service	140
Voice of the Arabs	130
Holy Koran	112
Middle East Service	100
Alexandria Service	98
People's Program	60
Musical Program	70
The Sudan Program	45
Palestine Program	42
Second Program	25
Youth Program	14

Sources: Figures, for 1979, from Egyptian Radio officials. In 1975 Egypt broadcast 896 hrs./week, while the USSR broadcast 1983, Peking 1402, VOA 775, BBC 728. Voice of America, *Statistics Book 1976.*

jor international broadcasters and the signal from Cairo is generally competitive on medium and short wave with that of BBC, VOA and Radio Moscow as well as RTF. For all of these reasons, Cairo is widely listened to. Although complete data on listener habits is not available, Table 13 gives some indication of the strong position Cairo holds, as well as the popularity of BBC among foreign broadcasters. Other Arab radio stations are also listened to outside of their home countries, particularly in neighboring ones. And Israeli Radio's Arabic Service is presumed to be widely listened to in the Arab world, particularly by those who tune in to more than one station and want to follow developments in the Arab-Israeli conflict. No reliable Arab listener figures exist, but observers note that listenership to Israeli Radio rises in periods of tension, when presumably audience size must run into the millions.

A major reason Arabs listen to foreign radio is to hear news, but also Arab television is a major source of news for Arab audiences. In Lebanon, where literacy is high, it ranks third behind newspapers and radio as a preferred source of news, but it still is used by 65 percent of

TABLE 13
Radio Listening Habits Among Arabs
Selected Survey Data

	Kuwait (1974)	Saudi Arabia (1975)	Lebanon (1974)	Morocco (1974)	Egypt (1975)
NON-ARAB BROADCASTERS					
BBC	23%	32%	40%	3%	6%
VOA	9	19	10	0.1	9
Moscow	2	1	1	0.1	0
ORTF (Paris)	0.3	1	1	3	0
EGYPTIAN STATIONS					
Voice of the Arabs	18%	22%	16%	2%	61%
Radio Cairo	18	17	20		85
OTHER ARAB BROADCASTERS					
Radio Damascus	4%	5%	45%	0	
Radio Baghdad	22	4	1	0	
Hashemite Broadcasting (Jordan)	3	5	3	0	11%
Radio Bahrain	3	16		0	
Radio Lebanon	2	5	74	0	

Sources: All data taken from USIA Office of Research, VOA audience estimate reports, done separately on the countries mentioned but in all cases of urban adults (usually over age 18) in selected major cities. Reports: Kuwait no. E-7-75, June 16, 1975; Saudi Arabia (adults in Jidda and Dammam) no. E-5-76, April 23, 1976; Lebanon no. E-9-75; September 30, 1975; Morocco (six cities) no. E-14-75, December 15, 1975; Egypt (five cities) no. E-14-75, December 15, 1975. Geographic proximity and transmitter power are also major influences on these figures. Percentages indicate listenership once a week or more.

the educated elite and more of the other groups.[40] In Jordan, TV is preferred over radio and newspapers as a news source.[41] The vast majority
of Arabs who watch TV news prefer to watch their own home station,
and most of them cannot even receive TV programs from other countries. But there are some border areas, and clusters of countries, where
TV news from abroad is important. The Persian Gulf is an area of high
television concentration, especially during humid evenings when atmo-
spheric conditions allow TV signal propagation along the coast and
Arab audiences can see several channels.[42] Viewers in Lebanon, Jordan,
Syria, and Iraq, as well as some in Egypt, can see each others' programs
at times in border areas, and North African TV viewers can often watch
television programs from neighboring countries including Southern Europe. Israeli Television, which did not begin until 1967, has developed
a regular Arab audience in Amman, where reception is consistently
good, and in some areas of Syria and Southern Lebanon. Israeli TV's
Arabic language news and feature programs are editorially aimed at
Arab audiences, and they have achieved some success in reaching those
within range. Israeli TV almost daily carries news items about America. Thus television, too, plays a role in the dissemination of news across
borders, including news about the United States.

Foreign Publications

Most Arab governments restrict the importation of foreign print
media in some way, by prohibition of entire publications, or of single issues, or by selective censorship of parts of issues. For this reason, and
because of the low literacy rates and low levels of foreign-language
competence in the Arab countries, this channel is a minor one for the
dissemination of foreign including American news. Nevertheless foreign print media do play a role here, especially for the educated elite in
the Arab countries.

The foreign publications which carry the most news related to the
United States and are imported into the Arab countries are the international editions of *Time* and *Newsweek*, and the *Paris Herald Tribune*,
but only a few thousand copies of each go into the area, mostly to the
eastern Arab states. British publications are also read by educated elites
in the latter countries, while *le Monde* and some other French publications are very popular among North African Arab elites. All of these
carry a good deal of non-Arab news including information relating to
the United States.

Some Arab publications are distributed and read outside of their countries of origin. The number of Arab daily newspapers that cross borders is small, because of technical and political distribution problems, and the perishable nature of dailies. The only dailies that are seen consistently throughout the Arab world are Cairo's *al Ahram* and *al Akhbar*, and leading Lebanese papers such as *al Nahar* and *l'Orient-le Jour* which tend to be less politically biased. Kuwait's *Ra'y al 'Amm* and *al Siyasah* began in the 1970s to have some success in the Near East, while North African dailies have circulated within that sub-region.

Several Arab weekly magazines, and one monthly, have developed audiences in the Arab world outside their countries of publication. Publishers in Cairo and Beirut have done particularly well in creating magazines that sell well throughout the area. But the most popular magazine of all is the monthly *al 'Arabi*, published by the Kuwaiti Ministry of Information, as Table 14 shows.

The foreign news content of these magazines is primarily related to the Arab world, but a portion of that usually relates in some way to Western countries including the United States because of Western involvement in the Middle East and North Africa. Such highly political magazines as *Rose al Yusif* frequently contain commentaries relating to the United States. However, the monthly *al 'Arabi*, for example, specializes in nonpolitical features. Occasionally, these relate to the United States, such as an article on the American space program, but most of the content does not concern America.[43]

The levels and characteristics of foreign print media imports into Arab countries fluctuates so much because of political and other factors

TABLE 14
Well-Known Arab Magazines
(1978)

Name	Est. circ. (1000s)			Location
	foreign	domestic	total	
Al 'Arabi	140	15	155	Kuwait
Al Hawadith	50	15	65	Beirut
Jeune Afrique	50	15	65	Tunis
Sabah al Khayr	30	55	85	Cairo
Al Sayyad	11	4	15	Beirut
Al Musawwar	25	60	85	Cairo
Hawa'	15	45	60	"
Akhir Sa'a	25	85	110	"
Rose al Yusif	20	90	110	"

that it is impossible to generalize for the whole area about this information source. But to give some idea of the relative importance of this source in some countries, the following is the approximate volume of foreign daily newspaper imports into Saudi Arabia in 1973, at a time when Saudi dailies were distributing between eight and ten thousand copies each:[44] Egyptian: 1500 *al Ahram* (the paper had been banned until 1970), 1000 *al Akhbar,* and 700 *al Gumhuriyah;* Lebanese: 3000 *al Hayat* (*al Nahar* was not permitted in at the time); Kuwaiti: 3000 *al Ra'y al 'Amm,* and 300 *al Siyasah* (delivery usually delayed by censors).

At the same time, the American publications *Time* and *Newsweek* were coming in to Saudi Arabia at about 1,100 copies weekly, and the *Herald Tribune* was selling about 600. In contrast, more than 17,000 copies of Kuwait's monthly *al 'Arabi* were sold in just a few hours after arrival in the kingdom. In countries like this, where the local press is not particularly strong on international news, literate Arabs depend to an important degree on foreign publications, particularly Egyptian and Lebanese, to broaden their picture of the world.[45]

Circulation of Arab publications, however, tends to follow patterns of foreign policy and ideological orientation. Thus Saudi Arabia, for example, banned all Egyptian publications from the start of the Yemeni war in 1962 until the Saudi-Egyptian reconciliation ten years later. Censorship of non-Arab print media tends to be not as strict as with Arab publications, since the audience is limited to the educated elite, and precisely those readers who would complain most about censorship are the ones able to read foreign publications. For example, even Algeria has always, since the achievement of independence in 1962, allowed large numbers of French publications in, although domestic media are quite strictly controlled. Foreign print media do, therefore, contribute to the dissemination of news and opinion, including that about the United States.

Information Distributed by Foreign Embassies

A third source of news which is used by Arab media and which also reaches Arab audiences in many cases directly, is information provided by foreign embassies in the Arab world. The United States and many other countries assign information officers to their embassies in an attempt to provide additional information about their countries to Arab audiences. This effort provides information to Arab editors for their use and to important Arab elite groups in each country. The Arab editors, however, usually publish these materials without attribution and tend to avoid any that might look too obviously like propaganda to Arab audiences. In some Arab countries, the government even restricts or filters embassy direct-mail distribution of information materials. It is a source which the government can fairly easily curtail if it wishes.

COMPARING THE NEWS SOURCES

There are five major sources of regular foreign news, including news about the United States, which are available to Arab editors: the international wire services, the Arab news agencies, foreign radio and television broadcasts, foreign publications, and information supplied by embassies such as the American. There are, of course, other sources of foreign information, such as films, resident foreigners, travel abroad, etc., but these do not provide the day-to-day news which is our concern in this chapter.

How do these sources compare as to usefulness and reliability? From the perspective of the Arab media editor, the world news agencies are the most complete, timely and efficient sources for non-Arab news, and the Arab agencies are useful for Arab news, but radio broadcasts are used to cross-check on both of them. Commercial print media and embassy releases provide helpful background material especially for editorials and features, although they are usually too late for inclusion in fast news coverage. Television is a supplemental source only in those areas where it is seen regularly.

Each of these sources of foreign news must be regarded, however, as part of a complex channel through which news and information flows from the originator to the audience. Gatekeepers who help regulate the flow of news and shape its form and content along the way include Arab editors and government officials as well as, in some cases, foreigners.[46] The series of filters or gatekeepers through which the news passes before it reaches the Arab audience varies, depending on the particular channel and the origin of the news item. Take, for example, news about America, for which the channels of the five major sources of foreign news could be summarized, with their gatekeepers, as follows:

1. *World news agencies*
   - Correspondents in the U.S. of international news agencies such as AP, TASS, AFP

- News agency bureau editors in the U.S.
- News agency home office editors in New York, Moscow, Paris
- Foreign bureau editors, or (in eight Arab countries) Arab government editors in national news agencies
- Arab media editors

2. *Radio broadcasts*
   - Correspondents in the U.S. of international radio broadcasting stations, such as VOA, BBC, Radio Moscow, RTF, Israeli Radio
   - Bureau editors of these stations
   - Home office editors, in Washington, Moscow, London, Paris

3. *Arab news agencies*
   - MENA correspondent in Washington
   - MENA editor in Cairo
   - Arab media editors

4. *U.S. embassy information program*
   - USICA reporters & information officials
   - Policy guidance officials, in Washington
   - Information officers in embassies in Arab countries
   - Arab media editors, (or direct dissemination to Arab audiences)

5. *Foreign print media*
   - Correspondents in the U.S. of American, British, and French publications, such as *Herald Tribune, le Monde*
   - Bureau editors of these publications
   - Home office editors in New York, Paris, London
   - Arab government censorship offices

In passing through these channels, the news may be shaped or distorted by many factors. One observer has said that the main barriers to the transmission of accurate information and ideas are incompetence, intentional or unintentional bias, commercialism (giving the consumer what he wants), censorship and other regulatory measures, and technical and economic factors.[47] Language barriers could be added. All of these are present in the networks that carry foreign news to Arab audiences.

We have seen that the economic factor and commercialism have influenced the development of networks in the Arab world. High costs helped create the world news agency cartels, which dominated the dissemination of news from America even after the monopoly was broken, and helped prevent the formation of an Arab world news agency or Arab news bureaus in America. Commercialism has apparently had an effect on the content of wire service copy, as has the choice of language for news distribution.

We have also seen that censorship and other regulatory practices have distorted the free flow of news to the Arab world. This applies not only to domestic Arab media, which are under varying degrees and types of government control, but also to incoming news agency materials, which are filtered by governments in eight countries. There is little attempt to prevent Arab audiences from listening to foreign radio broadcasts, and these are a major source of foreign news, but the dissemination of print media is restricted. Incompetence is also undoubtedly a factor, although this is very difficult to measure except for illiteracy and lack of foreign language competence on the part of the audience, both of which are important barriers to dissemination of American news to Arabs.

The most important barriers to news dissemination in the Arab world probably fall under the rubric of bias, both unintentional and deliberate. Bias is very difficult to measure or describe accurately, and often it cannot be determined whether the bias was deliberate. But it is clear that the Arabs have perceived bias in the reporting of the world news agencies and that this perception was a major reason behind the establishment of the Arab national news agencies, of the ASBU and of the Arab satellite project.

8

Conclusions

THIS BOOK has examined the news media in the Arab world, as these media relate to the societies in which they function, and especially to the political process. In the above chapters we have described in some detail: the structure of the daily newspaper as an institution, the structure of radio and television, and Arab newsgathering mechanisms. Now it is time to develop a typology of typical Arab press forms, and ask what conditions have led to the emergence of each sub-type, and what conditions are likely to cause perpetuation of the status quo or, alternatively, lead to transformations in the system.

Our underlying assumption has been that newspapers, radio and television respond in many ways to their environment, both in content and in functioning of institutional structure. This assumption has certainly been borne out in our analysis of the Arab media. The Arab news media can only be understood in terms of the economic conditions, cultural milieu, and political realities of the societies they serve.

As for content, the readers of an Arab newspaper or listeners to an Arab radio broadcast would agree that the medium usually carries unmistakeable local identification of some kind, reflecting local conditions. The items that presumably have the most political impact, such as commentaries on current events, seem to reflect local conditions most clearly, but often headlines and even fictional pieces do too. To be sure, the news media carry out their functions to a large extent the way news media do anywhere in the world. They convey local and international news, information, opinion, entertainment and advertising to a mass audience. Much of this material originates from the same common sources, and is processed by the same news agencies and other international services, as the material used outside of the Arab world. Arab media report on important events at the same time as American media, and to some extent in similar fashion. Advertising and entertainment material also has some international interchangeability. But Arab news media content usually carries the stamp of the originating institution in one way or another, which alert audiences can detect. The message provides them with clues about the origin and control of the medium.

This book, however, is not about content of the media. The above observations are made on the basis of opinions of experienced consumers of these media and not on the basis of an objective content analysis of press, radio and television in all eighteen countries. Such a study has not yet been done, and would be an enormous undertaking. This book, instead, has analyzed the news media as institutions, to see what forms they have taken in the independent Arab states, how the self-governing Arab societies have chosen to control them, and how they relate to the political processes in the Arab world.

Arab media have characteristics which can be found elsewhere in non-Arab developing countries. The electronic media, especially radio, have become true instruments of mass communication, reaching the bulk of the population across barriers of literacy, geography and economy, while print media still generally reach only elite groups. The commercial side of the media is still relatively weak, and neither the wide-circulation newspaper dependent on advertising revenues nor fully commercialized television and radio, U.S.–style, have appeared. But the political side is relatively strong, and the role of government quite prominent.

GOVERNMENT-MEDIA RELATIONS

We have seen that Arab government-media relations are quite complex. The Arab media do play a role in the political process and are affected by it, but it is clear that the role cannot be described accurately by using one of the theories that have been used to describe other media systems. The one which comes closest to fitting is the authoritarian theory, by which the media are controlled by the elite who believe they understand truth better than the masses do, and who assume they should use the press, radio, and television to convey information and interpretation downward. That theory has many adherents in the Arab world, where one sees in many places its most common practical consequence, the strong influence of government on the media. But there are also manifestations of the libertarian and social responsibility theories, by which the media are supposed to present a variety of viewpoints, a clash of opinions, and some criticism of government. The extent to which this occurs, however, varies from country to country and over time.

In any case, the actual performance of the media on the Arab political stage cannot be judged on the basis of the prevailing law or formal structure alone. More important are such factors as the existence of real and open opposition to the government, the legitimacy and actual strength of the ruling group, the stability of the political system, the existence of perceived external threats, the economic base of the media, and the vigor of an independent journalistic tradition in the country. As these vary, so does the behavior of journalists, regardless of the media laws which invariably, in one way or another, proclaim freedom of the press, speech and information.

Crucial to understanding the dynamics of Arab media structures is a comparison of the three distinct sub-types of organization for the daily press which have emerged in the Arab world in the third quarter of the twentieth century. Radio and television organization is much more uniform throughout the area primarily because their broad reach and their potential for instant mass political impact have persuaded Arab regimes to insist that they be under direct governmental control, particularly since for technical and economic reasons there are usually only one or two broadcasting stations serving the entire country. Newspapers, which theoretically could be published by many different people but which reach smaller audiences, have been organized in one of three basic systems in the independent Arab countries. A given system emerges at different times and places, depending on certain conditions.

PRESS SUBTYPES AND POLITICAL OPPOSITION

First, a system we have called the mobilization press has emerged in countries where the ruling group is aggressively dedicated to revolutionary change, and it has managed to eliminate all real organized public opposition domestically, but requires active support from the media to help achieve its stated goals and combat its declared enemies. All the newspapers of any political consequence are owned by agents of the ruling group, and control over newspaper content is assured primarily through personnel control, but also on occasions by censorship, legal sanctions, rewards, and indirect means made possible by the existence of a political environment in which the regime is unopposed.

Secondly, the loyalist press exists in countries where a more traditional political system prevails; all are monarchies except for Tunisia, which is a republic but dominated overwhelmingly since independence by one man. No real organized public opposition exists, but the government, more satisfied with the status quo than intent on change, is content with passive acquiescence from the public and does not require the press to generate public action. The press is loyal to the regime and its fundamental policies but newspapers often avoid the most controversial issues rather than engaging them with the zeal of a mobilization type newspaper. The loyalist press is privately owned. The government uses several means to obtain its support, including financial inducements and legal sanctions but the primary reason for press loyalty is the consensus that prevails in public debate on important issues: the regime's basic policies are not criticized in public, so the press does not dissent either.

The third system, the diverse press, functions in a political environment where the public expression of a variety of opinions and viewpoints, including criticism of the government, is possible, and where the regime does not intervene to suppress all open dissent. The press is in private hands and there are more daily papers than in other countries. The government may occasionally take action against a newspaper but these interventions are used sparingly and done through the courts, since the government prefers to exercise restraint in dealing with the press.

Table 15 puts these three systems together into an overall typology and shows the countries in which they are found as of the 1970s. Within these groupings there are some differences. In Lebanon, there is more diversity among newspapers, and more criticism of the government, than exists in Kuwait or Morocco, although the latter two clearly belong in the grouping with Lebanon rather than with either of the other groups. Among mobilization systems, Iraq and the People's Democratic Republic of Yemen have the most mobilized press, while Egypt has the least, although they all can be put in this category.

Diversity among newspapers is a key criterion in determining the nature of the relationship between the government and the press. In all of the Arab countries, at least some of the press reports and supports government policy. But the newspaper reader is better informed about

TABLE 15
Typology of Arab Press Systems

	Mobilization	Loyalist	Diverse
PRESS CHARACTERISTICS			
Ownership	agents of regime	private	private
Variety among papers	non-diverse	non-diverse	diverse
Attitude toward regime	support	support	pro and con
Style and tone	active, contentious	passive	varied
POLITICAL CONDITIONS			
Ruling group	revolutionary	traditionalist	various
Public debate	none	none	active
Public opposition	non-existent	non-existent	institutionalized
COUNTRIES WHERE SYSTEM PREVAILS			
(1970s)	Algeria	Bahrain	Lebanon
	Egypt	Jordan	Morocco
	Iraq	Qatar	Kuwait
	Libya	Saudi Arabia	
	The Sudan	Tunisia	
	Syria	UAE	
	Yemen (PDRY)		

any given subject, and has more of a chance to discern the true facts and make up his own mind without relying on what the government tells him, if there is genuine diversity in the newspapers available to him. Different newspapers will print different versions and interpretations of the story, and taken together, they provide more to choose from. Thus considered as a whole, a diverse press system is likely to be freer than the others even though individual papers may be biased, because the reader has greater access to a spectrum of information and opinion.

The essential factor behind a diverse press is the existence of genuine opposition to the ruling group which is able to function openly. If no real public opposition to the regime is permitted in the political system, then it follows that the press speaks with one uniform voice and the individual newspaper reader is less able to make up his own mind about important issues of the day. The existence of public opposition is, in turn, usually related to the existence of representative political parties. The parties must be representative of truly different policies including some not espoused by the regime. For example, Lebanon and Iraq both have political systems in which several political parties function, but the Lebanese parties represent truly contrasting policies and points of view, while the Iraqi parties do not disagree in public on any issues of major consequence; Lebanese press diversity and Iraqi press uniformity are to a great extent dependent on this important distinction.

It is, on the other hand, also possible to have a diverse press backed by genuine opposition groups rather than parties, as is the case in Kuwait for example, where formal parties do not exist. But again, the essential requirement is that the opposition must differ substantially and publicly with the policies of the regime. The differences do not have to include every issue of consequence but they must be sufficiently comprehensive so as to provide a distinction between the regime and the out-group on matters of national importance. The more comprehensive the list of differences, the more diverse the press is likely to be.

A second important factor in government-press relations is whether the press has developed the status of an independent institution (the so-called Fourth Estate) and the profession of journalism has become a prestigious one. The press has acquired some institutional prestige in Lebanon and in Egypt, for example, during more than a century of development in these countries. In Lebanon, this combines with factors in the political environment which help keep the press diverse and relatively independent. In Egypt, it helps the press withstand some of the pressures of the political system and cause newspapers there to show more vitality and character than the mobilization type of press elsewhere.

The Arab press systems cannot be divided into neat categories. The three-fold division, for purposes of analysis, into mobilization, loyalist and diverse systems is a rough one. In fact, a kind of spectrum exists from the highly mobilized newspapers in Algeria to the rather diverse and independent press in Lebanon, with the others in between. The Algerian system is not as mobilized as are totalitarian ones in the Soviet Union, and the Lebanese press is not as independent as, say, British newspapers. All of the Arab countries have some elements of an authoritarian press system, in which the ruling elite in the country, has considerable influence over newspaper content and the independence of journalists is periodically abridged.

DYNAMICS OF CHANGE

The three basic types of press system which we have identified are not static and permanent, but depend very much on existing conditions.

The diverse type of press exists in only three Arab states in the 1970s, but it appeared at earlier times in the seven countries which now have mobilization systems. The press in those countries also went through a nonpartisan stage, somewhat similar to the loyalist type of press that exists in six Arab countries in the mid-seventies. Thus it is possible for a country to move from any one of the three types to any other, provided conditions are right. One can to a certain extent predict the type of media system by looking at the conditions and key indicators. If there are changes in the status of political parties and opposition groups, in the attitude of the government toward the press, and in the ownership of the newspapers, their role in the political process could be converted into another type.

The type of press system is not merely the accidental byproduct of political realities, however, but is itself an object of political calculations. Rulers know well that if they encourage a freer debate and competition on the political scene, they are encouraging the growth of newspapers some of which will criticize them. So although most Arab governments pay lip-service to a free press, in practice they make attempts to control it. If the regime is determined to make the press a political tool and conditions are just right, it will be able to create a mobilization system out of a loyalist or even a diverse one.

Professional journalists, on the other hand, tend to pull in the other direction and seek more independence from government controls. Backed by powerful enough political factions, they can succeed in gaining at least a measure of freedom. But in the Arab world in the 1970s, with enormous problems of economic development and of foreign policy (Arab-Israeli conflict) to deal with, it is more difficult for independent-minded journalists to resist the pressure for submergence of press freedom under the regime's demands for national unity needed to face the common problem. In these circumstances it seems easy for people to accept the authoritarian rationale.

RADIO AND TELEVISION: DOMESTIC UNIFORMITY, INTERNATIONAL COMPETITION

This rationale has been most forcefully put forward, and most universally accepted, in the case of radio and television. A government monopoly controls radio in each country in the Arab world and it controls television in every one but Lebanon. Governments insist on controlling the electronic media because of their obvious political importance in communicating with most of the population across the literacy barriers that prevail in the area. The seven mobilization states control the electronic media more strictly and they have pushed radio and television development faster in order to use them more, but radio and TV structural forms are more similar in the Arab world than are the forms of press organization.

Paradoxically it is radio, the medium most tightly controlled by Arab governments, which gives the Arab public its greatest choice and variety of information and opinion. This is so because Arab radio listeners with simple transistor receivers can hear not only their own national broadcasting stations but those of other countries as well. The close proximity of many countries in the area to each other, and the fact that radio broadcasts do not stop at borders, make it possible for the average Arab to tune in to broadcasts by Arab stations, Israel, etc., presenting other points of view than his government's.

FOREIGN NEWS: TEST OF A SYSTEM

Arab audiences receive foreign news, information and opinion through several channels. While most of them have some access to foreign news via international radio broadcasts, it also comes to them primarily through their own national media. The international wire services, foreign newspapers, magazines and other sources pour foreign news in great quantities into the Arab world every day. But much of it never reaches the Arab public at all, or only after being revised and reshaped by one of the governmental or media gatekeepers. The means by which it is screened and the criteria applied by the gatekeepers are indicators of the nature of the domestic media system and its response to the political environment.

In Iraq, for example, where only the government is allowed to subscribe to a foreign news agency, and incoming print media are censored, a government official screens all incoming foreign news before passing it on to the Iraqi editors, who screen it again before giving it to the public. In Jordan, on the other hand, the media editors can subscribe to foreign wire services directly so the screening process is less severe, although the editors are themselves subject to cultural, economic, political, and other pressures of their environment. And in Lebanon, the public has an even better chance of obtaining foreign news because the channels are more open. The media editors not only have direct access to foreign news sources but because of the media system they have more freedom, and the government's censorship of imported print media is much lighter.

The information available to Arab audiences on a daily basis, therefore, varies considerably from country to country, depending on the nature of the local media system. This system depends, in turn, on various conditions prevailing in the country, as we have seen. Foreign news is treated in various ways, by editors and other journalists who are interested in doing a professional job but who are also consciously and unconsciously influenced by their environments.

The mass media in the Arab world, whether dealing with foreign or domestic issues, participate significantly in the political process, and political and other factors shape the press, radio and television as institutions. Neither the media nor their environments can be understood properly without reference to the other.

NOTES

PREFACE

1. Tom J. McFadden, *Daily Journalism in the Arab States* (Columbus, Ohio: Ohio State University Press, 1953). This book covers only Lebanon, Syria, Jordan, Iraq, and Egypt.

2. Adib Mruwa, *al Sahafah al 'Arabiyah* (Beirut: Dar al Hayat, 1961).

3. Scholars are not in complete agreement on the definition of "who is an Arab," but for the purposes of this particular book a definition based on language, culture, and subjective judgment seems appropriate. The Arab League, which admitted the new state of Djibouti as its twenty-second member on September 4, 1977, and also includes Somalia, Mauritania, and Palestine, has a broader definition, partly for political reasons, to give the League more weight through maximum membership.

4. The Foreign Broadcast Information Service (FBIS) is a department of the CIA which monitors foreign radio broadcasts around the clock and issues translations of them for use by governmental and other analysts. Translations of Arabic broadcasts are printed in the FBIS "Daily Report, Middle East and North Africa," FBIS, Washington, D.C. A similar report is BBC Monitoring Service, "Summary of World Broadcasting," London.

INTRODUCTION

1. Mass communication media are all those means of transmitting messages or meaning publicly to "large, heterogeneous and anonymous audiences." Charles R. Wright, *Mass Communication* (New York: Random House, 1962), pp. 11–16.

2. Detailed studies have been made of this issue in the U.S.; to cite just two examples: Walter B. Emery, *Broadcasting and Government* (East Lansing: Michigan State University Press, 1961); John Tebbel, *The Media in America* (New York: Crowell, 1974).

169

3. Fred S. Siebert, Theodore Peterson, and Wilbur Schramm, *Four Theories of the Press* (Urbana: University of Illinois Press, 1963), p. 1.

4. These observers — journalists, diplomats, and others — typically make quick analyses on a daily basis rather than long-term systematic studies, and their conclusions are usually not made public. However, one published a case study of Arab attitudes based on media sources is William A. Rugh, "Arab Perceptions of American Foreign Policy During the October War" (Washington, D.C.: Middle East Institute, 1976).

5. See, for example, Siebert, Peterson, and Schramm, *Four Theories*; Wilbur Schramm, "Two Concepts of Mass Communication," in Bernard Berelson and Morris Janowitz, eds., *Reader in Public Opinion and Communication* (New York: The Free Press, 1966), pp. 206–19; or Raymond Williams, *Communications* (New York: Barnes and Noble, 1966), pp. 124–32.

CHAPTER 1—Arab Information Media

1. Every Arab country has a Muslim majority, and that majority is overwhelming in all but Lebanon and the Sudan. Every Arab country has a majority whose mother tongue is Arabic; other languages are discussed below.

2. Sami Aziz, "al Tatawwur al Sahafah fi al 'Alam al 'Arabi" (Cairo: al Ma'had al Qawmi li al Sahafiyin al 'Arab, 1969, mimeographed), pp. 2–3; see below for details. Napoleon took printing presses to Egypt at the end of the eighteenth century, and his occupying regime published the two newspapers *Le Courrier de l'Egypte* and *La Decade Egyptien*, in French, but these were not Arab papers. In 1799 Napoleon had ordered the making of Arabic type, but he never used it for newspapers.

3. Iraq TV began broadcasting in late 1956, Lebanon in 1959, Egypt and Syria in 1960, and the others after that. Egypt began radio broadcasting in the early 1920s and has continued to this day as the most active Arab broadcaster. See Chapter 6 for details.

4. UNESCO, *Mass Media in Developing Countries*, Reports and Papers on Mass Communications, No. 33 (Paris: UNESCO, 1961), p. 16.

5. Data on eighty nations compiled by Frederick Frey show that 85 percent of them surpassed the minimum standards in radio receivers but only 58 percent passed it in TV receivers. Frey, "Communications and Development," in Ithiel Pool and Wilbur Schramm, eds., *Handbook of Communication* (Chicago: Rand McNally, 1973), pp. 348–49.

6. Tom J. McFadden, *Daily Journalism in the Arab States* (Columbus: Ohio State University Press, 1953), p. 26.

7. Selaheddine Boustany, *The Press During the French Expedition in Egypt 1798–1801* (Cairo: al Arab Bookshop, n.d.), pp. 16–19.

8. The latter point is endorsed by Adib Mruwa, *al Sahafah al 'Arabiyah* (Beirut: al Hayat Press, 1961), p. 143.

9. Aziz, "al Tatawwur," p. 3.

10. McFadden, *Daily Journalism*, pp. 4 and 14; see also pp. 40 and 6. The political importance of the media in developing countries elsewhere has been studied by others.

Frey, "Communications and Development," pp. 383–4, 387, says "The mass media constitute excellent bases for political operations. Hence the mass media themselves become objects of political conflict and embroiled in partisan dispute."

11. McFadden, *Daily Journalism*, pp. 32–33, 28, 30, his analysis is still valid. He found 55 percent of the papers operated ostensibly in the red, and each accused the other of taking subsidies; this writer found exactly the same reaction in Beirut in May 1973 to questions posed to a variety of Lebanese newspaper editors.

12. The phrase and analysis are from ibid., p. 16.

13. Ibid., pp. 36–37; and Wilton Wynn, "Western Techniques Influence Party Newspapers in Egypt," *Journalism Quarterly* 25(4):391.

14. Frank Luther Mott, *American Journalism* (New York: Macmillan, 1942), p. 253; see also pp. 113–14, 168, 215–16, 411–12.

15. McFadden, *Daily Journalism*, pp. 28, 84, 94; Wynn, "Western Techniques," pp. 291–93.

16. Wynn, "Western Techniques," p. 392.

17. Wynn, "Western Techniques, . . ." p. 392, who says that in Cairo in the late 1940s "fly-by-night" and other low-overhead operations were common; today they are much less so, but even in wealthy Saudi Arabia low budget papers are the rule. See also on this subject an MA thesis by Louis Greiss, American University of Cairo, Cairo, 1955, no. 55/53.

18. Ghassan Tueni's *al Nahar* and its French-language sister paper *l'Orient-Le Jour*, both published in Beirut, achieve a remarkable level of objectivity in news reporting; and with their diverse spectrum of columnists they manage to present opinions on events from widely different perspectives. *Al Ahram*, for example, has not achieved that kind of objectivity, contrary to the trends described by Helen Kitchen in "*Al Ahram—the Times* of the Arab World," *Middle East Journal* 4(2)(April 1950):155ff.

19. The names *shilla* and *bashka*, or *dawra, halghah*, and others seem to refer to the same general phenomenon. See references to it in, for example, the following: Robert Springborg, "Patterns of Communication in the Egyptian Political Elite," in George Lenczowski, ed., *Political Elites in the Middle East* (Washington, D.C.: American Enterprise Institute, 1975), p. 96; William Rugh, "Emergence of a New Middle Class in Saudi Arabia," *Middle East Journal* 27(1)(Winter 1973):18–19; and James Bill, "Dialectics of Modernization in the Middle East," *International Journal of Middle East Studies* 3(4)(October 1972):426–27. Bill points out that non-Arab societies have similar groupings also.

20. Hamid Mowlana, "Mass Media Systems and Communication Behavior in the Middle East," in *Handbook to the Middle East* (London: Blond, 1970), pp. 58–60. For a discussion of communication in the mosque, see Bruce M. Borthwick, "The Islamic Sermon as a Channel of Political Communication," *Middle East Journal* 21(3)(Summer 1967):299–313.

21. Charles R. Wright, *Mass Communication* (New York: Random House, 1959), p. 16; Wright expanded on Harold Lasswell's categories; I have added advertising.

22. McFadden, *Daily Journalism*, pp. 25–26, reports the average size before World War II was 8–10 pp., but material shortages forced cuts. *Al Ahram* was exceptional with 32 pages, although some other Egyptian dailies such as *al Balagh* had 12 to 16.

23. Ibid., pp. 4, 14, 28, and 65; Wynn, "Western Techniques," pp. 391–92; Mowlana, "Mass Media Systems," p. 56; and Nabil H. Dajani, "The Press in Lebanon," *Gazette* 17(3):169—all stress the prominence of commentary in Arab media. Observations on the part of the author and others who follow the media also support these conclusions.

24. The Commission on Freedom of the Press, *A Free and Responsible Press* (Chicago: University of Chicago Press, 1947), pp. 23–28.

25. Wynn, "Western Techniques," pp. 391–92; see also McFadden, *Daily Journalism*, p. 65. According to *A Free and Responsible Press*, p. 22, "Of equal importance with reportorial accuracy are the identification of fact as fact and opinion as opinion, and their separation, so far as possible."

26. Mowlana, "Mass Media Systems," pp. 56–57, says that the core of an Arab newspaper is its political flavor, and that Arab audiences do not expect the media to be neutral but rather to be politically combative.

27. *A Free and Responsible Press*, p. 21. Herbert Brucker, in *Freedom of Information* (New York: Macmillan, 1949), pp. 149–50, reports that the American Society of Newspaper Editors adopted some Canons of Journalism which included: "By every consideration of good faith a newspaper is constrained to be truthful. . . . Headlines should be fully warranted by the contents of the articles which they surmount." See also Brucker's Chapter 18, "America's Contribution: Objective Reporting." Whether Americans have met these ideals is another question.

28. This important point is made by W. Phillips Davison, *International Political Communication* (New York: Praeger, 1965), p. 80.

29. This is not unusual. According to Herbert Passin, "Writer and Journalist in the Transitional Society," in Lucien Pye, ed., *Communications and Political Development* (Princeton: Princeton University Press, 1963), pp. 97–98, Japan, China, India, and Korea have experienced a similar evolution in journalism because literary development was well advanced when journalism arrived there also.

30. The popular novelist and short story writer Yousif Siba'i was, until his death in February 1978, Chief Editor and Board Chairman of *al Ahram*, a post held earlier by prominent writer Ihsan Abdel Quddus. See Kitchen, "Al Ahram," p. 157, on Muhammad Abduh and his contemporaries. Quddus, whose actress mother Rose al Yusif founded the magazine of that name in 1925, himself became editor of *Akhbar al Yawm* newspaper at the peak of his career. The writings of these three authors are discussed briefly in Trevor LeGassick, "A Malaise in Cairo: Three Contemporary Egyptian Authors," *Middle East Journal* 21(2)(Spring 1967):145–56.

31. Saudi television, for example, always begins with a passage from the Koran, goes dark at the time of the evening prayer, and carries religious discussions with some regularity. In the mid-seventies it also carried a very popular program by a religious shaikh discussing practical everyday problems with references to the Koran.

32. Philip K. Hitti, *The Arabs, a Short History* (Princeton: Princeton University Press, 1943), p. 21, quoted also in Raphael Patai, *The Arab Mind* (New York: Scribners, 1973), p. 49. The phrase "intimate interdependence" is from an excellent short article by E. Shouby, "The Influence of the Arabic Language on the Psychology of the Arabs," *Middle East Journal* 5(3)(Summer 1951):284. Albert Hourani has pointed out that not religion but language "emerged as the common good of the Near Eastern people." Hourani, in

"Democracy and the New States," Rhodes Seminar Papers (New Delhi: Congress for Cultural Freedom, 1959).

33. Shouby, "Arab Language," pp. 288, 295, see also pp. 289, 296–99, and see Patai, *The Arab Mind*, pp. 41–49.

34. Edward Atiyeh, *The Arabs* (Baltimore: Penguin, 1955), p. 96.

35. Shouby, "Arab Language," p. 293, says: "A successful Arab writer, so long as he pays attention to the grammatical and idiomatic aspects of his writing, has only to make it diffusely comprehensible; his duty does not extend so far as to make his meaning clear-cut and unequivocal." See also pp. 291–93, 298–99, and Patai, *The Arab Mind*, pp. 49–59.

36. Zubayr Sayf al Islam, *Tarikh al Sahafah* (Algiers: Sharikah al Wataniyah li al Nashr wa al Tawzi', 1960), shows very strong influence of the French people and culture including language on Algeria in the nineteenth and twentieth centuries.

37. *L'Orient-le Jour* in Beirut is a leading daily newspaper; there are no significant French dailies outside of the four countries mentioned. Several countries have English dailies but they are mostly read by the resident foreign community—Cairo's *Egyptian Gazette*, Kuwait's *Daily News* and *Kuwait Times*, Jidda's *Arab News*, and Baghdad's *Baghdad Observer*.

38. There are a few purely entertainment-oriented magazines, such as the Egyptian weekly *Sabah al Khayr*, which is primarily satirical. But most magazines do more than entertain, and even some children's "comic" books are heavily political in content, supporting the Palestinian "resistance," etc.

39. William Hachten, "Ghana's Press Under the N.R.C.," *Journalism Quarterly* (Autumn 1975):462–63. The television stations in Dubai and Lebanon are the only commercial ones in the Arab world; see Chapter 6.

40. Fred S. Siebert, Theodore Peterson, and Wilbur Schramm: *Four Theories of the Press* (Urbana: University of Illinois Press, 1953), pp. 1–37.

41. *Ibid.*, p. 2.

42. Ghassan Tueni, *Freedom of the Press in Developing Societies* (Beirut: al Nahar Press, 1971), pp. 2–3.

43. Wilbur Schramm, "Two Concepts of Mass Communication" in Bernard Berelson and Morris Janowitz, eds., *Reader in Public Opinion and Communication* (New York: The Free Press, 1966), pp. 213, 216; see also Siebert, Peterson, and Schramm, *Four Theories*, Chapter 2.

44. Siebert, Peterson, and Schramm, *Four Theories*.

45. Ithiel Pool, "Communication in Totalitarian Societies," in Pool and Schramm, *Handbook of Communication*, p. 467.

46. Passin, "Writer and Journalist," p. 111.

47. These categories are basically those of Siebert, Peterson, and Schramm, *Four Theories*, but his fourth category, "Soviet totalitarian," has been broadened to include all totalitarian systems because other analysts have done so persuasively: see William Ebenstein, *Totalitarianism* (New York: Holt, Rinehart and Winston, 1962), pp. 7, 14–17, 25–30, 52, 64; and Carl J. Friedrich and Zbigniew K. Brzezinski, *Totalitarian Dictatorship and Autocracy* (New York: Praeger, 1961).

CHAPTER 2—The Mobilization Press

1. Interview no. 105, Egyptian journalist, May 5, 1975. Interview no. 30, Sudanese official, May 14, 1973. Interview no. 22, Egyptian journalist, May 10, 1973; for example, in 1974 the two Damascus dailies began carrying a column called "Popular Control," which may criticize a lower-level engineer at a match factory for allowing production of defective matches but would never blame top Syrian leadership for shortcomings; NY *Times* Magazine, May 18, 1975, p. 85.

2. Interviews no. 12 and 32, Egyptian and Tunisian journalists, May 7 and 15, 1973, among others.

3. Karl Deutsch, "Social Mobilization and Political Development," *American Political Science Review* (Sept. 1961):493–94.

4. David E. Apter, *The Politics of Modernization* (Chicago: University of Chicago Press, 1965), pp. 36, 240, 359.

5. Daniel Lerner, "Toward a Communication Theory of Modernization," in Lucien Pye, ed., *Communications and Political Development* (Princeton: Princeton University Press, 1963), p. 344.

6. Preamble to Law no. 155, Government of Iraq, December 1967, as broadcast by Baghdad Radio December 13, 1967, at 1500Z.

7. Program of the Arab Ba'th Socialist Party, 1965, art. 4 "The Party and the System of Government," cited in Roy E. Thoman, "Iraq Under Ba'athist Rule," *Current History* (January 1972):32.

8. Sudan News Agency, "Revolution, Information and News" (Khartoum, 1971); see also Gamal al Din al 'Utaifi, *Hurriyit al Sahafah* (Cairo: al Mutabi' al Ahram al Tijari, 1971), p. 40, quoting Egyptian press law.

9. Declaration of the Central Committee of the National Front Political Organization, February 28, 1974, published in *al Thawri* (Aden), March 7, 1974, pp. 6–7.

10. Final communiqué of the Seminar, published in *Revolution Africaine* (Algiers), January 31–February 6, 1975, p. 20.

11. The findings on African media parallel these; William Hachten, "Ghana's Press Under the NRC: an Authoritarian Model for Africa," *Journalism Quarterly* 52(3) (Autumn 1975):459–60.

12. One clear instance of this occurred during the October 1973 Arab-Israeli war when the Iraqi press attacked the other Arab oil-producing countries, including Saudi Arabia, by printing editorials, cartoons, and headlines designed to show that these countries were helping the Israeli enemy by not placing an embargo on oil to the U.S. William A. Rugh, "Arab Media and Politics During the October War," *Middle East Journal* 29(3) (Summer 1975):319–22.

13. Apter, *Politics of Modernization*, p. 360; other writers have also made the important contrast between totalitarian and authoritarian; see, e.g., Carl J. Friedrich and Zbigniew Brzezinski, *Totalitarian Dictatorship and Autocracy* (Cambridge: Harvard University Press, 1965), espec. Chapters 1 and 4.

14. Ithiel Pool, "Communication in Totalitarian Societies," in Pool and Wilbur Schramm, eds., *Handbook of Communication* Chicago: Rand McNally, 1973), p. 468; see also pp. 463–66.

15. Apter, *Politics of Modernization*, pp. 181–202, 363. Algerian President Houari Boumedienne declared on May 1, 1975: "If we want to talk about democracy we should understand among ourselves the real meaning of the word. There is, first of all, bourgeois democracy based on the multiplicity of parties and the game of influence. There is now that which we call true democracy, which is that based on economic and social factors. For our part, we say 'yes' to the democracy of the workers, the peasants and the revolutionary youth." *El Moudjahid*, May 2, 1975.

16. Apter, *Politics of Modernization*, p. 363, says the solidarity party is the main instrument of control in a mobilization system; he adds (p. 383) that the media there are "controlled by the government," but he does not elaborate.

17. Law for the Organization of the Press (qanun tanzim al sahafah), sections 1, 3, 6, 7 and 8. This law is decribed and analyzed by an Egyptian expert in 'Utaifi, *Hurriyit al Sahafah*, pp. 39, 59 and 87.

18. A few Egyptian weeklies, still in private hands, are allowed to function outside this system because they are not politically significant—*Journal d'Egypte* and the Copt-owned *Watani*; Interview no. 18, Egyptian journalist, Cairo, May 9, 1973.

19. 'Utaifi, *Hurriyit al Sahafah*, pp. 41, 43, 63, and 73, citing the 1956 and 1964 constitutions and other laws; also Interviews no. 18 and 106, Egyptian journalists, May 1973.

20. Interview no. 12, Egyptian journalist, Cairo May 7, 1973; according to 'Utaifi, *Hurriyit al Sahafa*, p. 76, *al Ahram* gives half of its profits to its workers and reinvests the other half in development.

21. Ben Bella was personally involved in the dramatic seizure of the European-controlled paper *La Depeche d'Algerie*, whose facilities were turned over to the FLN daily *Le Peuple*; New York *Times*, September 18, 1963.

22. Merger reported in *ibid.*, June 5, 1965. Previously *Alger Republicain* had been Communist-backed but the CP was illegal at this time, and the paper's Communist editor, Henri Alleg, had resigned in August 1964; *ibid.*, August 4, 1964; see report in *ibid.*, June 28, 1964.

23. "Numeri Outlines Organization of Sudanese Press Corporation," *Sudan News*, September 8, 1970, p. 5. Al Ayyam publishing house also issued a weekly, *Sudan al Jadid*, and provincial and women's papers. The al Sahafah publishing house issued the daily *Sudan Standard* starting November 24, 1970, a weekly (formerly daily) *Ra'y al 'Amm*, and a monthly *al Khartum*. The newspapers *Ahrar* and *Sudan News* suspended publication.

24. Sudanese Press and Publication Act of 1973, Act. no. 6 of May 10, 1973, paras. 5, 8, and 4, respectively. Since 1970, the armed forces publish a weekly *Quwwat al Musallahah*, and the Southern Regional Ministry of Information, Culture, and Youth publishes the weeklies *al Iza'a* (Broadcasting) and *al Shabab* (Youth).

25. Interview no. 29, Sudanese official, May 14, 1973, Khartoum.

26. The Iraqi Revolutionary Command Council promulgated Law no. 98 in 1971, which established al Jamahir House for Press as a "public utility connected with the ministry" to publish newspapers, etc. RCC resolution no. 117 of 1972 established al Wataniyah publishing house for the same purpose. See official gazette no. 17 of April 25, 1973 (in English), p. 6, and gazette of November 11, 1972 (in Arabic), p. 3, resp. The Communist paper is *Tariq al Sha'b* and the Kurdish paper is *Taakhi*.

27. Foreign Area Studies, American University, *Area Handbook for Syria* (Washington, D.C.: USGPO, 1965), p. 115. Syria has three provincial dailies—*al 'Urubah, al Jamahir,* and *al Fida'*—and the newest daily *Tishrin* (October) was started to commemorate the October 1973 war; all are centrally controlled. In South Yemen, the Marxist-oriented ruling National Front joined with the Democratic Peoples Union Party and the Popular Vanguard Party in October 1975 because there were no real differences between them.

28. The two met in 1948. For a description of the relationship, see Edward R.F. Sheehan's introduction to Muhammad Hassanain Haykal's *Cairo Documents* (Garden City, N.Y.: Doubleday, 1973).

29. For example, the "exceptional times" of the Arab-Israeli conflict of 1947–50 were cited as a justification for censorship, as were the January–June 1952 period of unrest between the Cairo fire and the colonels' coup d'etat; the 1956–58 Suez Crisis and its aftermath; and the 1967–73 period of Arab frustration with the Arab-Israeli problem; Interview no. 18, Egyptian journalist, Cairo, May 9, 1973. Publications other than dailies in Egypt were censored too, but more lightly in some cases, such as *al Ahram al Iqtisadi,* an economic journal; interviw no. 15, Egyptian journalist, Cairo, May 8, 1973. In 1973 the military censor visited each publication before an issue went to press to check copy for sensitive material, but this practice ceased after the October War.

30. Interview no. 17, Egyptian journalist, Cairo, May 8, 1973. The Sudan Press Directory 1974, refers to censorship, but typically in these countries the practice is not formalized in law.

31. Interview no. 102, June 1973.

32. Interview no. 12, Egyptian journalist, Cairo, May 7, 1973. When this interview was conducted, Egypt was still in a state of war with Israel and tension was high—this was the primary reason for the close attention by military censors.

33. *Ibid.;* one editor told this writer he carefully reads the discussions of the People's Assembly, looking for detailed guidance on specific issues.

34. Interviews no. 12, 13, 22, May 7 and 10, 1973, respectively, Egyptian journalists, May 1973.

35. Interviews no. 12, 15, 17, 22, Egyptian journalists, Cairo, May 1973, and interview no. 105. President Sadat cites these three principles often; see his speech quoted in *al Ahram,* June 27, 1977.

36. Interview no. 17, Egyptian journalist, Cairo, May 8, 1973.

37. Interviews no. 13 and 22, Egyptian journalists, Cairo, May 1973.

38. Editorial "A Thought," published on May 3, 1965, by Ali Amin in *al Ahram;* this was the day he left *al Akhbar.* The great fiction writer Naguib Mahfuz managed to convey his discontent with the situation after the June 1967 War. On *al Ahram al Iqtisadi:* interview no. 15, Egyptian journalist, May 8, 1973.

39. Interview no. 13, Egyptian journalist, Cairo, May 8, 1973. On the history of *al Ahram,* see Dr. Ibrahim 'Abdu, *al Ahram, Tarikh wa Fann 1875–1964* (Cairo: Mu'assasat Sijl al 'Arab, 1964).

40. Interview no. 17, Egyptian journalist, Cairo, May 8, 1973.

41. Haykal's especially critical articles were published in *al Ahram* on January 11 and February 1, 1974. For biographical information on Haykal, see his book *Cairo Documents* (Garden City, N.Y.: Doubleday, 1973), pp. i–xxvii, and Desmond Stewart, "The Rise and Fall of Muhammad Haykal," *Encounter* (June 1974):87–93.

42. On February 1, 1974, Cairo Radio announced that Ali Amin had replaced Haykal as Chief Editor of *al Ahram* and Abdal Qadir Hatim had replaced him as Board Chairman. He subsequently has written for publications in Kuwait, Jordan, Lebanon, and Europe.

43. Mustafa Amin, jailed in 1965 on charges of spying for the U.S., and his twin brother Ali, who went into exile, were rehabilitated in January 1974. Mustafa became Board Chairman of *Akhbar al Yawm*, which he and his brother had built up in the 1940s and 1950s.

44. On February 8, 1974, *al Ahram* announced the government's easing of press restrictions. Examples of discussion of Nasserism: Badawi in *al Gumhuriyah*, March 21, 1974; Bathi and Gawdat in *al Musawwar*, March 14 and 28, 1974. On parties: 'Utaifi in *al Ahram*, March 9, 1974; Gawdat in *al Musawwar*, April 12, 1974; Sa'dah and Ali Amin in *Akhbar al Yawm*, August 24 and September 21, 1974. On press freedom: Mahfuz in *al Akhbar*, February 22, 1974; Abu al Fath in *Akhbar al Yawm*, January 18, 1975; Ghallab and Aziz in *al Tali'ah*, February 1975. On student concerns: *al Ahram*, January 6, 1975. On corruption, *Akhbar al Yawm* published a long series of articles by its reporter Tahani Ibrahim accusing Ahmad Yunis, chairman of the Central Union of Agricultural Cooperatives, of corruption; they appeared on July 3 and 24, August 20 and September 14, 1976.

45. Following a disagreement over the March issue, the editor of *al Tali'ah* was fired by the publishing house, which then converted the magazine. The changes at *Rose al Yusif* were made in April.

46. One example among many is his speech to the ASU Central Committee on July 22, 1978, reported in all Cairo newspapers the next day.

47. A fourth party, the New Wafd, which emerged in early 1978, dissolved itself the same year without having started to issue a newspaper.

48. For example, in 1977, *al Ahram*'s Board Chairman was the well-known short story writer Yusif al Siba'i, who had on his staff the outstanding Arab novelist Naguib Mahfuz, the creator of modern Arab literary theater, Tawfiq al Hakim, and perhaps the Arab world's most popular fiction writer, Ihsan Abdal Quddus. The other major publishing house, Akhbar al Yawm, had Mustafa Amin, Ahmad Abul Fath, and Galal al Hamamsi, three of Egypt's leading professional journalists.

49. Musa Sabri, *Akhbar al Yawm*, October 4, 11, and 18, 1974; Mamduh Rida and Anwar Za'luk, in *al Ta'awun al Siyasi*, April 7 and May 1, 1977, respectively. See also Fu'ad Matar, *al Nahar* (Beirut), February 4, 1974.

50. Sadat's speech on the third anniversary of Nasser's death, *al Ahram*, September 29, 1973. President Sadat's speeches at Alexandria University and to the ASU Central Committee, *al Ahram*, May 4 and July 17, 1977.

51. Sadat's speech on the fifth anniversary of Nasser's death, *al Ahram*, September 28, 1975.

52. President Sadat to the Higher Press Council, *al Ahram*, May 27, 1975.

53. President Sadat's speech at Mersa Metruh, *al Ahram*, August 9, 1977.

54. In March 1975, President Sadat, in his capacity as ASU president, announced creation of the council to which the ASU would transfer 49 percent ownership of publications. But the ASU retained 51 percent, the press members are all appointed by the president, and the council by law includes a majority from positions bound to be loyal to the regime, such as ASU officials, editors, and the Information Minister.

CHAPTER 3—Mobilization Press: Development Stages

1. Even Syrian writers, chafing under stricter Ottoman governors in Beirut and Damascus, moved to Egypt where they were able to begin private newspapers under Ismail's regime. For example, *al Ahram* was established in Alexandria, the commercial center, in 1875 by two brothers from Beirut, Salim and Bishara Taqla. Adib Mruwa, *al Sahafah al 'Arabiyah* (Beirut: Dar Maktabah al Hayat, 1961), p. 193. See also Helen Kitchen, "Al Ahram—The Times of the Arab World," *Middle East Journal* 4(2)(April 1950):155–60. Adnan Almany, "Government Control of the Press in the United Arab Republic, 1952–1970," *Journalism Quarterly* 49(2)(Summer 1972):340; and American University, *Area Handbook for the United Arab Republic* (Washington, D.C.: USGPO, 1970), p. 255; also Anwar al Gindi, *Tatawwur al Sahafah al 'Arabiyah fi Masr* (Cairo: Matba' al Risala, n.d.), Chapter 1.

2. Quotations from Henry Ladd Smith, "The Egyptian Press and Its Current Problems," *Journalism Quarterly* 31 (2) (Summer 1954):333; see also Rosalynde Ainslie, *The Press in Africa, Communications Past and Present* (New York: Walker, 1967), p. 142, and Almany, "Government Control of the Press," p. 341.

3. Interview with Dr. Sami Aziz, professor of Journalism, Cairo University, May 8, 1973; other examples are *al Balagh* of Abdal Khaliq Hamza and Dr. Haykal's *al Siyasah*.

4. Interview no. 22, Cairo, May 10, 1973.

5. Almany, "Government Control of the Press," p. 341, describes *al Liwa'* newspaper as an instrument of nationalism used by Mustafa Kamil and his Nationalist Party. Mruwa, *al Sahafah*, pp. 306–14, describes the growth of nationalist papers in the 1920s in Syria as it emerged from Ottoman restrictions, but some nationalist writers were jailed by French authorities. Sayf al Islam Zubir, *Tarikh al Sahafah* (Algiers: al Sharikah al Wataniyah li al Nashr, 1960), p. 52, describes the heavy French influence and the "imperialist press." Tom J. McFadden, *Daily Journalism in the Arab States* (Columbus: Ohio State University Press, 1953), pp. 8–9, describes *al Mu'ayyid*, established in 1889 as Egypt's first party paper. See also Shams al Din al Rifa'i, *Tarikh al Sahafah al Suriyah* (Cairo: Dar al Ma'rif, al Juz' al Thani, 1969) pp. 11–15. American University, *Area Handbook for Iraq* (Washington, D.C.: USGPO, 1971), p. 223; Mruwa, *al Sahafah*, pp. 216 and 322–35.

6. American University, *Area Handbook for Algeria* (Washington, D.C.; USGPO, 1965), p. 324; Mruwa, *al Sahafah*, p. 223; al Islam, *Tarikh al Sahafah*.

7. OAS terrorism closed the pro-Socialist paper *Oran Republicain* in the 1950s after it called for government reforms, and OAS bombs closed the moderate *Journal d'Alger* in 1961 after it dared to make overtures to moderate Arabs. Ainslie, *The Press in Africa*,

p. 147. A new liberal daily appeared in Algiers in early 1960 which was reportedly backed by Paris in an attempt to break the monopoly of the conservative *colon* dailies that opposed independence, according to the *New York Times*, April 29, 1960.

8. Helen Kitchen, ed., *The Press in Africa* (New York: Ruth Sloan Associates, 1956), p. 1.

9. *Area Handbook for Algeria*, p. 325; al Islam, *Tarikh al Sahafah*.

10. In the Sudan, Kitchener in the 1890s had had the *Dongola News* produced for his army on its way up the Nile, according to Bashir Mohamed Saeed, "The Press in the Sudan," Khartoum, December 1971, manuscript, p. 1. In Aden, the first paper and the only one published prior to World War I was the mimeographed Reuters news bulletin according to *World Press* (Paris: UNESCO, 1964), p. 83. In Libya, the only papers between 1945 and 1950 were those published in Arabic and Italian by the British Information Service.

11. Saeed, "The Press in the Sudan," pp. 1–5; see also Mahjub Muhammad Salih, *al Sahafah al Sudaniyah fi Nisf al Qarn* (Khartoum: Jam'at Khartum, 1971).

12. For example, Muhammad 'Abbas Abu al Rish started a literary magazine, *Nahdat al Sudan* (Sudanese Renaissance), in 1930; a few years later, when the magazine ceased upon his death, 'Arafat Muhammad 'Abdullah started a bi-monthly called *al Fajr* (The Dawn) to promote Arab literature.

13. Saeed, "The Press in the Sudan," pp. 5–8.

14. UNESCO, *World Press*, p. 83.

15. C. Wilton Wynn, "Western Techniques Influence Party Newspapers of Egypt," *Journalism Quarterly* 25(4)(December 1948):391–94; see also McFadden, *Daily Journalism*, p. 6, and Kitchen, "*Al Ahram*—The *Times* of the Arab World," p. 160, cites nonpartisan papers in Egypt. According to Gamal al 'Utaifi, *al Ahram* board member interviewed in Cairo on May 9, 1973, the government censored the press during 1948–49. See also Dr. Rif'at al Said, *al Sahafah al Yasariyah fi Masr, 1925–1948* (Beirut: Dar al Tali'ah, 1974).

16. Mruwa, *al Sahafah*, pp. 309 and 319 describing the 1954 law passed by the Syrian regime to abolish the press which cooperated with Shishakli.

17. Gordon Torrey, *Syrian Politics and the Military* (Columbus: Ohio State University Press, 1964), pp. 41–43.

18. *Area Handbook for Iraq*, p. 224; the moderate socialist paper *al Ahli* and the pro-government paper *al Akhbar* at that time had the highest circulations.

19. William Quandt, *Revolution and Political Leadership: Algeria 1954–1968* (Cambridge: MIT Press, 1969), pp. 193–95, 200.

20. For a description of the political situation, see Majid Khadduri, *Modern Libya: A Study in Political Development* (Baltimore: Johns Hopkins University Press, 1965), pp. 318–19.

21. American University, *Handbook on Libya* (Washington, D.C.: USGPO, 1969), pp. 175–77; and Mruwa, *al Sahafah*, pp. 383–84.

22. For example, when General Za'im came to power in Syria in 1949 he suspended eleven of the nineteen Damascus newspapers, including the leading dailies which had op-

posed him; in 1952 the regime took similar steps, according to the *New York Times*, April 4, 1949, March 14, 1952, and July 9, 1952. In Iraq, the government of Nuri al Sa'id suspended some party newspapers in 1954 that opposed his rightist policies, but later after the monarchy was overthrown, the Qasim regime took actions which favored leftist writers, according to *Area Handbook for Iraq*, pp. 223–24.

23. For example, in Egypt the government made use of the power in the constitution basically to prevent attacks on royalty. Sometimes this was interpreted broadly, in order to jail an editor for criticizing an Egyptian official, or to suspend an editor for complaining about the gap between the rich and the poor, but normally it was interpreted more narrowly than that. *Area Handbook for the United Arab Republic*, p. 225.

24. Interview with Mustapha Bahgat Badawi, Chief Editor of *al Gumhuriyah*, May 8, 1973; Badawi, who in 1952 was working in army public relations, was one of the founders of al Tahrir publishing house.

25. Ainslie, *The Press in Africa*, p. 143, and Almany, "Government Control of the Press," pp. 342–43.

26. Badawi interview, May 8, 1973. McFadden, *Daily Journalism*, p. 88, and Smith, "The Egyptian Press and its Current Problems" p. 335, give estimates of 110,000 and 150,000 respectively.

27. Interview no. 106, Egyptian journalist, April 1973.

28. Don Peretz, "Democracy and the Revolution in Egypt," *Middle East Journal* (Winter 1959):37.

29. *Ibid.*, Bribes reportedly went up to as much as 48,000 pounds. Almany, "Government Control of the Press," p. 34.

30. Ihsan 'Askar, *Tatawwar al Sahafah al Suriyah* (Cairo: Dar al Nahda al 'Arabiyah, 1973), p. 325. The merger was a double blow to the Syrian press, which suffered also under competition from the Egyptian newspapers that flooded Syrian news stands—they were generally stronger to begin with, and in addition received favored treatment by Egyptian officials.

31. *Area Handbook for Iraq*, p. 225.

32. Quandt, *Revolution and Political Leadership*, pp. 193–95, 200.

33. The NLF began a French daily named *El Chaab* in Algiers, then in December 1962 renamed it *Le Peuple* when it began an Arabic edition called, by the same name, *al Sha'b* (The People); *Area Handbook for Iraq*, p. 327.

34. This issue was debated briefly in the press at the time; see *al Yawm*, February 5, 1970, and *al Thawrah*, February 7, 1970, both published in Tripoli.

35. RCC press law announced on June 18, 1972 (Libyan News Agency bulletin of 12:45 P.M.).

36. American University, *Area Handbook for the Sudan* (Washington, D.C.: USGPO, 1960), p. 200; and Mruwa, *al Sahafah*, p. 376.

37. The political climate in such a situation has been analyzed for Algeria by Clement H. Moore, *Politics in North Africa* (Boston: Little, Brown, 1970), pp. 118, 128, 130; and for Syria by P. J. Vatikiotis in Paul Y. Hammond, ed., *Political Dynamics in the*

Middle East (New York: American Elsevier, 1972), pp. 227 ff; also confirmed for the Sudan by interview no. 31, Khartoum, May 14, 1973.

38. President Ja'far Numeiry, interview with *al Quwwat al Musallahah*, August 29, 1970, broadcast on Radio Omdurman on the same day at 6:00 P.M.

39. In the Sudan, it was particularly concerned about Communist ideas surfacing in some of the newspapers. Interview no. 31, Khartoum, May 14, 1973.

40. *La Depeche* had a circulation of 80–90,000 while *Le Peuple* was in the 10–15,000 range; *Area Handbook for Algeria*, p. 328. While *al Ahram* and *al Akhbar* quite quickly passed the 100,000 mark, *al Gumhuriyah* always remained well below it.

41. Interview with Gamal al 'Utaifi, *al Ahram* editor and People's Assembly Member, Cairo, May 9, 1973.

42. Gamal al 'Utaifi, *Huriyyit al Sahafah* (Cairo: Mutabi' al Ahram al Tijari, 1971), p. 40.

43. Preamble to Law no. 155, Baghdad Radio December 3, 1967, 1500 GMT.

44. Numeiry speech, broadcast on Omdurman Radio, August 26, 1970, 1050 GMT; and Numeiry statement published and on August 29, Omdurman Radio, 1600 GMT.

45. Algiers Radio, September 18, 1973, 1303 GMT.

46. Interview no. 31, Khartoum, May 14, 1973.

47. Interview no. 18, Cairo, May 9, 1973.

48. 'Utaifi, *Hurriyit al Sahafah*, p. 41, says the Arab Socialist Union is not a party; also confirmed by interview no. 106, April 1973; the Algerian Press is controlled by the "National Liberation Front"; see *New York Times*, July 19, 1964.

49. *Taakhi* existed before the 1967 "nationalization" but disappeared at that time; it reappeared in February 1968 when the government was moving toward reconciliation with the Kurds in their conflict which had been going on since 1961, but it came and went with the ups and downs of that conflict. It resumed publication in May 1970, a few weeks after five Kurds were included in the Iraqi Cabinet of March 29, but after 1976 was replaced by *al Iraq*. *Tariq al Sha'b* had similar varying fortunes, but in 1973 it became a daily newspaper, in the same year that the Ba'thists invited Communist leaders to join the National Front and the Cabinet. Since then, the newspaper has done reasonably well. Roy E. Thoman, "Iraq Under Baathist Rule," *Current History* (January 1972): 32–36; *New York Times*, July 13, 1973, and *Christian Science Monitor*, June 8, 1971.

50. For a discussion of solidarity and representational parties, and a definition of party, see David E. Apter, *The Politics of Modernization* (Chicago: University of Chicago Press, 1965), pp. 181, 199.

CHAPTER 4—The Loyalist Press

1. Interview no. 6, Tunisian journalist, Tunis, May 3, 1973; The Chief editor of *al 'Amal*, for example, is a Central Committee PSD member.

2. In 1930, at the age of twenty-seven, Bourguiba was writing for the Destour Par-

ty's paper *La Voix Tunisienne*; in 1932 he established his own paper, but the French closed it in 1933 along with others like it. Then after the Neodestour was split from the Destour in 1934 the new party began publishing *l'Action* which Bourguiba wrote for.

3. U.S. Information Service Abu Dhabi, "Media Directory, United Arab Emirates," Oct. 15, 1974, typescript. Interview no. 119, UAE official, June 1976.

4. Interviews no. 6, 7, 34, 36, 37, 58, Tunisian, Saudi, and Jordanian journalists, Tunis, Jidda, Riyadh and Amman, May 1973. See also Lars Rudebeck, *Party and People, a Study of Political Change in Tunisia* (Stockholm: Almqvist and Wiksell, 1967), p. 45 and Clement H. Moore, *Politics in North Africa* (Boston: Little, Brown, 1970), p. 150.

5. Interviews no. 34 and 37, Saudi journalists, Jidda and Riyadh, May 17 and 18, 1973.

6. Interviews no. 60 and 91, Jordanian official and journalist, May 24, 1973, Amman.

7. Interviews no. 6 and 7, Tunisian journalists, May 3, 4, 1973.

8. Interviews no. 36 and 37, Saudi journalists, Riyadh, May 18, 1973.

9. *Ibid.*, interview no. 36.

10. *al Ra'y* tends to be more optimistic on the Arab-Israeli problem than is *al Dustur*, which tends to emphasize problems in foreign and domestic policy more, but can, at times, express more pro-government sentiments even than *al Ra'y*. Interview no. 57, Jordanian journalist, May 23, 1973.

11. For example the weekly *al Sabah*, which specializes in Palestinian and West Bank news, refers to organized Palestinian groups in headlines and the "resistance" policies in its editorials. *Al Urdun* is much smaller in circulation, weaker on news, but is outspoken on some issues. Interview no. 55, Jordanian journalist, May 23, 1973 Amman.

12. Interview no. 37, Saudi journalist, Riyadh, May 18, 1973.

13. *Al Madinah* and *'Ukaz* tend to have more foreign news and more editorials; *al Bilad* tends to pick up stories helpful to the government more frequently than most, while *al Madinah* and sometimes *'Ukaz* seem to take chances on that score. *Al Nadwah* is strong on features and literature, *'Ukaz* is popular with educated Saudis. *Al Riyadh* and *al Jazirah*, published in Riyadh, are strong on reports of ministry activities. Interviews no. 36, 40, and 89, Saudi Arabia, May 1973.

14. Interview no. 7, Tunisian journalist, Tunis, May 4, 1976; the two independent sister dailies *al Sabah* and *Le Temps*, published by a wealthy businessman Habib Cheikh-Rouhou, have good editors and tend to be written in a somewhat more aggressive, interesting style; they also tend to be more critical of U.S. foreign policy. Interview no. 85, Tunis, May 1976.

15. Preamble and para. 8 or the 1963 Law, printed in Muhammad Nasir bin Abbas, *Mujiz al Sahafah fil Mamlakah al 'Arabiyah al Sa'udiyah* (Riyadh: Mu'assasa al Jazirah, 1971), pp. 231–37. Paras. 10, 11, 13, 16, 17, 24.

16. Interviews no. 34 and 37, Saudi journalists, Jidda and Riyadh, May 17 and 18, 1973.

17. Press and Publication Law no. 33, articles no. 10, 23 and 38, which replaced Law No. 16 of 1955 (qanun al matbu'aat of March 30, 1955), articles 6, 20, 21, and 25; see also 'Adib Mruwa, *al Sahafah al 'Arabiyah* (Beirut: Dar al Hayat, 1961), p. 347.

18. Tom Brady article in *New York Times*, March 26, 1967. *Filastin* and *al Manar* merged into *al Dustur* and moved to Amman, while the personnel of *al Difa'a* and *al Jihad* arranged to publish a new daily, *al Quds*. Interview no. 56, Jordanian journalist, Amman, May 23, 1973.

19. On another occasion, on December 3, 1975, the government closed *al Akhbar* after its editorials said that the new Jordanian currency carried "the Star of David . . . Israel's flag"; the other papers that day carried the government's denial of that charge.

20. Interview no. 60, Jordanian official, May 24, 1973, Amman.

21. Press Code of February 9, 1956, as amended in April 1975, chapters 2 and 4, cited in JPRS 65003 U.S. Commerce Dept., of June 13, 1975. The amendment was intended to "bring it up to date" and in line with "Tunisification" of the legal system and "to promote the national press."

22. For example, in 1962 the Communist monthly *al Tali'ah* was closed as was the pro-Communist-monthly *Tribune de Paris*, following an attempt on Bourguiba's life. In January 1957 the weekly *l'Action* was suspended for a week for criticizing the government and the trials of former Protectorate collaborators; it was closed again in September 1957 after the PSD Political Bureau denounced it for "using the prestigious name of the paper founded by the Party leader" for waging an "insidious campaign of confusion." I. William Zartman, *Government and Politics in Northern Africa* (New York: Praeger, 1963), pp. 73–74. Interviews no. 6 and 7, Tunisian journalists, Tunis, May 3 and 4, 1973.

23. January 1974 law, articles 5 and 8; article in *al Ittihad* (Abu Dhabi), January 28, 1974, pp. 1-2.

24. For example *al Madinah* (Jidda), half, and *al 'Amal* (Tunis) 60 percent interviews no. 34 and 6, Jidda and Tunis, May 17 and 3, respectively.

25. Interviews no. 6, 7, and 34, Tunisian and Saudi journalists, Tunis and Jidda, May 3, 4, and 17, 1973.

26. The press was run mostly by Syrians, Turks, and others; the major exception was *Barid al Hijaz* in Jidda. Dr. Muhammad al Shamikh, *al Sahafah fi al Hijaz 1908-1941* (Beirut: Dar al Imana, 1971), pp. 60–133.

27. *Ibid.*, pp. 133, 198, 201–206, 209, 213, 217, 220. *Sawt al Hijaz* became an organ of Hijazi writers; *al Madinah* in 1939 became a news bulletin, but it was suspended in 1941; *Umm al Qura* at first had Syrian editors Muhammad Abdul Maqsud and Fu'ad Shakir. 'Abbas, *Mujiz al Sahafah*, pp. 61-62, 119–24.

28. Interviews no. 34, 35, 36, 37, Saudi journalists, Jidda and Riyadh, May 16 and 17, 1973. The opinion was expressed in interviews that most Saudi journalists treat their job like a routine in a bureaucracy rather than as a skilled individual profession, and they are timid, unadventurous, and lacking in desire to produce a product they can be proud of. The level of professionalism of course varies and generalizations are difficult.

29. Egyptians, Palestinians, Lebanese, and Jordanians are well represented, according to "Media Directory, United Arab Emirates."

30. *Filastin* was established in 1911 by a Christian Arab family of 'Isa al 'Isa, and *al Difa'a* was established in 1933, also in Jaffa; both were moved to East Jerusalem during the first Arab-Israeli war.

31. *Al Urdun* is published in the 1970s by Dr. Hanna Nasr, the son of the founder; in 1949 it became a daily and did not hesitate to criticise the government on policy. Inter-

view no. 56, Jordanian journalist, May 23, 1973; see Raphael Patai, *The Kingdom of Jordan* (Princeton: Princeton University Press, 1958), pp. 52–53. The dailies *Al Jihad* and *al Manar* were established in 1959 and 1960, respectively; weeklies that continue to exist are *'Amman al Masa'*, *Akhbar al Usbu'*, *al Sabah*, and *al Hawadith*.

32. Interview no. 56, Saudi journalist, Riyadh, May 23, 1973; see fn. 8, above.

33. *Al Dustur* was formed by a merger of *Filastin* and *al Manar*, arranged before the war, and *al Difa'a* was the third reincarnation of that paper originally founded in Jaffa in 1933.

34. Interviews no. 56, 57, and 59, Jordanian journalists, May 23 and 24, 1973, and no. 60, Jordanian official, May 24.

35. Kuwait, Abu Dhabi, and Qatar have brought a large number of Jordanian, Palestinian, and Egyptian journalists in to help boost their media: Jordan's prominent journalist Mahmud Sharif was for many years the DG of Qatari radio and TV; see fn. 29, above.

36. Helen Kitchen, *The Press in Africa* (New York: Ruth Sloan Associates, 1956), pp. 13–14; American University, *Area Handbook for the Republic of Tunisia* (Washington, D.C.: USGPO, 1970), pp. 218, 221. The Neodestour Party broke off from the Destour in 1934 and later began publishing its own paper, *l'Action*.

37. Interview no. 56, Jordanian journalist, May 23, 1973. For details see L. Carl Brown, "Historical Constants in Tunisian Political Culture," September 1972, U.S. State Dept. colloquium on Tunisia, unpubl. paper; and Zartman, *Government and Politics*, p. 35, Moore, *Politics in North Africa*, p. 218, Rudebeck, *Party and People*, p. 44 and Patai, *The Kingdom of Jordan*, p. 50.

38. Interview no. 6, Tunisian journalist, Tunis, May 3, 1973.

39. Interviews no. 34 and 39, Saudi journalists, Jidda and Riyadh, May 18 and 19, 1973.

40. Interviews no. 35, 36, and 57, Saudi and Jordanian journalists, Jidda, Riyadh, and Amman, May 17, 18, and 23, 1973.

41. Zartman, *Government and Politics*, p. 12.

42. Interview no. 55, Jordanian journalist, Amman, May 23, 1976.

43. Rudebeck, *Party and People*, pp. 44–45, Moore, *Politics in North Africa*, p. 150; interview no. 34, Saudi journalist, Jidda, May 17, 1976.

44. Interview no. 7, Tunisian journalist, Tunis, May 4, 1976.

45. Minister Muhammad Abdu Yamani quoted in *al Jazira*, May 13, 1976, p. 12.

46. Shamikh, *al Sahafah*, pp. 67, 73, 81; *Shams al Haqiqah* and *al Islah al Hijazi*, respectively; both were established in 1909.

47. *Al Falah* was established in Mecca in 1920 by a Syrian, 'Umar Shakir; Muhammad Nasif established *Barid al Hijaz* in November 1924 for his National Hijazi Party, and it clashed with the Saudi-supported *Umm al Qura*, established in Mecca in 1924; *ibid.*, pp. 119, 194. *Sawt al Hijaz* in 1932 became the organ of Hijazi writers; *al Madinah al Munawwarah* was established in 1937 with a strong literary, social, and historical orientation. The style was partly influenced by contemporary Egyptian newspapers which were

available in the Hijaz at the time and also had a literary emphasis, 1922–42; *ibid.*, pp. 221–23, 209–13, 217–19.

48. Interview no. 56, Jordanian journalist, May 23, 1976.

49. For example, on May 12, 1976, Saudi Information Minister Muhammad Abdu Yamani paid a visit to one of the daily newspapers, *al Bilad*, and his comments of praise for the paper's objectivity and balance were well reported in the press the next day, implying to Saudi editors that *al Bilad* was a model to follow.

50. Tunis Afrique Presse, Jordan News Agency, Saudi News Agency, and Qatar News Agency were established in 1961, 1965, 1971, and 1975, respectively, Bahrain and the UAE in 1976; see Chapter 7 for details.

CHAPTER 5—The Diverse Press

1. M. H. Mukhaibir in "Ashghal wa Ayyam" (Beirut: l'Universite St. Josef), 11 (October–December 1963), reporting on a survey conducted by the Lebanese Broadcasting Center, gives the figure 77 percent of adults. A 1970 survey found the figure to be 68 percent, 73 percent in Beirut, according to Nabil H. Dajani, "The Press in Lebanon," *Gazette* 17(3)(1971):173. *Al Anwar, al Bayraq, al Hayat, al Jumhuriyah, al Liwa', al Muharrir, al Shams, al Sharq,* and *al Yawm* in 1974 sold more copies outside Lebanon than inside; see further discussion of this below, Chapter 7. The civil war in Lebanon diminished the export of papers considerably.

2. Interview no. 61, Lebanese journalist, Beirut, May 28, 1973; other observers call it a "prostitute press."

3. *Al Nahar*, December 1, 1974, p. 3, quoting Minister Majid Hamadah and Syndicate President Riad Taha. Others agree that most papers take subsidies and that this is a sensitive subject to discuss in public; interview no. 65, Lebanese journalist, Beirut, May 29, 1973.

4. These figures and the political and religious orientations of Tables 1 and 2 were given to the author by independent, qualified observers in 1974 and 1975, but because real figures are tightly held and much exaggeration takes place around them, they should be considered estimates. For the dates of the first publication see Adib Mruwa, *Al Sahafah al 'Arabiyah* (Beirut: Dar Maktabit al Hayat, 1961), pp. 166–90, 259–82. Papers in Arabic, French, English, and Armenian are published in Beirut.

5. Tom J. McFadden, *The Daily Press in the Arab States* (Columbus: Ohio State University Press, 1953), pp. 1–4; and Mruwa, *Al Sahafah;* Dajani, "The Press in Lebanon," pp. 163–67, has a good brief description of the leading dailies, and a table (p. 171) of the papers published during the first thirty years, 1858–88. Ghassan Tueni, *Freedom of the Press in a Developing Society* (Beirut: al Nahar, 1971), pp. 5–8.

6. Dajani, "The Press in Lebanon," pp. 157–58.

7. *Ibid.*, p. 58; Tueni, *Freedom of the Press*, part II p. 1.

8. Malcolm H. Kerr, "Political Decision Making in a Confessional Democracy," in Leonard Binder, ed., *Politics in Lebanon* (New York: Wiley, 1966), pp. 188–91.

9. *Ibid.*, pp. 188–91.

10. Ghassan Tueni, "Democracy and the Challenge of Jerusalem" (London: Anglo-Arab Association, 1971), p. 13; the first quote is from interview no. 61, Lebanese journalist, May 28, 1973.

11. Dajani, "The Press in Lebanon," p. 59.

12. *New York Herald Tribune*, June 14, July 24, 1952; *New York Times*, July 25, August 19, 1952; Dajani, "The Press in Lebanon," p. 159.

13. Dajani, "The Press in Lebanon," p. 159.

14. Sam Pope Brewer, "Beirut Tightens News Censorship," *New York Times*, April 16, 1958. Another occasion of an import ban was *Time* magazine article on Lebanese religious dissent, November 5, 1973.

15. Press Law of September 4, 1962, article 62. Dajani, "The Press in Lebanon," pp. 160–61.

16. Three such editors expressed this in interviews no. 61, 62, and 65, May 28 and 29, 1973. The quote is from Baha Abu-Laban, "Factors in the Social Control of the Press in Lebanon," *Journalism Quarterly* 43(3)(Autumn 1966):513; see also Dajani, "The Press in Lebanon," p. 161.

17. *L'Orient-le Jour* article on the new press law, July 4, 1974, p. 4. A famous case which occurred in 1973 was the arrest of *al Nahar's* publisher-editor Ghassan Tueni, a prominent personality and former minister, along with his foreign editor for printing the Algiers Arab League Conference secret resolutions; *al Nahar* Arab Report v. 4 no. 51, December 17, 1973. Examples of others were reported in *al Nida'*, December 22, 1973, p. 4.

18. The Lebanese government, for example, asked the press on January 16, 1972, not to publish reports on the bombing of *Lisan al Hal* newspaper. Examples of censored stories—the U.S. resumption of arms aid to Jordan as published in the *Daily Star*, July 23, 1967, and an editorial on Western journalists acting as Israeli spies in *Muharrir*, September 21, 1972, both partially censored.

19. Sa'b Salam, Beirut Radio at 1500Z, June 28, 1972; also President Franjieh on Beirut Radio 1600Z, June 14, 1972, appealed to "national responsibility."

20. On January 31, 1976, the offices of *al Muharrir* and *Bayrut* were attacked by a large force, apparently of the Syrian-backed Palestinian group, Saiqa. *Muharrir* Chief Editor Shublaq and *Bayrut* Deputy Chief Editor 'Amir died as a result of the attack, which many suspected was intended by Syria as a blow to two papers which support Syria's archrival, Iraq. Information Minister Tueni denounced the act, said he was against violence and for freedom of speech and an "honest press" (Beirut Radio 1300Z, February 2, 1976, *Bayrut* and *al Muharrir*, February 1 and 20, 1976). The *Daily Star* was the only major daily paper to disappear completely in the winter of 1975–76.

21. *Arab Report and Record*, January 1–15, 1977, p. 9; Prime Minister's announcement of January 2, 1977. Prime Minister's statement of January 3, 1977. Prime Minister's statement, Beirut Radio, 1200 GMT, January 2, 1977, FBIS, January 3, 1977, p. G-2.

22. Abu-Laban, "Factors in the Social Control," pp. 515–18; Dajani, "The Press in Lebanon," pp. 162–70; interview no. 65, Lebanese journalist, May 29, 1973, Beirut.

23. William A. Hachten, "Moroccan News Media Reflect Divisive Forces While Unifying," *Journalism Quarterly* (Spring 1971):103. Hachten also cites heavy competition from imported French publications.

24. USIS Kuwait, "Kuwait Media Directory," Kuwait, August 1974 and April 1977, mimeo. USIS Kuwait, "Kuwait Press," Kuwait, 1971, mimeo., pp. 17–18. In an interview with Masa'id in Kuwait, May 19, 1973, he said, "I'm a Westerner *(ana gharbi)*. The only thing I object to about America is its Middle East Policy." Also interviews no. 46, 47, 48, and 52, Kuwait, journalists and government officials, May 20 and 21, 1973. *Al Siyassah's* chief editor quarrels with the left and with the Arab nationalists as well as with the right.

25. *Al Nahdah* is conservative pro-Establishment, *al Hadaf* is liberal, *al Tali'ah* is Arab nationalist and trade unionist, *al Risalah* tends to support the Ba'th, *al Ra'id* is Marxist, and *al Mujtama'* supports extreme religious (Muslim) conservative positions; *al Siyassah* however, includes Marxist and other tendencies on its writing staff. Interviews no. 46 and 48, Kuwaiti journalists, Kuwait, May 20, 21, 1973.

26. Interviews no. 2 and 3, Moroccan journalists, Rabat, May 2, 1973.

27. Law no. 3 of 1961 on printing and publishing *(Qanun al Matbu'at wal Nashr)* amending Kuwait's first publishing law of 1957—articles 23, 25, and 30. It is also prohibited to publish official secrets (art. 24), harm public morality, or belittle religion (26 and 30) or slander and defame individuals (26 and 29), as in Lebanon.

28. Interview no. 45, Kuwait government official, May 20, 1973; Law no. 9 of 1972 amending art. 35 of the press and publication law, *Kuwait al Yawm* (gazette), 869:18.

29. Amiri Decree of August 29, 1976, Law no. 59, article 1, amending article 35 of the existing press law.

30. Radio and TV address to the nation, August 31, 1976, by Prime Minister Jabir al Ahmad al Sabah, FBIS, September 1, 1976, p. C-1.

31. During the two-year period following the decree, the Minister suspended newspapers nineteen times, but only six of those were for the full three months, and editors were able to complain publicly. A column in the June 14, 1978, issue of *al Ra'y al 'Amm*, for example, protested continuing suspensions. Several had been suspended before: *al Siyassah* in 1973 and early 1976, *al Watan*, 1964–65, *al Hadaf*, 1965 and 1967, *al Risalah*, 1965, 1967, and 1970, *al Ra'id*, 1971, and *al Tali'ah*, early 1976 several times.

32. Schaar, "Mass Media in Morocco," quotes this in his footnote 13.

33. Hassan interview in *La Nation Africaine*, June 6, 1962, quoted in *ibid.*, pp. 11–12.

34. *New York Times*, October 5, 1959, December 6 and 16, 1959, and September 8, 1960; interview no. 3, Rabat, Moroccan journalist, May 2, 1973. The government actions against newspapers have been too numerous to catalog; following are some examples: in April 1974 *al Kawalis* had four issues seized and *al Ittihad al Watani* (UNFP union paper) lost one; *al Muharrir* disappeared March 1973 to November 1974. Early 1974 was a period of frequent seizures; by March *Maghreb Informations* had been seized thirteen times, *l'Opinion* ten times, and its sister paper almost as many; in April 1975 *al Muharrir* was seized twice and *al 'Alam* once, and two months later issues of *al 'Alam*, *al Muharrir*, and *al Bayan* were all seized. But they kept on publishing.

35. American University, *Area Handbook for Morocco* (Washington, D.C.: USGPO, 1972), pp. 121–148.

36. Hachten, "Moroccan News Media,"p. 102. *Le Monde Diplomatique*, Paris, January 1972, p. 10. Rosalynde Ainslie, *The Press in Africa, Communications Past and Present* (New York: Walker, 1967), p. 149.

37. *Le Monde Diplomatique*, Paris, January 1972.

38. *Al 'Alam*, October 8, November 2, 1971. A Spanish daily was also taken over and a new Moroccan daily in Spanish, *Atualidad*, appeared in its place.

39. Abdul Aziz Masa'id owns *al Ra'y al 'Amm*, and Ahmad Jarallah is Chief Editor of *al Siyassah*; the Chief Editor of *al Tali'ah* is a former MP with connections on the left and with the Arab nationalists; Jarallah is seen as a nonconformist, more daring and professional. Interviews no. 46, 48, 52, Kuwait.

40. Interviews no. 3 and 4, Rabat, Moroccan journalists, May 2, 1973.

41. Interview no. 2, Rabat, Moroccan journalist. The UNDP was recently restricted and the CP is now illegal, though its leader Ali Yata leads the "Party of Progress and Socialism" and controls in effect the editorial line of *al Bayan* newspaper.

42. Interviews no. 46, 47, and 50, Kuwait, Kuwaiti journalists and officials, May 20, 21, 1973. The tribal structure appeared to be fading in the 1970s, though the tribes still retain half the seats. The left and the Arab nationalists lost ground in the January 1975 elections because, apparently, their rhetoric was no longer effective. Arab Nationalist leader Ahmed Khatib is close to *al Tali'ah*; *al Qabas* speaks for the Chamber of Commerce; Jarallah is thought to be close to Deputy Premier and Information Minister Jabir al Ali.

43. Speech by Amir Sabah to the Kuwaiti people, and message from Prime Minister Sheikh Jabir to the Amir, both August 29, 1976; *al Siyassah*, August 30, 1976. *Arab Report and Record*, May 1–15, 1977, p. 348.

44. I. William Zartman, *Government and Politics in Northern Africa* (New York: Praeger, 1963), p. 35.

45. The earlier history of the Moroccan press can be found in Mruwa, *Al Sahafah*, pp. 224 and 397–402; in Helen Kitchen, *The Press in Africa* (New York: Ruth Sloan Associates, 1956), pp. 8–9 and 11; in *Area Handbook for Morocco*, pp. 145–46; and in Zayn al Abdin al Kitani, *al Sahafah al Maghribiyah, al Juz' al Awwal, 1820–1912* (Rabat: Nashrah Wazarat al Anba', n.d.).

46. Schaar, "Mass Media in Morocco," p. 7; see also Schaar's table of political orientations of leading dailies, p. 8.

47. *Al Kifah al Watani* was Communist, *al Harakah* was Mouvement Populaire, and *l'Avant-Garde* was UMT-oriented. Maghreb no. 17, September–October 1966, pp. 30–41, and Schaar, "Mass Media in Morocco," pp. 8–11.

48. Clement H. Moore, *Politics in North Africa* (Boston: Little, Brown, 1970), p. 218; see also pp. 107–109 and 207, and Zartman, *Government and Politics in Northern Africa*, p. 12.

49. Hachten, "Moroccan News Media," p. 101.

50. Interviews no. 2 and 4, Moroccan journalists, Rabat, May 2, 1973. Interviews no. 47, 48, and 49, cited. Palestinians are the most prominent, but there are many Syrians, Egyptians, Lebanese, and Adenis. *Al Siyassah* has at least one of each. See "Kuwait Press 1971" for details.

CHAPTER 6—Arab Radio and Television

1. Jordan's Hashemite Broadcasting Service is one of the few stations that conducted audience surveys on contract, for example, Associated Business Consultants Ltd. (Beirut), research reports dated July 1965, February 1972, and January 1970, issued by the Jordanian Information Ministry, Amman. However, even the HBS in the mid-seventies had no more data to judge audiences than by listener mail, just like the other Arab broadcasters. Interviews no. 53 and 54, Amman, May 23, 1973, Jordanian broadcast officials; also interviews no. 8, Tunis, May 4, 1973, and 46 and 50, Kuwait, May 20, 21, 1973, broadcast officials. Douglas A. Boyd, "Development of Egypt's Radio: 'Voice of the Arabs' Under Nasser," *Journalism Quarterly* 52(4)(Winter 1975):651; interview no. 120, July 1976, Egyptian broadcaster; and A. Saad, "Report on Sudan TV," Khartoum, May 11, 1973, p. 4, unpublished paper, which says the Sudanese first attempted to survey their audience in 1971 but failed. One of the few attempts to gauge radio listener reaction among Arabs was that by Ilya F. Harik, "Opinion Leaders and the Mass Media in Rural Egypt," *American Political Science Review* 65(3):731.

2. Jordan and the Sudan, for example, have receiver license fees in addition to allowing limited broadcast advertising. Revenues from Egyptian sales of TV programming abroad have been tabulated by Christopher Jamieson, "Television and Radio in the Arab Republic of Egypt," unpublished paper, Cairo: American University in Cairo, 1972, Appendix 10.

3. Dubai had television in 1968 under government auspices, but the Palestinian station manager a few years later was allowed to open a separate commercial color station which—with some light government supervision—was broadcasting 6 to 11 P.M. nightly by the mid-seventies. Similarly Dubai Radio, a government station, was later joined by a separate commercial one.

4. Jamieson, "Television and Radio in Egypt," pp. 4–5. Douglas A. Boyd, "Egyptian Radio: Tool of Political and National Development," *Journalism Monographs* 48 (February 1977):3–5.

5. Boyd, "Development of Egypt's Radio," p. 645. In 1951, for example, the radio receiver fee was 110 piasters per set plus 5 piasters per tube, annually; Europa Publications, *"The Middle East and North Africa 1971-72* (London: Europa, 1971), p. 102.

6. A 1975 survey of urban Egyptians 18 years of age and over found that 85 percent hear the General Program, 78 percent Middle East Radio, and 61 percent Voice of the Arabs at least weekly; USIA, Office of Research, Report no. E-13-75 p. 5, Washington, D.C. See also Boyd, "Development of Egypt's Radio," pp. 645–53, on Voice of the Arabs, and Sydney W. Head, ed., *Broadcasting in Africa* (Philadelphia: Temple University Press, 1974), p. 19.

7. Quoted in Head, *Broadcasting in Africa*, p. 19. A good survey of the different

Egyptian radio services is in Boyd, "Egyptian Radio: Tool of Political and National Development," pp. 13–23.

8. The information on these countries is from various interviews, from American Embassy sources including USIS country data sheets (mimeographed, updated annually), and Europa Publications, *The Middle East*, 1953, 1962, and 1971. See Chapter 7 for a discussion of external broadcasting.

9. Radio Libya was established in 1957 by the monarchy, and had studios in Tripoli and Banghazi. The Aden Broadcasting Service opened in August 1954 with a government-run broadcast assisted by the British, in Arabic, and an English-language station was opened the same year by the British. Both were damaged in the fighting, and the British took with them every moveable piece of equipment when they left in 1967. The new service was named "Broadcasting Service of the People's Republic of South Yemen." Arab States Broadcasting Union, *"A.S.B.U. Review"* (January 1972):70–71; *New York Times*, November 10, 1970, p. 8.

10. Limited-range TV stations were established in Dhahran, Saudi Arabia, in September 1957 by Aramco, at Wheelus in December 1954 by USAFRTS, and in Algiers in 1957 by the French government, but these were not indigenous systems. They broadcast primarily in the language of the foreign country that controlled them, and they were closed or (for Aramco) restricted to non-Arabic programs when the national systems were established. The two American stations broadcast in the U.S. 525-line standard, but many Arabs watched their programs, though Arab TV is now in 625-line. For details on Saudi TV, see Douglas A. Boyd, "An Historical and Descriptive Analysis of the Evolution and Development of Saudi Arabian Television: 1963–1972," unpublished Ph.D. dissertation, University of Minnesota, 1972, pp. 80–82.

11. Head, *Broadcasting in Africa*, p. 24. Egyptian TV receivers grew to 200,000 by 1961 and to one million by the late seventies.

12. Interviews no. 27 and 28, Khartoum, May 13, 1973, broadcasting officials.

13. "Report on Sudan T.V.," p. 3.

14. Quoted in Head, *Broadcasting in Africa*, p. 29. See also the RCC-promulgated "Law for the Establishment of a General Authority for Broadcasting the Popular Revolution," *al Fajr al Jadid* newspaper (Tripoli), November 19, 1973, p. 4.

15. The author has observed many such programs in most of these countries, for example, one broadcast on Sudanese TV on May 10, 1973; no systematic analysis of the content of such broadcasts has yet been made.

16. The author watched these programs on Egyptian TV; for details, see the Cairo press September 4–11 and 26–29, October 11, and special features in *al Akhbar*, September 25–29.

17. Boyd, "Development of Egypt's Radio," pp. 645–53, for details on some foreign campaigns. Muhammad Abdel-Kader Hatem, *Information and the Arab Cause* (London: Longmans, 1974). Hatem discussed the policy issues behind them.

18. The quote is from Information Minister Dr. Kamal Abu al Magd, cited in *al Ahram*, June 30, 1974, p. 4. The August 13, 1970, presidential decree said "Radio and Television are to be used only in the national interest." One program that often carries critical material is "Two Words and Nothing More" of comedian Fu'ad al Muhandis.

19. "The Voice of Palestine, Voice of the Palestinian Revolution" (Sawt Filastin, Sawt al Thawrah al Filastiniyah) name has been used in all stations since June 5, 1972, before which it was Voice of Fatah or Voice of the Storm (al 'Asifah). In Oct. 1973 for example VOP broadcast from Cairo daily 1630–1830 GMT, Baghdad 1730–1830, Algiers 1830–1930, Damascus 1530–1630, and a clandestine station, perhaps in Syria, 1000–1100. A few other countries have had VOP programs briefly but discontinued them. Algeria also apparently supports Voice of the Free Canaries and Voice of the Free Sahara; Aden has had Voice of Oman also. For details on VOP see Donald R. Brown "The Voices of Palestine: A Broadcasting House Divided," *Middle East Journal*, 29(2)(Spring 1975):133–50.

20. For example, Cairo's VOP service on June 18, 1972, strongly attacked King Husayn at a time when Egyptian leaders did not object, although the following year that was discontinued, and on September 13, 1975, the program itself stopped. Meanwhile the Algiers VOP commentaries on September 12, 1975, were attacking President Sadat for the Sinai II agreement.

21. Recent examples are the 1975–76 Egyptian-Syrian disagreement over the Sinai II accord with Israel, and the Egyptian-Libyan controversy over that and other ideological issues, 1974–76. See *al Ahram*, July 26, 1974, *al Akhbar*, July 23, 1974, *Bayrut* newspaper, December 21, 1974.

22. Baghdad TV has used the same technique as in Cairo, broadcasting confessions of saboteurs before they are executed; *al Thawrah* (Baghdad), May 1, 1974, pp. 1, 7. Baghdad and Aden radio continually rail against "imperialist policy and the campaign of American lies . . . racialist, Zionist, and imperialist designs on the Arab homeland" and cheer for "the struggle of the forces of liberation and progress in the world and the cause of the people"—Aden Radio 1730 GMT, June 28, 1975, and Baghdad Radio 1130 GMT, December 29, 1971.

23. Syria, for example, signed a radio-TV agreement with Poland in 1976 to exchange broadcasts, and South Yemen signed one with Bulgaria in 1973; *al Ba'th* (Damascus), January 28, 1976, p. 4; Aden Radio, 1730 GMT, December 9, 1973.

24. The author had observed this in most of these countries personally. See also Head, *Broadcasting in Africa*, pp. 26, 49, "Report on Sudan TV," p. 3. Jamieson, "Television and Radio in Egypt," Appendix 9, reported that Egyptian TV's 1971 imports of film series were 97 percent American, feature films 40 percent U.S. and only 52 percent Communist, despite the poor state of U.S.–Egyptian relations then.

25. Muhammad al Sakni, *al Thawrah* (Tripoli), January 6, 1970. Libya has also on occasion apparently jammed the BBC, as has Egypt; see Information Minister Hatem's statement that Egypt had decided to stop jamming the BBC, Cairo MENA 1235 GMT, January 18, 1972; the Egyptians have also made diplomatic representations to the UK about the content of the BBC, see *al Ahram*, November 12, 1972.

26. Boyd, "Analysis of Saudi TV," p. 57; interview no. 41, Riyadh, May 18, 1973, Saudi broadcaster. In 1962 Saudi Radio, as "Radio Mecca," broadcast 7½ hours daily in Arabic, one in Urdu, and one in Indonesian, but since has added Swahili and other languages.

27. All of these stations have a majority of non-local Arab staffers who frequently made their own decisions on content and succeeded so long as local taboos were not violated. Abu Dhabi Radio became Voice of the UAE but in fact remained under Abu Dhabi

control; it broadcast twelve hours a day, Dubai seventeen, Qatar twelve, and Oman six by 1972; Ras al Khaimah then built its station.

28. Three private stations were operating then—Radio Tangier International, Radio Africa Maghrib (in Tangier), and Radio Dersa (Tetuan). RTM now has studios in five major cities doing programs in Arabic, French, and Berber.

29. USIA, Office of Research, Report no. E-7-74, p. 6; in 1972 Tunisian Radio was broadcasting nineteen hours/day in Arabic, 4½ in French, and one each English and Italian.

30. Boyd, "Analysis of Saudi TV," pp. 107–109; see also Douglas A. Boyd, "Saudi Arabian Television," *Journal of Broadcasting* 15(1)(Winter 1970–71):74–78. A Saudi prince, Khalid bin Musa'ad, was killed in 1965 as a result of a protest against the opening of the Riyadh TV station. Jidda and Riyadh TV signals began on July 17, 1965, Medina on December 30, 1967, and Dammam on November 5, 1969.

31. Boyd, "Analysis of Saudi TV," pp. 59–62, 150–53.

32. The U.S. firm RTV operated Bahrain TV starting in 1971 under a contract which gave it 80 percent of the shares, but the Bahrain bank withdrew its credit in 1975 and the government took over the station. Interview no. 117, Bahrain, May 1976, government official. Sultan Qabus opened Omani "Information City" and color TV on national day, November 17, 1974, and is reportedly spending $10 million per year on TV. Interview no. 116, Muscat, May 1976, broadcast official.

33. *Al Thawrah* newspaper (Sana'a), December 9, 1975, quoting a Yemeni official that Shaikh Zayid had promised to bear the full cost of a nationwide network.

34. TV came to Morocco in 1954 under the auspices of the private firm Compagnie Marocaine de Television, which failed financially by 1956 despite Protectorate help; the government bought the facility in 1960. By 1961 there were already 95,000 TV receivers in Morocco, 3,000 in Tunisia.

35. Interview no. 81, Rabat, April 29, 1973, Moroccan observer; no. 50, Kuwait, no. 53, Amman and no. 8, Tunis, May 21, 23, 24, 1973, broadcast officials. See also Boyd, "Analysis of Saudi TV," p. 242, on censored subjects.

36. Interview no. 84, Tunis, May 3, 1973, observer; the author also observed representative samples of programming.

37. Interview no. 41, Riyadh, Saudi broadcaster, May 18, 1973.

38. Interviews no. 39, 46, and 49, Riyadh and Kuwait, Saudi inside observer and Kuwaiti information officials, May 18, 20, and 21; and author's personal observations.

39. Quote from Qatari Radio official A. R. Ma'dadi in *al Ahd* magazine (Dawha), July 23, 1974, p. 7; on Saudi TV see Boyd, "Analysis of Saudi TV," pp. 72–73, 83–85, 121–23, 150, 233.

40. Boyd, "Analysis of Saudi TV," pp. 234, 242, 238–40, 262–63, 295; interviews no. 36 and 41, Riyadh, Saudi journalists, May 18, 1973, and author's personal observations. Saudi TV allowed a few Saudi women to appear briefly in plays in 1968 and on a children's show in 1969, but complaints from conservative elements ended that experiment. State of Qatar Weekly Program Schedule, Dawhah.

41. Nabil H. Dajani, "The Press in Lebanon," *Gazette* 17(3)(1971):172.

42. USIA, Office of Research, Report no. E-9-75, p. 9, Washington, D.C.; a 1972 survey of just urban adults showed 84 percent listened once a week or more; USIA, Office of Research, Report no. E-14-73 p. 3, Washington, D.C. In 1962 the government installed a pair of 100 kw transmitters to cover the country, and from 1962 to 1967 receivers increased from 120,000 to 450,000.

43. Interviews no. 65 and 66, Beirut, May 29, 1973, Lebanese journalists, and author's observations; also information from American embassy observers.

44. Interviews no. 65, 66, and 67, Beirut, May 29, 1973, Lebanese journalists.

45. The firm Advision was created in 1963 to handle ads for CLT; at first owned by Lebanese businessmen and CLT, in 1967 it became French-owned (government and private); Tele-Orient's studios and transmitters are owned by a Lebanese-British partnership, Thompson-Rizk.

46. See FBIS broadcast reports for this period: FBIS, September 30, 1975, V-G-2 on Voice of Arab Lebanon September 29 at 0500 GMT, and FBIS, March 5, 1976, V-G-1 on Voice of Lebanon March 4, 1976, at 1200 GMT.

47. The pro-Franjieh transmitter at Amshit north of Byblos (100 kw) was in competition with the pro-coup auxiliary transmitter in central Beirut (10 kw) especially on the shared 836 kcs frequency. See FBIS V-G-1-15 (March 12, 1976) and G-1-30 (March 15, 1976) for details. Information also from U.S. Embassy sources, as are the conclusions in the following three paragraphs.

48. Program and frequency details for "Voice of Lebanon" in "Editorial report," *FBIS Daily Report*, January 11, 1977, G-4.

CHAPTER 7—Sources of Foreign News

1. Francis Williams, *Transmitting World News* (Paris: UNESCO, 1953), p. 39; UNESCO, *News Agencies, Their Structure and Operation* (Paris: UNESCO, 1953), pp. 15, 35–36.

2. Submarine cables to the Arab world from England opened first in 1856 (Crete-Alexandria), then expanded in 1860 (Egypt-Sudan-Aden-Muscat-Karachi) and 1861 (Malta-Tripoli-Alexandria). England had been connected by cable with the Continent since 1851. UNESCO, *News Agencies*, p. 147.

3. Rosalynde Ainslie, *The Press in Africa, Communications Past and Present* (New York: Walker, 1967), p. 201; Tom J. McFadden, "News Agencies and Propaganda in Five Arab States," *Journalism Quarterly* 30(Autumn 1953):482. Havas was discredited during the war because of its association with Nazi Germany. AFP was created in 1945 as an autonomous public body whose director is appointed by the government and whose budget is subsidized from government funds.

4. Both AP and UPI are private companies which had overseas connections since 1870 and 1909, respectively, and which became more aggressive abroad in the 1930s as the news agency cartel agreements collapsed. Williams, *Transmitting World News* p. 24.

5. Information on AP and UPI activities was taken from many issues of the USIA's

"Country Data Sheets" and "Communications Fact Books" and from the author's personal knowledge.

6. McFadden, "News Agencies and Propaganda," p. 485; UNESCO, *News Agencies*, p. 57. TASS is a Soviet government bureau directly responsible to the Council of Ministers, and it follows guidance laid down by the Soviet Communist Party.

7. Evron M. Kirkpatrick, *Year of Crisis* (New York: Macmillan, 1957), p. 136.

8. USIA, "Communist News Agency Operations Abroad," Office of Research Report No. R-27-70, November 18, 1970, p. 2. By the end of the 1950s, the Near East and North Africa had become the primary target area, while Western Europe had become a secondary one. Simon Costikyan, "Twelve Years of Communist Broadcasting 1948-1959," USIA, Office of Research and Analysis, Washington, D.C., n.d., p. 8. Interview no. 112, Arab journalist, Washington, D.C., January 1973.

9. L. John Martin, "Analysis of News Agency Coverage of the U.S. Supplied to the Near East and North Africa," USIA, Office of Research, document R-1-76, January 20, 1976. Interview no. 26, SUNA journalist, May 13, 1973, Khartoum.

10. This service, which provided six 45-minute Arabic bulletins daily, was to some extent a successor for the Cairo-based "Arab News Agency" which had just closed. The ANA was established in 1941 by the Hulton Press Organization, a private British firm, to distribute news to the Middle East, half of which was in Arabic. It was very successful until it closed in 1964. In the 1950s, ANA was the leading foreign news source in Iraq, Jordan, Egypt, and Syria. McFadden, "News Agencies and Propaganda," pp. 485-87; UNESCO, *News Agencies*, pp. 52, 137-38.

11. AFP's Arabic service began in March 1969. AFP officials decided to sign the contract because of its low cost and the high quality of the translations. Interview no. 68, AFP officials Paris, June 1, 1973. The AFP and Reuters contracts are described in *al Fann al Iza'i*, No. 62 (January 1974), Radio and Television Federation (Cairo), p. 79.

12. Arab States Broadcasting Union, *ASBU Review* (January 1972):18-20. See below for a discussion of Arab efforts to share TV material.

13. DPA officials clearly had political motives in mind when they signed the DPA-MENA agreement in 1968, since at that time West Germany had no diplomatic relations with several key Arab states, and Bonn sought to improve relations. Interview no. 23, news agency journalist, Cairo, May 10, 1973.

14. It is virtually impossible to determine with any precision actual wire service usage patterns. Arab newspapers often cite only "wire services," or they omit the source entirely. In countries where the foreign wire services are subscribed to only by the national news agency, the latter is usually given as the source even when the story originates abroad. Ibrahim Abu-Lughod, "International News in the Arabic Press: A Comparative Content Analysis," *Public Opinion Quarterly* 26(Winter 1962):603-12.

15. This comparison was made in July 1975 in a study under contract with USIA. Martin, "Analysis of News Agency Coverage of the U.S.," pp. 14, 16, 39-43.

16. Interview no. 9, TAP official, Tunis, 5/4/73.

17. Maghreb Arabe Presse, "MAP: Maghreb Arabe Presse: Two years of Activity" (Rabat, n.d., ca 1962), p. 1.

18. Arab States Broadcasting Union, *ASBU Review* (January 1972):18–20 and appendix.

19. MENA began operation on February 28, 1956, before the Suez crisis actually came to a head, but the feeling was already very strong. MENA was taken over by the government in the wake of developments that led to the ASU's becoming owner of the press. MENA, "Dalil Wakalat Anba' al Sharq al Awsat" (Cairo: MENA, 1977), pp. 3–4. A smaller-scale private effort had been launched by some journalists in 1950 in Cairo, but it was in effect replaced by this larger-scale one. Interview no. 21, Egyptian journalist, Cairo, May 10, 1973.

20. McFadden, "News Agencies and Propaganda," pp. 489–90.

21. President Ben Bella in a 1963 speech, quoted in American University, *Area Handbook for Algeria* (Washington, D.C.: USGPO, 1965), p. 34.

22. WAFA statement broadcast on Baghdad's Voice of Palestine, May 27, 1974, 1700 GMT.

23. Interviews no. 9 and 26, TAP and SUNA officials, Tunis and Khartoum, May 4 and 13, 1973, respectively.

24. In 1962, for example, the Orient News Agency and Akhbar Lubnan were thought to be pro-Egyptian, while al Mashriq, the Lebanese Publishing Agency and the Local News Agency were seen to be conservative and pro-West. Two others had changing orientations.

25. Television agreements are with West Germany's Wiesbaden station, England's Visnews, and UPI. MENA, "Dalil Wakalat," pp. 7–11. *Al Fann al Iza'i* No. 62, Radio and Television Federation, Cairo, pp. 69–89.

26. McFadden reports these early efforts in "News Agencies and Propaganda," pp. 489–90.

27. General Secretariat, Arab States Broadcasting Union, "Convention of the Arab States Broadcasting Union" (Cairo: Dar al Nafih Press, 1973), p. 4.

28. Arab States Broadcasting Union, *ASBU Review* (January 1973), p. 44 and appendix, p. 3.

29. The 5 percent and 15 percent figures are for April 1976, and are probably typical for Cairo TV in the mid-seventies. The comparable January and February 1976 figures were 142 and 149 items sent to Cairo from Eurovision, of which 8 and 11 were used, respectively. The remaining 80 percent is local news production. Most other Arab stations, except North African ones, are probably lower than 5 percent. William Amin, "The Role and Means of the Arab States Broadcasting Union in Retribalizing the Arab Audience," unpublished paper, American University in Cairo, Spring 1976, pp. 24, 40.

30. The criticism was published by ASBU. *ASBU Review* (January 1972):44 and appendix no. 3. The story of the creation of MAP has only partly been published. Maghreb Arabe Presse, "MAP," pp. 3, 4, 9, and interview no. 5, MAP official, Rabat, May 2, 1973. Amin, "ASBU in Retribalizing," p. 42. On April 1, 1978, six Arab states on the Persian Gulf opened the Gulf News Agency in Bahrain, but it seemed to have little impact.

31. The "Project for Arab Space Communications for Arab Telephone, Telegraph, Radio and Television Communications," named "Arabsat" by some, was agreed to in a

February 10, 1974, resolution, and then an April 4, 1976, meeting in Cairo of Arab League Communications Ministers agreed on a budget and on locating it in Saudi Arabia. *Ibid.*, pp. 30–39. As of 1977, North Africa had microwave links to Europe, while the rest of the Arab world, except the two Yemens, had satellite ground stations. Algeria had both. *Middle East Economic Digest* 20(13)(March 26, 1976):14.

32. Dr. Gamal al 'Utaify, speech of January 10, 1977, quoted the same day by MENA, Cairo. For a description and analysis of this pool, see Edward T. Pinch, "The Third World and the Fourth Estate," monograph, Senior Seminar in Foreign Policy (Washington, D.C.: U.S. Department of State, April 1977).

33. *Ibid.*, pp. 6, 11–12. The Middle East problem took up 17 percent of the pool, which, compared to worldwide news flow, is quite high, as Pinch shows.

34. This office is run by Levon Keshishian, whose primary customers have been Cairo's *al Ahram* newspaper, plus the media in Kuwait, Abu Dhabi, Saudi Arabia, and Morocco. Interview with Keshishian, New York, September 1972.

35. Interview no. 112, Arab journalist, Washington, D.C., January 1973, and several other interviews. By 1979 eight Arab countries were represented by correspondents in New York but five of those were by Keshishian; only four Arab countries had correspondents in Washington. Israeli media, for example, had seven in Washington and seventeen in New York.

36. UNESCO, *News Agencies*, p. 35.

37. For example, Jordan arrested the Iraqi News Agency Bureau Chief in Amman in October 1972, Syria closed the Damascus MENA office in July 1973, and Libya closed the Tripoli MENA office in March 1976. In April 1979 Jordan closed the MENA office in Amman.

38. The BBC Arabic Service began in 1938. During the 1956–57 Suez Crisis it grew from 3¾ to 66½ hours per week and then reached the 70-hour level. VOA, which began Arabic later than BBC, by 1955 was transmitting 21 hours per week and 49 by the 1970s. Voice of America, *VOA Fact Book* (Washington, D.C., 1971). BBC broadcasts to the Arabs from transmitters on Cyprus and Masira, while VOA broadcasts from Rhodes.

39. It is common knowledge in the Middle East that these stations are rarely listened to; the listener surveys that have been conducted either have shown that or have omitted these stations from consideration because they are insignificant in the area. Monte Carlo seems to be very popular with younger Arabs, but there is little survey data on this newer service.

40. Middle East Marketing Research Institute, "Media Habits Among USIA Target Groups in Beirut, Lebanon" (Beirut, 1969), mimeo.

41. Of the Jordanians living in six main cities 54 percent preferred TV news, 34 percent radio, 12 percent newspapers; Associated Business Consultants, "A Media Penetration Survey in Jordan" (Beirut: ABC, January 1970), pp. 40–41.

42. TV viewers in this area can watch programs from Iraq, Kuwait, Saudi Arabia, Qatar, Abu Dhabi, and Dubai, all in Arabic, when conditions are right. The Iranian stations and the Aramco station in Dhahran can be seen by viewers with 525-line-standard sets. Also, Egypt exports about 2000 hours/year of TV programming to other Arab countries, but none of this is news or public affairs.

43. Interview with the chief editor of *al 'Arabi* (Kuwait), March 1972; some of this information is from personal observation by the author.

44. Interviews no. 42 and 43, Saudi publication distributors, Riyadh, May 18, 1973.

45. A 1965 study of six Jordanian cities showed that six foreign publications outsold two Jordanian dailies; Associated Business Consultants, "A Media Penetration Survey Conducted in the Cities of Jordan" (Beirut: ABC, July 1965), Tables 80 and 83.

46. There have been many gatekeeper studies. The first application to journalism of Kurt Lewin's "gatekeeper" concept was in: David Manning White, "'The Gate Keeper': A Case Study in the Selection of News," *Journalism Quarterly* 29 (Fall 1950):383–90.

47. W. Phillips Davison, *International Political Communication* (New York: Praeger, 1965), pp. 14–21.

INDEX

Abboud, Gen. Ibrahim, Sudanese leader, 58, 64
Abdal Karim Qasim, Iraqi leader, 58
Abdul Nasser, Gamal, Egyptian leader: and Haykal, 12, 41; use of language, 22; and *al Gumhuriyah*, 44–45, 61; and newspapers, 45, 48; and censorship, 61; view of private press, 66–67; use of radio and television, 121
Abdul Quddus, Ihsan, Egyptian writer and journalist, 62, 172n30, 177n48
Abdul Salam Arif, Col., Iraqi leader, 63
Abu Dhabi. *See* United Arab Emirates
Action, L' (Tunisian newspaper), 72–73. 83
Aden News Agency, 42
Advertising in media, 11, 16, 23–24, 125, 129
Agence France Presse, 134–35, 137, 139–40
Ahali, Al (Egyptian newspaper), 46–47
Ahram, Al (Egyptian newspaper): early beginnings, 13, 53, 178n1; fiction in, 19–20; circulation, 32, 66; style and readership, 44; editorial change, 45; nonpartisan, 57; popularity in 1950s, 62; exports, 153. *See also* Haykal, Muhammad
Ahram Publishing House, Al (Egypt), 5, 10, 37–38, 45–46
Ahrar, Al (Egyptian newspaper), 46–47
Ahrar, Al (Lebanese newspaper), 99
Akhbar, Al (Egyptian newspaper), 32, 44, 66, 153
Akhbar al Yawm Publishing House (Egypt), 37–38, 62
Akhir Sa'a magazine (Egypt), 153

'Alam, Al (Moroccan newspaper), 104, 107, 109
Alger Republicain (Algerian newspaper), 39
Algeria: first newspapers, 2, 6; media statistics, 3; language of media, 23; media types, 28, 31–49 passim; newspapers in, 31–70 passim, 163, 164; government view of press, 35; press law, 39; newspaper ownership, 39; nationalism and newspapers, 53–54, 63; expatriate journalists, 53–54; imports of foreign publications, 54; political parties and press, 58–59, 63; censorship, 63; radio, 113–23 passim; television, 119; news agency (A.P.S.), 141–42
Amal, Al (Lebanese newspaper), 92–94, 99
'Amal, Al (Tunisian newspaper), 72–73
American media, compared with Arab, 9, 26
American news agencies. *See* Associated Press; United Press International
American news in imported print media, 153–54
American publications, 152
American television films on Arab T.V., 122
American-controlled television in Arab countries, 2–3, 120, 190n10
Amin, Ali, Egyptian publisher and journalist, 44, 177n42
Amin, Mustafa, Egyptian publisher and journalist, 177n48
Anba', Al (Kuwaiti newspaper), 102–103, 105, 108
Anba', Al (Moroccan newspaper), 104

199

THE ARAB PRESS

was composed in 10-point Compugraphic Caledonia and leaded two points,
with display type in Compugraphic Caledonia,
by Metricomp Studios, Inc.;
printed on 55-pound Warren Antique Cream paper stock,
Smyth-sewn and bound over boards in Holliston Roxite B Linen,
also adhesive bound with Wyomissing Corvon covers,
by Maple-Vail Book Manufacturing Group, Inc.;
and published by

SYRACUSE UNIVERSITY PRESS
SYRACUSE, NEW YORK 13210